Supported Em

D0166973

DATE DUE			

Supported Employment
A Community Implementation Guide

by

G. Thomas Bellamy, Ph.D.
Director, Office of Special Education Programs
U.S. Department of Education
Washington, D.C.

and

Larry E. Rhodes, Ph.D.
David M. Mank, Ph.D.
Joyce M. Albin, M.Ed.
Specialized Training Program
Division of Special Education and Rehabilitation
University of Oregon
Eugene, Oregon

with invited contributions

·P A U L·H·
BROOKES
PUBLISHING CO.

Baltimore • London • Toronto • Sydney

Paul H. Brookes Publishing Co.
Post Office Box 10624
Baltimore, Maryland 21285-0624

Typeset by Brushwood Graphics Inc., Baltimore, Maryland.
Manufactured in the United States of America by
The Maple Press Company, York, Pennsylvania.

This book was prepared while Dr. Bellamy was director of the Specialized
Training Program of the University of Oregon, Eugene. This book was written
by Dr. Bellamy in his private capacity. No official support or endorsement by
the Department of Education is intended or should be inferred.

Library of Congress Cataloging-in-Publication Data
Supported employment.
  Bibliography: p.
  Includes index.
  1. Handicapped—Employment—United States.
2. Vocational rehabilitation—United States.   I. Bellamy,
G. Thomas.   II. Title.
HD7256.U5S86   1987   362'.0425   87-14367
ISBN 0-933716-83-4 (pbk.)

Contents ─────────────────

Contributors

Joyce M. Albin, M.Ed.
Senior Research Assistant
Specialized Training Program
135 Education Building
University of Oregon
Eugene, OR 97403

G. Thomas Bellamy, Ph.D.
Director, Office of Special Education
    Programs
U.S. Department of Education
Room 3086 MES Building
400 Maryland Avenue SW
Washington, DC 20202

Jay Buckley, Ed.D.
Research Associate
Specialized Training Program
135 Education
University of Oregon
Eugene, OR 97403

David M. Mank, Ph.D.
Assistant Professor
Division of Special Education and
    Rehabilitation
135 Education Building
University of Oregon
Eugene, OR 97403

John J. McDonnell, Ph.D.
Assistant Professor
Department of Special Education
229 Milton Bennion Hall
University of Utah
Salt Lake City, UT 84112

Kenneth D. Ramsing, Ph.D.
Graduate School of Management
College of Business Administration
University of Oregon
Eugene, OR 97403

Larry E. Rhodes, Ph.D.
Associate Director
Specialized Training Program
135 Education Building
University of Oregon
Eugene, OR 97403

Heidi Rose, Ph.D.
Coordinator of School Integration
Episcopal Church
bei Viedrock
Uhlandstr. 37
28 Bremen 1
Federal Republic of Germany

Barbara Wilcox, Ph.D.
Associate Professor
Indiana University
2853 East Tenth Street
Bloomington, IN 47405

___ Acknowledgments _____

While the writing itself was mercifully shorter, this book was in a real sense 10 years in the making. A decade ago, our research group at the University of Oregon, having just completed a text on procedures for vocational training for persons with severe mental retardation, began working to implement those procedures in conjunction with a variety of community employment programs. The resulting experiences focused on the organizational and policy variables that affected employment outcomes and led through a series of program development and evaluation activities. Our thinking was shaped to a great degree during this time by the employment service providers with whom we had the opportunity to work, the businesses that shared our confidence that persons with severe disabilities contribute to company productivity, the state and federal agencies that implemented and modified the ideas, and the work of parallel research and development groups with whom we have shared important mutual influence in the development of supported employment concepts.

To acknowledge adequately the contribution of important members of all these groups to the development of supported employment and of our own thinking would require a separate volume. A few individuals' contributions and personal support have been so great, however, that we could not honestly publish without recognizing their impact.

Our most important learning came from efforts to provide assistance to individuals who managed and supported the development of employment services for persons with severe disabilities. The difficulties and insights that resulted from their efforts to provide training and to support integration provided the foundation for all the organizational design work. Particular contributions were made by several individuals with whom we enjoyed such relationships over several years: Trish Borden, Paula Johnson, Teri Johnson, Mark Jewell, Lee Valenta, Anne O'Bryan, Maria Gomez, Joe Turner, Dennis Sandow, Vicki Whitney, Jeff Miller, Marcia DeLorme, Gwen Sither, Joan Maura, Elena Boyer, Chuck Dady, Angela Zimmer, Patti Ghiossi, Kathy Moore, Candace O'Neill, Marge Hauritz, Harriet Yaffe, Anne Paradis, Liissa Carroll, Rosemary Hennessy, Marcia Dwonczyk, and Michael Collins.

Our challenges to design service programs that fit the needs of labor markets came as a result of the confidence and support of key business leaders. We want particularly to thank Dave Jay and Brenda Graesser of Physio Control, Jim Harper of Wacker Siltronic, Monie Burnett of Tektronix, Thomas Eder of A-Dec, Inc., Tim Weyer of NEC America, Beverly Osborn of Photon-Kinetics, and Kenneth Ramsing of the University of Oregon.

The concept of supported employment is a synthesis of our own work and that of many other important research and development efforts. Over the last several years, we have been fortunate to have an active exchange of ideas with many professional colleagues in all parts of the United States. Their impact on our work has been invaluable and is greatly appreciated.

Isolated model services were gradually formed into the present program of supported employment because of the interest and commitment of many public officials with responsibility for administering employment services. We want particularly to acknowledge the contribution of individuals with whom we worked: John Stern, Ralph Larsen, Madeleine Will, William Jones, Justin Dart, Jr., Sue Warth, and Dick Melia.

We are particularly indebted to our colleagues at the University of Oregon's Specialized Training Program. The luxury of working in a supportive environment of committed and insightful professionals cannot be fully described. From help in solving specific problems to continuous support for rigor, sensitivity to needs of individuals with disabilities, and personal support, we thank Rob Horner, Barbara Wilcox, Roz Slovic, Shawn Boles, Dianne Ferguson, Jay Buckley, Brigid Flannery, Phil Ferguson, Steve Newton, Kris Smock, and Howard Loewinger.

Finally, we want to thank those who helped directly with the preparation of the book. For reviews of early drafts, thanks to Kathy Moore, Marcia Dwonczyk, John Berendt, Michael Collins, Marge Hauritz, Lee Valenta, Marion Jay, Phil Ferguson, and Dennis Sandow; for editing that significantly improved our writing, Polly Ashworth; and for preparation of the manuscript itself, Terri Reese, Stacey McCormack, and Tammy Aho.

This book is dedicated to the many individuals with severe disabilities who endured our learning about successful employment, and to the many parents and advocates who sustain a persistent vision of an employed, integrated life-style for persons with disabilities.

Supported Employment

Chapter 1

Supported Employment

John Harrison will finish special education at his high school next year. His family, teacher, and other advocates have been talking with him about job possibilities. John has completed several months of training as a dishwasher in a small restaurant near his high school, two semesters on a work crew that did groundskeeping for the school district, and one year in an office, where he learned to operate duplicating machines.

John has been labeled severely mentally retarded. As his family and friends plan for his future, they recognize that he will need some support both at home and work throughout his life. Fortunately, his community has several employment services that offer just such support at work. One, Olympic Personnel Systems, places persons with severe disabilities in individual community jobs, provides on-site training, and maintains the level of support each employee needs to keep his or her job. Another service, Metro Employment, supports small groups of persons with severe disabilities in the community's larger industries. A third, Chocfactory, a small chocolate company, employs four persons with disabilities and three without. A new employment opportunity is also being developed in the city parks department that will enable persons needing ongoing support to work on two three-person crews that maintain public parks and playgrounds.

After assessing John's interests and skills, the group decides that a job involving machine operation and frequent coworker contact would be ideal. A review of local options reveals a vacancy at Precision Connectors, a large manufacturing company that employs five persons with severe disabilities, in cooperation with Metropolitan Enclaves. An interview is arranged for John, and he is hired on probation to do part-time work during his last year of high school. The high school special education staff provides the initial on-the-job training, and upon John's graduation, Metro Employment, an organization funded by the state's developmental disabilities agency, takes responsibility for ongoing support.

Working at about 40% of normal productivity during his first year of full-time employment, John makes about $500 per month. Recent legislation has enabled him to remain eligible for Supplemental Security Income (SSI) and Medicaid, just in case the job doesn't work out. John is now developing a few friendships with coworkers at the plant, and his earnings allow him to choose how to spend his time and money. For now, it appears he has found his niche in the work-life of the community.

But this story is fiction, not fact. This dream of successful employment has sustained many teachers, parents, and professionals as they have fashioned employment-preparation programs for youth with severe disabilities in the schools. This dream also motivates many who seek to return persons from institutions to community settings, for work is an important part of community life. The same dream is shared by providers of adult services, who know that the people they serve could do much more than pass the hours in conventional day programs.

The means is within grasp. A public policy framework now exists for transforming this dream into local realities. Federal and state initiatives to establish *supported employment services* now provide the opportunity to replace conventional day programs with work opportunities specifically designed for persons with severe disabilities. By combining work opportunities and ongoing support in an integrated work setting, supported employment offers a new future for persons with disabilities so severe that they require ongoing services. Previously served in activity programs, viewed as totally dependent on public programs for income support, and given no role in the work force, persons with severe disabilities have been segregated, impoverished, and hobbled by their dependency. Supported employment offers the employee the alternative of participating in a community's work-life and achieving at least partial self-support while needed public assistance and service is maintained. With supported employment, the price of the needed ongoing support is no longer segregation and dependency for persons with disabilities.

Supported employment is possible today for people like John because of significant federal initiatives. Actions by Congress, federal agencies, and a majority of states have produced many investments in the development of supported employment opportunities. Although this activity has helped promote a groundswell of interest in supported employment, there are limits to what will be accomplished through federal, or even state, action. Supported employment is neither a mandate nor a service to which individuals with severe disabilities are entitled. It is, rather, an opportunity for local communities to develop alternative services that express the employment aspirations of persons with severe disabilities and their families.

This book is about making that opportunity a local reality. Its purpose is to provide a guide to implementing supported employment, so that readers can take better advantage of federal- and state-supported employment initiatives to improve local services. As an *implementation guide*, the book is neither a review of related research nor an exhaustive discussion of the logical foundations of the supported employment concept. Instead, the book offers practical advice on how to develop, organize, operate, manage, and evaluate supported employment efforts.

Implementing supported employment requires the coordinated efforts of several groups, each of which approaches the task with unique perspectives, needs, and responsibilities. Employers provide job opportunities; state and local agencies fund, regulate, and evaluate programs; service providers offer the needed training and support; parents and advocates choose among services and provide assistance outside the work place; persons with disabilities choose whether or not to participate in particular jobs or programs. The efforts of all these groups, and more, are needed to implement supported employment. The essence of coordination among them is the sharing of a vision of the supported employment opportunity that should result from each group doing its part while appreciating the importance of the work of the others. The need for this coordinated effort is an underlying theme of this book. After describing various supported employment options and how these are established, the book addresses the tasks and issues from the perspective of state agency administrators, service program managers, teachers, parents, and employers. Although implementation of supported employment is discussed from each perspective separately, the intended result is the coordinated effort of all these groups.

This chapter introduces the concept of supported employment. A brief review of the problems of current services is followed by an analysis of the current federal supported employment initiative. The chapter then addresses how this program relates to other concepts in vocational and related programs, and illustrates the kinds of benefits that are expected when conventional day programs are replaced with supported employment.

Because different definitions of severe disabilities are used in special education, vocational rehabilitation, and Social Security, considerable confusion naturally results when communication is attempted with persons working from these different perspectives. Since the intention behind this book is to provide useful information to all these groups, it is important to be explicit at the outset about those to whom the authors refer. Throughout the book, the term *severe disabilities* is used to describe persons who need intensive, ongoing support to live and work in community settings. These are individuals who have not typically been served in vocational rehabilitation and other job-training programs. Instead, when services have been available, they have been for lengthier programs in institutions, day-activity services, or adult training programs. In the group considered to have severe disabilities, the discussion includes persons labeled moderately, severely, and profoundly mentally retarded, autistic, multiply handicapped, and chronically mentally ill. The discussion of eligibility for supported employment, which appears later in this chapter, provides a more detailed treatment of this issue.

THE NEED FOR CHANGE

Why has supported employment emerged as a new federal and state initiative at a time when cutback, not expansion, is the norm for social services? At least part of the reason is the widespread concern about conventional service models for persons with severe disabilities. This section briefly examines the logic and results of those conventional services.

The Continuum of Employment Services

Community-based day and vocational programs for persons with disabilities have developed since the 1960s as a continuum of levels through which individuals have been expected to progress toward competitive employment. Different levels on this continuum are funded by different federal and state agencies and are designed to offer different kinds of services. At the top of the continuum, persons with the least severe disabilities are included in *regular program workshops*, where sheltered work is intended as a means of preparation for competitive work. Work evaluation and work adjustment in these sheltered workshops are typically funded by the state vocational rehabilitation agency and other agencies responsible for time-limited services. Consequently, the admission standards for these programs often reflect the funding agencies' emphasis on offering services to those most likely to benefit in terms of employability. Surveys of workshop entry requirements by Johnson and Mithaug (1977) and Mithaug, Hagmeier, and Haring (1977) illustrate this characteristic. The workshops they studied had similar entry requirements, ranging from the ability to communicate basic needs and move safely about the shop to the ability to work for sustained periods without leaving the work station, responding to interruption, or disrupting others. These entry requirements typically apply, although some workshops may choose to emphasize employment in the workshop rather than preparation for competitive employment.

Individuals who cannot gain entry into these regular program workshops (either because of the criteria of the funding agency or because of the expectations of the workshops themselves) have been served in a variety of work-activity and day-activity programs. In many states, there are two separate program levels below workshops on the continuum. One includes work activity as a component of the program, but is designed to build work-related skills that will allow later entry into a regular program workshop. The other level may have no work component at all, but may focus instead on skills for daily living, self-care, and recreation. These latter services are funded by a mix of federal and state funds, including the Social Service Block Grant, Medicaid, and the Developmental Disabilities Program. Most states administer programs at the bottom of the continuum through mental retardation and mental health agencies, and several provide state funding for administration of intermediate program levels by vocational rehabilitation agencies.

Results from the Continuum

Whatever success may have been enjoyed by regular program workshops and other programs serving persons at the top of the continuum of services, there has been little success in moving persons with severe disabilities from lower program levels toward employment. Studies of progress from day-activity programs to higher-level programs have been completed in a number of states, and the resulting data indicate movement rates of 1%–3% per year (California Department of Finance, 1979; Minnesota Developmental Disabilities Council, 1982; Zivolich, 1984). If an individual with a severe disability entered the continuum in a day-activity program and progressed through the continuum at the estimated average rate, he or she would spend 37 years preparing for a work-activity center, another 10 years in such a center before moving to a workshop or job, and 9 more years in a regular program workshop. In other words, an individual who entered this continuum upon completing school at age 21 would begin his or her first job at age 77.

These data clearly indicate that day- and work-activity programs can be best understood as a source of ongoing services which any consumer can be expected to receive over an extended period, perhaps throughout an entire adult career. When the costs and benefits of day services are evaluated from this perspective, attention necessarily shifts from data on advancement to what is received by consumers while they are in these programs. The results are no more encouraging from this perspective, however. Earnings in these programs range from none in the many states' programs that disallow work to an average of less than $2.00 per work day in certified work-activity centers. Even lower wages are earned by persons with mental retardation (U.S. Department of Labor, 1979). The pervasive segregation of persons with disabilities while they are served in day-activity programs is compounded by the poverty that results from these low earnings. Although these programs may indeed have provided a stopgap alternative to even more restrictive institutional care, it is clear from their performance to date that they are ineffective at moving people to higher-level services or employment, providing employment opportunities within the programs, or supporting meaningful integration into community life.

Program Growth and Costs Although the unsatisfactory outcomes of day-activity and work-activity programs have been well-publicized, these programs have grown explosively in recent years. Between 1979 and 1984, the population served by day programs administered by state mental retardation or developmental disabilities agencies increased from 105,000 to 185,000, a 76% rise in 5 years (Buckley & Bellamy, 1985). Data from the U.S. Department of Labor (1977, 1979), presented in Figure 1.1, indicate a similar trend. Whereas programs at the top of the service continuum (regular program workshops and training and evaluation centers) experienced no growth in number of people served, work-activity centers served about four times more people in 1984 than in 1976. Work-activity centers until late 1986 were described in the federal law as programs in which work is not the main purpose, and a pay ceiling of 25% of the minimum wage is set. There is some overlap between day programs administered by state mental retardation agencies and those certified as work activity centers, but many persons with severe disabilities are served in programs where work is disallowed.

Rapid growth has been accompanied by significant escalations in both per-person and total-program costs. As Table 1.1 shows, the annual cost per person served in day programs administered by state mental retardation agencies increased from about $3,000 in 1979 to $4,963 in 1984, an undiscounted increase of 65%. The total cost of these programs is now almost $1 billion annually, and this includes only the public funds used to support service providers, not the cost of program administration within government agencies. This means

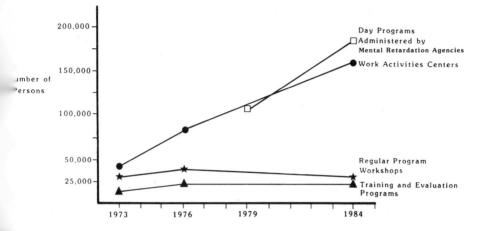

Figure 1.1. Number of persons served in various day and vocational services in the United States, 1973–1984. (*Sources:* U.S. Department of Labor, 1977, 1979; Buckley & Bellamy, 1985).

that in the last 5 years, day- and work-activity programs administered by the state mental retardation agencies have grown larger than those funded through the state-federal vocational rehabilitation program. When similar services for persons with chronic mental illness are added, it becomes clear that the nation's investment in vocational services is shrinking in comparison to its commitment to nonvocational programs. Of course, the cost of direct services is only one of many government expenditures on behalf of individuals with disabilities so severe that they must be served in these day programs. Most also qualify for transfer payments—Supplemental Security Income (SSI), Social Security, or both, together with state supplements to these programs—as well as Medicaid or Medicare, food stamps, and various housing programs.

The problems of lack of movement, low wages, segregation, program expansion, and cost escalation have persisted despite national

Table 1.1. Growth of day and vocational services administered by state mental retardation agencies, 1979–1984

	1979	1984	Change by %
Estimated number of persons served	105,500	185,536	76%
Average public support per person	$3,000	$4,963	65%
Total public support	$330,000,000	$921,000,000	179%

Sources: Buckley and Bellamy (1985); Bellamy, Sheehan, Horner and Boles (1980).

studies, legislative changes, interagency agreements, curriculum innovations, improvements in training procedures, and ongoing federal investments in research and demonstration. Supported employment has emerged as a response to the same problems, but with a novel approach: instead of trying to fix the continuum to promote greater movement, supported employment structures an *alternative* to the continuum logic itself. As will be seen, supported employment involves a complete redefinition of the purpose of programs at the bottom of the continuum.

FOUNDATION FOR CHANGE

While problems in day and vocational services for persons with severe disabilities prompted public consideration of alternatives, important advances in those same programs led to the genesis of the supported employment concept that has emerged as an alternative to conventional services. Supported employment is the product of three separate developments. The first is the growing evidence, from both research projects and community services, that most persons with severe disabilities are able and willing to work. Initial research documented the training procedures that produced needed work skills and the supervision procedures that led to competent work performance. Later efforts demonstrated service procedures for teaching skills required in regular work settings, where special supervision was not always available. Coupled with an increasing emphasis on community-based work training for secondary school students with severe disabilities, these employment demonstrations have radically raised the expectations of professionals, parents, and other advocates concerned with the employment of persons with severe disabilities. Instead of settling for day-activity programs, or even sheltered workshops, many parents of persons with severe disabilities share the feelings, if not the resources, of a participant in a recent national parents conference, who, exasperated that the employment services in his area offered nothing but perpetual training and sheltered work, threatened that he would *buy* a business to ensure his son's employment in a regular workplace upon his completion of school.

The second development that underlies the concept of supported employment is the emphasis on *integration*. As persons with severe disabilities attained the right to a free, appropriate public education in the least restrictive environment, the benefits of regular, daily involvement with persons without disabilities became increasingly apparent. Both professional and advocacy organizations have focused attention on the development of service approaches that allow persons with severe disabilities to learn, work, and play alongside peers who are not disabled. Although the results have not been automatic, the expectation has been that supportive friendships, informal support networks, and needed social skills can develop more easily in integrated settings. The extension of this concern for integration from schools to adult services has led several authors to advocate individual placement in community jobs as an alternative to conventional vocational services (Rusch, 1986; Wehman, 1981). The commitment to integrated services has become so strong that some have even argued that placement in individual jobs is always superior to conventional day services, even if this means working without pay (Brown et al., 1984; Tizard & Anderson, 1979).

The supported employment concept's third basis is the demonstrated need for ongoing support. Whereas federal vocational services have generally been designed and funded as time-limited services, data on service expansion suggest that an increasing number of persons receiving community services need ongoing support. That is, given a choice between time-limited vocational services and ongoing but nonvocational programs, parents, case managers, and service providers have chosen the latter option for many individuals with disabilities.

Supported employment is the combination of these three developments. It involves paid employment in an integrated work setting in which the individual receives ongoing public support. As Figure 1.2 illustrates, supported employment exists only when all three features—employment, integration, and ongoing support—are present. Consequently, supported employment breaks the traditional link between ongoing support and nonvocational services, and combines the emerging advocacy for employment opportunities and integration. Unlike previous efforts to extend employment opportunities to persons with severe disabilities, supported employment addresses the ongoing support needs of these individuals, rather than merely seek access to the time-limited services offered by vocational rehabilitation. Unlike earlier efforts to achieve integration, supported employment affirms the importance of equitable pay for work, and can help persons with severe disabilities enjoy all the benefits of working.

THE FEDERAL SUPPORTED EMPLOYMENT INITIATIVE

Supported employment has emerged in a variety of federal contexts since its initial definition in the regulations of the Office of Special Education and Rehabilitative Services in 1984 (34 CFR 373). The Developmental Disabilities Act of 1984 established supported employ-

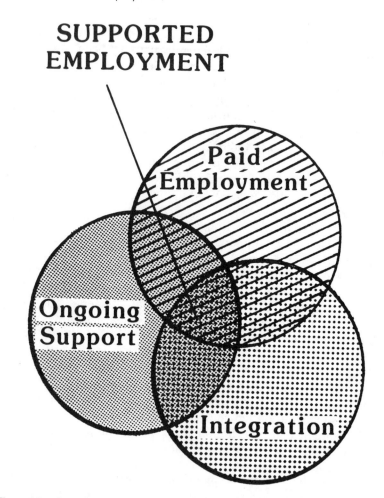

Figure 1.2. Supported employment can exist only when paid employment, ongoing support, and integration are present.

ment as a priority for state planning councils funded under that act (Federal Register, 1984); the Omnibus Budget Reconciliation Act of 1986 listed supported employment as a reimbursable service under the Home and Community Waiver Program of the Health Care Financing Administration; and supported employment has been added to amendments to the Rehabilitation Act (PL 99–506 [1986]). In addition, agency initiatives in both the Department of Education and the Department of Health and Human Services have focused discretionary funds on supported employment by providing state and local agencies the funds to build the capacity to offer supported employment as an alternative to conventional services.

Supported employment is defined in much the same way across these various programs. The Developmental Disabilities Act defines supported employment as:

> Paid employment which (i) is for persons with developmental disabilities for whom competitive employment at or above the minimum wage is unlikely and who, because of their disabilities, need ongoing support to perform in a work setting; (ii) is conducted in a variety of settings, particularly work sites in which persons without disabilities are employed, and (iii) is supported by any activity needed to sustain paid work by persons with disabilities, including supervision, training, and transportation. (Federal Register, 1984)

It is instructive to examine how the three developments that led to the supported employment concept are embodied in this definition. Each creates a standard by which both the presence and quality of supported employment can be assessed. The following brief discussion of paid employment, integration, and ongoing support is presented to clarify these standards. Additional features of the supported employment concept are then discussed to show the range of program flexibility, explore the issue of eligibility, and describe the phases of implementation from the perspective of a service recipient.

Paid Employment Supported employment is, first of all, paid employment. To be engaged in supported employment, an individual must be working for pay and other benefits. This standard contrasts sharply with the objectives of traditional services for persons with severe disabilities, which have focused on the development of skills that might allow later entry into paid work. It is not skill development, but work performance, that is the object of supported employment. Unless one accepts that persons with severe disabilities deserve less than others, the success of supported employment can be evaluated with the same general factors that society uses to evaluate the quality of employment situations: income level, working conditions, and benefits. Although these regular work outcomes serve as important quality indicators, the definition of supported employment is further clarified by standards for what constitutes a minimum level of paid employment. In its initial grant application materials, the U.S. Department of Education (1985) established *20 hours of paid work per week* as the minimum standard for engaging in paid work, without specifying productivity or wage levels.

Continuing Support The behaviors of many persons with severe disabilities are incongruent in important ways with the demands of most workplaces. Earlier program models treated this discrepancy as a readiness problem, and attempted to build the skills and behaviors that appeared to be missing in order to prepare the individual for work. The supported employment model acknowledges the same discrepancy but interprets it differently. Instead of a readiness problem, the discrepancy is treated as a need for continuing support in the work setting. This emphasis on support during employment greatly expands the range of service options beyond preparation. Included are a variety of on-the-job supports, such as periodic supervision, personal-care assistance, retraining, and supervised transportation. To meet the minimum standards of the Department of Education, such service options must be *ongoing, and involve the continuing expenditure of public funds to provide support in the work setting.*

Integration   With its emphasis on work in settings where persons without disabilities are also employed, supported employment provides a distinct contrast with traditional vocational services, which have become known by the "facilities" in which groups of persons with disabilities are separated from others in the community. Integration with others in regular workplaces has several potential benefits for persons with disabilities, including the opportunity to develop friendships, share interests and activities, and have access to normal community resources. Regular workplaces promote contact in several ways with persons without disabilities who are not paid caregivers. Depending on the type of work and location of the job, an individual with disabilities may have contact with coworkers, customers, and supervisors who are not disabled, and may have the opportunity to share work breaks, commuting, and mealtimes with others in the vicinity of work. Not all jobs offer optimum integration possibilities, but there are very few regular workplaces that do not offer some opportunities for interaction with others. The Department of Education's (1985) minimum standard is that a work-site can only be considered integrated when *eight or fewer persons with disabilities work together in a location not adjacent to another disability program.* This does not ensure contacts with persons without disabilities, but can reasonably be seen as necessary to foster such contacts.

Flexibility   There are many ways to organize and provide supported employment. The minimum standards—that an individual work for pay for at least 20 hours weekly in a setting where eight or fewer persons with disabilities are employed, and that the individual receive continuing, publicly funded support—can be applied to individual job placements or small work groups. The ongoing support may be provided by a nonprofit service organization or by a coworker or employer. The work itself may be provided by an employer distinct from the service organization, or may be generated by the organization itself. Many strategies for providing supported employment will no doubt emerge as adaptations are made to particular kinds of jobs, funding levels for continuing support, and individual support needs.

Rather than attempt to define the features of one best model, supported employment offers a challenge to find the support approaches that match individual needs, job opportunities, local conditions, and available funding.

Eligibility A residual population has been either explicitly or implicitly excluded from all previous employment programs for persons with disabilities. For example, the regulations of the vocational rehabilitation program mandate that services be provided to persons who are believed capable of benefitting from them in terms of employability. Even the Rehabilitation Act of 1973's much-publicized priority on services to persons with severe disabilities included this feasibility criterion. Other employment services effect the same exclusion by creating wage or productivity expectations for those completing the program, thereby creating incentives for local providers to select the most capable service recipients. Supported employment breaks with this tradition with the explicit purpose of including any individual whom the state funds for ongoing day services. The policy assumption is that no one is too severely disabled to participate in supported employment. Of course, individual program decisions may be made that work is not an objective of service, but the type or severity of disability is not itself grounds for denying supported employment services.

Having argued that supported employment need not exclude anyone with a severe disability, it is important to emphasize that, to date, the federal supported employment initiatives have not directly defined eligibility for supported employment services. Instead, the current programs let individual states decide who gets supported employment. Who gets funds for ongoing services is entirely a matter for state and local decision-making. Whether an individual with chronic mental illness, severe mental retardation, or a severe physical disability can participate in supported employment is determined by his or her state's decisions about who will receive ongoing services. As a result, although the concept of supported employment may apply to many different groups and may provide a way to include persons with very severe disabilities in the workplace, the final eligibility decisions will be made at the state and local levels as scarce resources for ongoing day services are allocated through political and administrative processes.

Phases of Supported Employment Because different agencies often have responsibility for time-limited and ongoing services, it is useful to distinguish two phases in the supported employment process for any given individual. Initial job location and training may require more support, and hence be more expensive than the second, continuing-support phase. An individual may hold several jobs during the course of a supported employment career, so the initial training phase may well be repeated.

SUPPORTED EMPLOYMENT AND THE SERVICE SYSTEM

Supported employment is a relatively new concept in federal policy; its relationships with other federal programs and services are, in part, a matter of interagency negotiation. Although these arrangements are not complete, a logical analysis of how the concept of supported employment fits with other programs may help clarify the purpose and scope of the program. This section provides a brief commentary on the apparent relationship between supported employment and other critical federal and state programs.

Vocational Rehabilitation Supported employment may be viewed as a continuation of efforts to offer vocational rehabilitation to persons with more severe disabilities. This concept is a direct extension of a longstanding commitment within the vocational rehabilitation system to the value of work, the importance of special provisions to help with disabilities, and the use of new technologies to help previously dependent people enter the work force. Supported employment differs from conventional vocational rehabilitation services in that it involves continuing support with the expectation that an individual will require services as long as he or she is employed. From the perspective of vocational rehabilitation, supported employment can best be viewed as an outcome of service. It is not a method of providing rehabilitation services, but rather a successful result of those services. After a time-limited training and placement program, an individual could be placed in supported employment for as long as public funding was available for ongoing support in the work setting. In some states, this ongoing funding might be administered by a mental health or mental retardation agency.

Mental Retardation and Mental Health Agencies Supported employment is an alternative way of providing the continuing day services offered in most states by mental retardation and mental health agencies. Supported employment simply substitutes support in the context of a work setting for the support that is now provided in nonvocational or prevocational services. This substitution shifts the purpose of these programs from treatment, therapy, nonvocational services, and progress to higher-level programs to outcomes associated with employment and integration. As detailed in later chapters, this shift requires changes in program administration, where new procedures are needed for funding, evaluating, and regulating programs, in service delivery, where different staff skills are needed and where the service context is moved from segregated facilities to integrated work places, and in the formulation of service goals, where the focus is shifted from preparation for employment and community participation to support in work and other community settings.

Social Security and SSI   Supported employment offers the opportunity for an individual to be partially self-supporting while continuing to receive ongoing support. The passage of the 1986 Employment Opportunities for Disabled Americans Act (PL 99–603) made permanent sections 1619(a) and (b) of the Social Security Act (42 USC 1382 et seq.). These sections allow continuing eligibility for assistance through the Supplemental Security Income (SSI) program, even though gross earnings exceed the level considered by the Social Security Administration to be *Substantial Gainful Activity*. Substantial Gainful Activity (SGA) is defined as a useful job paying a significant amount of money. When given the opportunity to work, many individuals are likely to earn between the SGA level and minimum wage—enough under the previous rules to eliminate SSI eligibility, but not nearly enough to support oneself. The 1619(a) and (b) provisions give at least a temporary structure within which an individual may reasonably engage in supported employment at or below minimum wage. Proposals have been advanced to make similar changes in the Retirement, Survivors, and Disability Income (RSDI) program.

Local Service Delivery   Supported employment is not a new system in the continuum of day and vocational services. Instead, it is an alternative to that part of the continuum of local services for which public agencies now provide ongoing support. Figure 1.3 illustrates

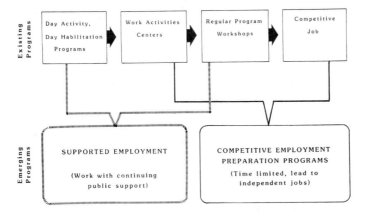

Figure 1.3. Supported employment provides an alternative to nonvocational and prevocational services provided by state and local agencies.

how the continuum discussed in preceding paragraphs is replaced by supported employment programs—those that have time-limited funding to prepare persons for independent employment. Different funding sources and different program labels across states will alter the mix of these two programs slightly, but the important points are that supported employment potentially includes all services at the bottom of the continuum and that it extends to any for which the state has made an ongoing funding commitment. It does not include those for which short-term funding is provided in conjunction with preparation for independent employment.

THE BENEFITS OF SUPPORTED EMPLOYMENT

Whereas the concept of supported employment is relatively new, there are several demonstration programs that provide a basis for initial estimates of how supported employment will benefit persons with severe disabilities and society at large. Evidence of the extent to which these benefits actually are achieved in most communities must necessarily await comprehensive evaluations of statewide implementation efforts. It is reasonable, nonetheless, to anticipate several effects of supported employment.

For individuals with severe disabilities, supported employment offers the opportunity to do work that has clear value in the economy—value that is made evident by someone's willingness to pay for its completion. Working offers structure to one's day, an opportunity to expand one's social circle, and the chance to contribute. It also produces income, which creates new opportunities for community participation and expands one's role as a consumer within the community. The personal, social, and economic benefits of working are well-documented within the general population, and there is reason to assume that persons with severe disabilities will experience the same benefits.

For employers, supported employment offers the possibility to contribute to a part of a community's welfare that heretofore has been impossible without incurring significant costs. Supported employment enables an employer to hire someone with a severe disability who would not otherwise be considered for employment in the competitive labor market. The employer is then protected from identifiable excess costs associated with training or supervising the individual, through ongoing public support. Furthermore, the employer is able to pay on the basis of productivity, so that labor costs per unit of work remain constant, whether the individual is an independent employee or receives continuing support. Given the growing concern for corporate responsibility and corporate culture, such an opportunity to have an effect on community issues can be an important benefit. For society at large, supported employment offers other benefits. In addition to the social benefits of allowing persons with disabilities to live and work in their own communities, supported employment offers the opportunity for persons with disabilities to become at least partially self-supporting. This translates directly into reduced dependence on public programs and income transfers. For example, an individual who earned only $300 per month in a supported job would save the government more than $100 per month in Social Security payments or SSI. Even greater benefits accrue to the public when an individual's earnings increase, income transfer programs become unnecessary, and the supported employee begins to pay taxes.

SUMMARY AND CONCLUSIONS

Supported employment is an important policy development that, although viewed as an extension of longstanding trends in vocational rehabilitation, must also be seen as a significant departure from current service delivery and policy. By combining ongoing services with employment opportunity in an integrated setting, supported employment offers very different options to those who require ongoing services. Implementation of supported employment will require significant adjustments among public agencies and private service providers. Local programs will need new organizational and staffing models, new relationships with employers, and new measures of program success. The funders of those services will need different funding formulas, new evaluation methods, and new strategies to facilitate the development of local service capacity.

Special educators will need to investigate an approach to work preparation that builds skills for integrated employment, regardless of the individual's level of disability. Existing vocational programs will need systematic plans for shifting from day- and work-activity models to supported employment alternatives. Because each of these changes will be somewhat dependent on changes in other parts of the system, a coordinated view of the implementation process is needed most of all.

REFERENCES

Bellamy, G. T., Sheehan, M. R., Horner, R. H., & Boles, S. M. (1980). Community programs for severely handicapped adults: An analysis of vocational opportunities. *Journal of The Association for Persons with Severe Handicaps, 5* (4), 307–324.

Brown, L., Shiraga, B., York, J., Kessler, K., Strohm, B., Rogan, P., Sweet, M., Zanella, K., VanDeventer, P., & Loomis, R. (1984). Integrated work opportunities for adults with severe handicaps: The extended training option. *Journal of The Association for Persons with Severe Handicaps, 9,* 262–269.

Buckley, J. T., & Bellamy, G. T. (1985). National survey of day and vocational programs for adults with severe disabilities: A 1984 profile. In P. Ferguson (Ed.), *Issues in transition research: Economic and social outcomes* (pp. 1–12). Eugene, OR: Specialized Training Program, University of Oregon.

California Department of Finance. (1979). *A review of sheltered workshops and related programs (Phase II): To Assembly Concurrent Resolution No. 2067, Volume II, Final Report.* Sacramento: State of California.

Federal Register (1984, September 25). Developmental Disabilities Act of 1984. Report 98–1074, Section 102 (11)(F).

Johnson, J., & Mithaug, D. (1977). A replication of sheltered workshop entry requirements. *AAESPH Review, 3,* 116–122.

Minnesota Developmental Disabilities Council. (1982). *Policy Analysis Series: Issues related to Welsch v. Noot (Paper No. 9).* St. Paul: Author.

Mithaug, D. E., Hagmeier, L. D., & Haring, N. G. (1977). The relationship between training activities and job placement in vocational education of the severely and profoundly handicapped. *AAESPH Review, 2,* 89–109.

Office of Special Education and Rehabilitation Services. (1984). *Supported employment for adults with severe disabilities: An OSERS program initiative.* Unpublished manuscript.

Rusch, F. R. (1986). *Competitive employment issues and strategies.* Baltimore: Paul H. Brookes Publishing Co.

Tizard, J., & Anderson, E. (1979, June). *The education of the handicapped people.* Paris: Organization for Economic Cooperation and Development, Center for Educational Research and Innovation.

U.S. Department of Education. (1985). *Special projects and demonstrations for providing vocational rehabilitation services to severely disabled individuals* (CFDA No. 84. 128A.). Washington, DC: Office of Special Education and Rehabilitation Services.

U.S. Department of Labor. (1977). *Sheltered workshop study, workshop survey, 1.* Washington, DC: Author.

U.S. Department of Labor. (1979). *Study of handicapped clients in sheltered workshops, 2.* Washington, DC: Author.

Wehman, P. (1981). *Competitive employment: New horizons for severely disabled individuals.* Baltimore: Paul H. Brookes Publishing Co.

Zivolich, S. (1984). *Regional Center of Orange County survey of day activity programs and developmental centers.* Unpublished manuscript, Regional Center of Orange County, Anaheim, CA.

Chapter 2

Program Models and Organizational Accomplishments

The previous chapter defines supported employment as paid employment in integrated settings that is supported by continuing public funding with the purpose of maintaining performance in the workplace. The chapter suggests that supported employment is superior to conventional nonvocational and prevocational program approaches from the perspectives of both individuals with disabilities and society.

This chapter begins to address the question of how to attain the benefits of supported employment. Specifically, approaches are introduced that have been used successfully to address the critical aspects of supported employment for individuals with severe disabilities. The chapter also addresses the common features of successful supported employment programs, identifying five things any program must do well to achieve the outcomes of supported employment.

PROGRAM APPROACHES

Many program approaches have been effective in providing supported employment to persons with severe disabilities. Four approaches are described in the following sections in the context of existing services. These approaches are not intended to constitute an exhaustive list of possible strategies, nor are they intended as complete descriptions of particular programs. Instead, they are provided as illustrative examples of known strategies in which variations have been used successfully under different economic and geographic conditions. These approaches represent only a few of an unlimited number of variations of supported employment.

Individual Supported Jobs in Community Businesses

Programs in several states, including Illinois, Maryland, Oregon, Vermont, Virginia, Washington, and Wisconsin, have adapted for supported employment the job training and placement strategies originally associated with preparation for independent competitive employment. These *supported jobs programs* typically locate full- or part-time jobs in conventional, private sector companies, and then place persons with severe disabilities in these jobs. A trainer usually performs the job for a few days to determine the exact job requirements and necessary social and personal skills. After this "job analysis," continuous on-site training is provided at the workplace until the new employee competently performs the job.

As the new employee gains skill and confidence, the trainer gradually spends less time at the site. Unlike training programs that provide short-term training for independent, competitive employment, however, supported employment programs never completely remove the support provided by the trainer. In order to maintain acceptable levels of performance by persons with severe disabilities in individual jobs in the community, adjustable levels of ongoing support are required. This continuing support may take a variety of forms: retraining when job assignments, quality, or rate requirements change, periodic consultations with coworkers and the employer to see that things are going well, regular evaluations of productivity levels to meet U.S. Department of Labor guidelines, assistance in adjusting challenging behaviors, orientation and training for coworkers, and working with home providers to coordinate transportation or other needed support. The kind and amount of ongoing support is as varied as the people who receive it.

A typical organization using this approach supports many persons in individual positions, with new employees with disabilities added as jobs and staff resources allow. The result, in a mature organization, is that a "job coach" or "employment training specialist" may be responsible for providing ongoing support to several persons who have already been trained in their jobs, while also being responsible for the primary training of a new individual in a new job.

Supported jobs programs appear to function effectively either as independent nonprofit organizations or as components of larger vocational services. Funding is provided for continuing support by public agencies that have traditionally been responsible for day services or extended sheltered employment programs. Costs for the more intensive, initial training may be met by these same agencies or by vocational rehabilitation, special education, or other agencies providing time-limited funds.

Supported jobs strategies have been successfully adapted to diverse circumstances, with many variations on the basic approach now in operation. A few significant differences among programs are:

Individuals with disabilities may be hired directly by the community employer or through an arrangement with the support organization. The latter strategy involves the support organization functioning somewhat as a temporary manpower organization for the business, receiving payment from the business to cover labor and other costs until the supported employee moves to the regular company payroll. This could be an ongoing arrangement with the employer.

The support organization may operate a central training site, providing some time-limited assessment and work behaviors training before placement.

The support organization may concentrate on one field, such as food service, or may support jobs among a range of businesses. Regular, private sector employment is most frequently sought by support organizations, although public sector jobs represent a significant job market in many communities.

The individuals with disabilities may receive regular wages or may be paid less than minimum wage based on actual productivity, per Department of Labor regulations.

Continuing support may be provided by the staff of the support organization, or the organization may contract with coworkers to provide part of the needed assistance.

Supported jobs approaches to providing supported employment are particularly attractive to many professionals and advocates because they reflect normal patterns of working in most communities. The approach does not require special groupings, special buildings, or other potentially stigmatizing arrangements. It enables persons with disabilities to work beside employees who are not disabled, and develop relationships based on that contact. Supported jobs approaches also mesh with aspects of the rapidly expanding service sector, the job market which appears to provide the greatest promise.

Communities must have the means to establish good jobs, with security and integration, for the maximum number of people with severe disabilities. It seems unlikely that developing supported jobs will fit the employment needs of all persons with severe disabilities in all employment contexts. An important drawback to supporting many employees and employers is the reliance of this approach on periodic support after the initial training period. This means that some persons with intensive support needs or challenging behaviors may be difficult to place or maintain in jobs.

Enclaves, or Work Stations, in Industry

Enclaves, or work stations, differ from individual jobs in that a group of persons with disabilities work in sufficient proximity to make coordinated training and support services available at all times, not just during the initial training period. An enclave approach does not require that workers be immediately adjacent to one another. The size of the group is limited by the supported employment criterion that permits no more than eight persons with disabilities to work together. Initial training and support are provided by an on-site supervisor who may work for a publicly funded support organization, the company providing the employment, or both. Unlike individual supported jobs, the enclave provides for the ongoing presence of a supervisor so that support can be continuous, more reliable and more intensive. The supervisor's responsibilities include securing work assignments for enclave members from the company, organizing the work to help enable job performance, training and supervising employees, managing workflow, and supporting the integration of enclave employees with other company employees.

Public funding for supporting individuals with disabilities within the enclave or work stations typically goes to a nonprofit corporation, which provides support at the work-site. As with other approaches, this corporation may be either a single-purpose agency, supporting several enclaves within a region, or a part of a larger organization with other components. Some costs of supervision are normally borne by the company providing the employment opportunity, just as it provides for support for all other employees. The proportionate share of costs borne by the support organization and the company may change as the productivity of enclave members increases.

Applications of enclaves for providing supported employment differ from more traditional uses of this approach which use work stations as a means of providing transitional training for future competitive jobs. The time-limited nature of services in traditional work station programs results in services to persons with less severe disabilities, who are expected to enter independent jobs after short-term training. Because those served in the programs are not necessarily expected to become regular employees of the company, there is a risk that the company will not be as involved in personnel selection and management decisions as is the case with supported employment enclaves.

Mobile Work Crews

Mobile work crews are small businesses that work for customers at their regular workplaces. The type of work may vary, but it often includes janitorial, groundskeeping, or related service industry jobs. Persons with disabilities achieve integration by working at regular work-sites with nonhandicapped persons present (for example, in offices, apartments, or boatyards), and by using typical community resources, such as stores and restaurants, during the work day. One of the advantages of the crew is that the company can control the volume and flow of work to any given crew to accommodate the training, work, and personal adjustment needs of each crewmember. The "mix" of job tasks can also be adjusted to address three goals: 1) give crewmembers enough jobs that they have previously mastered, to maximize wages and productivity; 2) increase the likelihood of individual choice in job selection; 3) have crewmembers continue to learn new jobs that will increase marketable skills. A mobile crew is a business that generates employment for its crew members by selling a service. Staff provide training and supervision after obtaining work contracts. Staff and other employees without disabilities work side by side as coworkers of crewmembers with disabilities. Staff responsibilities in a mobile work crew include all the training and continuous supervision responsibilities of an enclave in industry, plus the additional tasks associated with marketing and managing a small business.

A mobile work crew meets the minimum standards for supported employment if each crew consists of no more than eight persons with disabilities and some without disabilities, if the crewmembers work for pay at least 20 hours per week, and if ongoing publicly funded support is provided for the crewmembers. A single-purpose organization may be formed to manage one or several crews, depending upon the amount of work available in the area, or a larger organization may choose to manage work crews as one of its programs.

The mobility of the crew, together with its grouping of persons with disabilities, creates barriers to the integration objectives of supported employment. In many communities, the effort required to overcome these barriers is balanced by the advantages of the approach in generating work opportunities and providing continuous and reliable ongoing support. A mobile crew approach allows an organization to "package" jobs from a number of smaller, dispersed tasks that need to be done in a community, and is thus worth considering in rural areas with few jobs.

Other Small Businesses

In *small business* approaches other than mobile crews, organizations provide supported employment to persons with disabilities by selling products or services. This approach is familiar because of its similarity to sheltered workshop strategies, but must be structured very differently from many sheltered workshops in order to meet the size and integration requirements of supported employment.

In any small business approach, the organization is responsible for generating enough work to provide paid employment opportunities, and for providing training and ongoing support to its employees with disabilities. Organization staff sell services or products either to other companies or to individual customers. The small business may subcontract with industry for providing products or services, or manufacture its own product for sale in a retail or wholesale market (e.g., a bakery). The work performed to meet the sales objectives provides the employment opportunity for persons with disabilities. Once work is created through successful sales, staff are responsible for organizing the work for performance, and providing training and supervision to meet work quality and rate requirements.

Having a stationary workplace where even a few people with disabilities work together creates extremely difficult obstacles to integration. Consequently, the strategies used to overcome those obstacles are critical components of any successful small business approach. Integration may be supported by employing a mixed workforce of persons with and without disabilities, by organizing work in a manner that fosters customer contact, and by ensuring the use of community resources in the vicinity of the workplace.

Small business models typically receive ongoing service funding from public agencies, and in return guarantee that daily supervision and activities will be provided whether or not work is available. A critical problem faced by small business approaches to supported employment, and shared by sheltered workshops, is generating enough work to maintain paid employment at levels that qualify as supported employment. The requirement that supported employment groups consist of no more than eight persons with disabilities and include some coworkers without disabilities makes it especially necessary that a small business approach be commercially successful. The company must be able to generate enough work to sustain all employees (both with and without disabilities), and do the work efficiently, so that public funding is not used to support commercial costs.

PERSONNEL AND ENTREPRENEURIAL MODELS

Another perspective for considering various supported employment approaches is provided by distinguishing between *personnel* and *entrepreneurial* models. Some supported employment organizations function by helping persons with disabilities locate and do jobs as employees in *other* companies. These are called personnel models, because the major tasks of the support organizations resemble those done by personnel placement agencies and the personnel departments of larger companies. In personnel approaches, the individual with a disability is often an employee of the community business rather than the support organization.

On the other hand, entrepreneurial models combine the functions of the support organization and the employer. These programs resemble any other small business engaged in selling services and products. It is through this entrepreneurial effort that the capacity is developed to offer employment to persons with disabilities.

Most supported jobs and enclave approaches typically fall within the personnel category, whereas most crews and small businesses are entrepreneurial. Exceptions exist. Some enclaves are managed as off-site components of workshop programs, and their operation treats the work as simply another contribution to the larger program's entrepreneurial goals. Similarly, mobile crews, which normally operate as small businesses, could function as personnel models. For example, a crew employed by a city parks department which receives training and assistance from a support organization might have the personnel characteristics of an enclave. Distinguishing between personnel and entrepreneurial models is particularly useful in a discussion of the planning and management of supported employment programs. Whereas both models must provide job analysis, training, and support, the added responsibility for operating a successful small business may make entrepreneurial models more complex and difficult to establish and operate effectively. Similarities and differences in planning and operating personnel and entrepreneurial supported employment programs are discussed in later chapters.

Each of the program approaches described so far is a strategy that has been used successfully in communities to provide supported employment. It is not the approach, however, that defines a program as supported employment. Many programs that do not provide supported employment are very similar to the four basic approaches just described. The issue in determining whether supported employment exists is not the use of a particular approach, but the capacity of a program to meet the requirements of *paid, integrated employment, with support.*

For example, many programs operate much like supported jobs, placing and training persons with disabilities in individual jobs. Those that receive public funding for the initial, intensive training, but not for continuing support, are *not* supported employment programs under the current federal definition. Such programs may produce valued outcomes for persons with disabilities, but should be labeled competitive employment programs. Programs that place and train people with disabilities in unpaid positions also do not match the definition of supported employment, although these positions may produce desirable opportunities for integration or lead to future supported employment.

Similarly, programs employing persons with disabilities in small groups in crews, enclaves, or small businesses qualify as supported employment only if: 1) sufficient work is available for each employee to work 20 or more hours per week, 2) eight or fewer people with disabilities work together, and 3) persons without disabilities who are not paid caregivers are actually present in the workplace. Many small group programs exist today that are funded as time-limited preparation programs intended to prepare persons with disabilities for positions elsewhere. Although they address an important need, these programs do not meet the definition of supported employment.

ORGANIZATIONAL ACCOMPLISHMENTS
FOR SUPPORTED EMPLOYMENT

Immediately apparent in the preceding program descriptions is the diversity of approaches that can be used to provide supported employment. Unlike so many public services that prescribe both what is to be done and exactly how local programs are to do it, the federal supported employment initiatives offer a framework for rich and varied program strategies that accomplish the goal of employing persons with severe disabilities. Indeed, there are many ways of achieving the dual goals of paid employment and integration with ongoing public support. The approaches described in the previous section represent the most widely used categories today, but they are by no means exhaustive. The potential range of supported employment options is limited only by the economic realities of a community and the creativity of program developers. In any given community, more than one option will likely be needed to meet the varying needs of the individuals who require employment support.

This diversity of supported employment options offers both an opportunity and a challenge. By defining supported employment as it has, the federal government has created an opportunity for program developers to match local needs and resources by designing unique local programs. A community can fit local program options to the specific support needs of identified individuals, adapt program location, staffing, and business specialization to the local job market, and arrange support approaches that fit local budgetary constraints and meet individual needs.

The challenge inherent in such a flexible definition is to maintain a coherent conceptual basis for supported employment. A conceptual framework that describes how these various program approaches are alike is needed to provide the basis for planning, initiating, funding, operating, and evaluating supported employment programs. This chapter provides a framework for an analysis of the commonalities among supported employment programs.

Organizational Accomplishments

The many program approaches in supported employment share a concern with responsibility for specified outcomes. Whatever the strategies adopted by a program, it must create both opportunity for and performance of paid work to be successful in providing supported employment. It must also provide integration with persons without disabilities and access to continuing support to maintain employment. These requirements of all supported employment programs focus on the essential outcomes of the service. Gilbert's (1978) method of analysis of organizational performance provides a useful conceptual tool for viewing these outcomes. Gilbert argues that the critical measures of performance in any organization are the results or products that remain when the task is done, rather than the procedures it uses or the behavior of its members.

There are many results or outcomes of an organization's work, some much more important than others. Gilbert distinguishes among these by defining *accomplishments* as the valued outcomes of an organization's efforts (i.e., as the subset of outcomes that the organization considers important). Accomplishments are measurable, reflecting quantity, quality, timelines, cost, or other important factors of a particular situation. Especially useful is Gilbert's process for analyzing the mission of any organization by generating a set of accomplishments that reflects all the organization's primary responsibilities. Gilbert has referred to these accomplishments as an "organizational accomplishment model" to be used as a basis for planning and managing the organization.

The notion of an organizational accomplishment model is particularly relevant to supported employment because of the focus on the valued outcomes of an organization, rather than on processes or behaviors that occur as organizations strive for these outcomes. This makes it possible to define an organizational accomplishment model for supported employment that applies across the wide variation in supported employment options. This focus on outcomes serves as the needed conceptual framework for clarifying the similarities across all supported employment approaches, and provides a foundation for program planning and management. For these reasons, it is used throughout the remainder of this book.

Organizational Accomplishments within Supported Employment

Although Gilbert's notion of accomplishments may seem complex because of its unfamiliarity to many readers, its application has exactly the opposite effect. By focusing on the accomplishments of any successful supported employment organization, it is possible to describe the complex concept of supported employment in terms of five simple things which all such organizations must do. Not surprisingly, the list of five is closely related to the requirements for supported employment discussed in the first chapter. To provide successful supported employment, an organization must: 1) create the opportunity to perform paid work, 2) see that the work is performed according to employers' requirements, 3) integrate employees with disabilities into the social and physical environment of the workplace, 4) meet the employees' ongoing support needs, and 5) maintain the organization's capacity to offer supported employment. If an organization accomplishes all five of these outcomes, it will succeed in its mission of providing supported employment. Each of the five accomplishments is elaborated in the following sections. The accomplishments are summarized in Table 2.1.

Table 2.1. Organizational accomplishment model for any supported employment approach

Accomplishments	Responsibilities	Duties
Paid employment opportunities are available.	Jobs or work contracts arranged and agreements are signed. Access to employment maintained.	Potential customers identified. Specific job/work commitments secured. Customer needs met. Customer satisfaction assessed and maintained.
Work performance meets employer requirements.	Jobs and tasks organized for performance.	Systems established for performing and monitoring work.

(continued)

Table 2.1. *(continued)*

Accomplishments	Responsibilities	Duties
	Work performed.	Job tasks designed and analyzed for individual performance.
		Employees trained to perform each job task.
		Job performance maintained.
Employees are integrated.	Integration opportunities available and identified.	Social and physical integration opportunities identified.
	Integration of employees maintained.	Normal routine and tasks designed to promote integration.
		Resources to support integration are identified and arranged.
		Integration activities taught.
		Integration outcomes tracked.
Ongoing support needs are met.	Employees with disabilities hired.	Employees screened and selected.
	Employee services delivered.	Individual service needs assessed.
	Employee services maintained.	Individual service plans developed.
		Support activities occur and are adjusted over time.
		Support services' impact is monitored and summarized.
Organization's capacity is maintained.	Organization's capacity to deliver support established.	Support organization set up.
	Capacity to deliver support maintained over time.	Operating policies and procedures established.
		External agency requirements met.
		Organization managed.
		Financial stability established.

Accomplishment 1: Paid Employment Opportunities Are Available Since supported employment does not exist without employment, one thing an organization must do is create the opportunity for individuals to work. A supported employment organization may develop paid work opportunities by securing job placements in regular businesses or by creating opportunities through operation of a business that hires persons with severe disabilities. Depending on the program approach used, this accomplishment involves activities such as identifying potential employers, making sales calls to develop job or contract opportunities, negotiating job commitments and logistics, maintaining ongoing contact with the employer to ensure that his or her needs are met, and monitoring changes in labor market conditions.

Whatever strategy is used to create the work opportunity, the required accomplishment is the same: individuals with severe disabilities will have access to paid employment opportunities. Indicators of an organization's success at achieving this accomplishment can be measured by the number of hours per month an individual does paid work and the potential earnings on the jobs that are available, as well as the characteristics of the jobs themselves.

Accomplishment 2: Work Performance Meets Employer Requirements This second accomplishment is attained when employees with disabilities perform the available work, meeting all quality, rate, and other specifications of the employer, and earn wages for that work. It is unlikely that job opportunities will result in the anticipated wages, benefits, and security normally expected of jobs if this accomplishment is not met. The support organization will achieve this accomplishment by engaging in such activities as analyzing the job tasks and requirements, teaching the required skills to employees, making adaptations in the work setting, redesigning job responsibilities, developing performance and work-flow systems, procuring necessary equipment, and designing quality assurance procedures. The difference between entrepreneurial and personnel models is largely one of the scope of tasks performed to reach this accomplishment. The task within a personnel approach is to adapt to the company's performance systems and procedures, generally with few modifications to these systems. Consequently, the focus in these approaches is on the training and supervision procedures needed to help an employee with a disability learn and do the job. For entrepreneurial models, this accomplishment typically entails creating and managing such systems as work flow, job design, equipment utilization, quality assurance, and shipping, in addition to the training, engineering, and supervision procedures used to increase each individual's performance.

The success of an organization in attaining this accomplishment is usually measured by the quality and quantity of work performed. Because of regulations that link productivity with earnings, at least at lower wage levels, a useful indicator for this accomplishment is the compensation received by workers with disabilities. Indicators such as average monthly wages, or wages plus benefits, are useful summary measures of the extent to which an organization ensures that work requirements are being met.

Accomplishment 3: Employees Are Integrated   The integration that accompanies supported employment encompasses both interactions with persons without disabilities in and around the workplace, and the regular use of other community environments and resources. To achieve this, an organization offering supported employment engages in such tasks as evaluating prospective job sites to determine the potential for social and physical integration, analyzing integration opportunities in selected jobs, teaching individuals the skills required to take advantage of those opportunities, helping others in the workplace interact comfortably with employees with disabilities, arranging normal schedules and methods of transportation, and fostering activities with fellow employees outside of work.

The success of a supported employment organization in creating integration for employees with disabilities is difficult to measure, although many researchers and program developers are addressing this problem. Measures for this accomplishment should assess the quality and expansion of an individual's social network as a result of employment, and the kinds of community-integrated activities in which the individual participates.

Accomplishment 4: Ongoing Support Needs Are Met   This accomplishment involves identifying support needs and providing the required level of support to maintain an individual's success in the workplace. Typical duties include screening, selecting, and hiring persons with disabilities to insure that persons are employed in the least restrictive and most appropriate job possible, completing individual habilitation planning cycles, evaluating performance to identify support needs, and enlisting assistance from other service providers, the individual's family, and others. If individual support needs are not met, any advances in job performance and integration are likely to be limited. Job losses, breaks between periods of employment, and unnecessary disruptions in employment all may result from the failure to meet ongoing support needs.

An organization's success at meeting ongoing support needs can be measured by the tenure or job maintenance of employees with disabilities. It may also be helpful in some circumstances to use measures of the extent to which individual plan objectives are met, as a related index.

Accomplishment 5: Organizational Capacity Is Maintained Maintenance of organizational capacity encompasses the responsibilities and duties related to establishing and sustaining an organizational structure for providing supported employment. Even if all other accomplishments are achieved in an exemplary fashion, the ongoing provision of employment with ongoing support depends on the stability and viability of the organization providing the support. Establishing and maintaining the support organization involves such tasks as requesting funds from public agencies; planning budgets; recruiting, training, and supervising staff; and activities of the agency's board of directors. These accomplishments can be assessed by many measures, including evaluation of the extent to which the organization meets the expectations of public funders for effectiveness, efficiency of operation, and compliance with regulations.

The organizational accomplishment model for supported employment provides a framework for planning, staffing, managing, and evaluating supported employment programs. The five accomplishments serve to organize tasks for planning and establishing organizations, to help identify problems that require management attention, to structure measures for program evaluation, and to identify staff competencies for training programs. As these topics are discussed in the remainder of the book, the five accomplishments will be used repeatedly to structure both the discussion of issues and the recommendations for program developers and managers.

SUMMARY

Many program approaches meet the requirements for supported employment. Four leading approaches are: 1) individual placements in jobs, where initial, on-site, intensive training is followed by periodic continuing support, 2) small enclaves in large enterprises, in which initial training and ongoing support are provided by a trained on-site supervisor, 3) work crews that function as distinct businesses but work in regular settings, and 4) other small enterprises that employ persons with and without disabilities. These approaches are often combined or varied. Many other untried strategies seem reasonable as well. Supported employment is a flexible concept that allows for considerable adaptation to local service needs, employment opportunities, and service funding levels. Most communities will probably require more than one approach to meet all service needs, given the unique constraints faced within each community.

What is common to all these approaches to supported employment is the need to provide paid employment in integrated settings to persons with severe disabilities, while providing ongoing support. To accomplish this, each of the many alternative approaches must do five things: 1) create the opportunity for persons with severe disabilities to do paid work, 2) ensure that performance of that work meets requirements, 3) integrate workers into the social life as well as the physical environment of the workplace and its surroundings, 4) meet individual needs for ongoing support, and 5) maintain a viable support organization. These five requirements of all supported employment organizations provide a framework that is used throughout this book to describe the issues and tasks required for community implementation of supported employment.

REFERENCE

Gilbert, T. F. (1978). *Human competence: Engineering worthy performance.* New York: McGraw-Hill.

_ Chapter 3 _____

Planning
a Supported
Employment
Program

This chapter describes a process for planning a supported employment program. Planning involves collecting information and making decisions that result in a plan or proposal to establish a particular supported employment program. The planning phase begins when an individual or group becomes sufficiently committed to development of a supported employment option that inquiries into its feasibility begin. For the purposes of this chapter, the planning phase is completed when a proposal for starting a supported employment program is prepared.

Planning requires three things: 1) forming a planning group for collecting information and making decisions, 2) collecting information on service needs, employment opportunities, and public agencies in the community, and 3) preparing the program proposal. This chapter highlights the major issues and activities of each of these three aspects of the planning process.

FORMING THE PLANNING GROUP

The role of the planning group is to review the service need for supported employment in the community, the public resources and constraints (or barriers) that are present, and the type of work most likely to result in integrated, paid employment. The planning group may take many forms, depending on the impetus for development. Frequently communities have an agency, or a position within an agency, that has responsibility for needs identification and program development. Just as frequently, innovation and new program development are initiated by parent and consumer advocate groups and service providers. In most communities, the planning group will be formed *ad hoc*, and will require organization and the development of shared values and goals.

Organize the Planning Group

The planning group should have broad community representation. It should consist of individuals who have time, energy, and the ability to manage and perform the array of necessary planning activities. In a community in the Pacific Northwest, for example, a small group began meeting to discuss the lack of employment opportunities for community residents with severe disabilities. The group initially consisted of family members and advocates of persons with disabilities, but soon included a member of the business community and professionals in vocational services. County funding personnel and other service providers were included after the need for additional employment opportunities was established and ideas were generated about possible solutions. In this situation, unpaid volunteers who were committed to creating employment opportunities for local citizens with severe disabilities were the driving force in the planning process.

In another community, a planning group was initially organized by a county employee whose job was to promote the development of supported employment. This resource developer began by contacting existing service providers and advocacy organizations, seeking individuals who were interested in the problem and willing to commit time, energy, and skills to such an enterprise. Over a few months, a small group emerged that began the process of determining local need and how supported employment would be established in the community.

The most successful plannning groups are broadly representative of their communities. They should include interested citizens who collectively bring knowledge of the business community, experience relating to supported employment, and understanding of consumer advocacy issues. Such groups should also include representatives of funding or regulatory agencies. Members should collectively bring to the group information about the community, experience within the community, and energy that will be valuable in planning and start-up activities.

Develop Shared Values and a Sense of Mission

Before embarking on the many tasks associated with establishing a supported employment option, the planning group must reach agreement on the values that bring the group together, and what it seeks to accomplish. To help ensure that the group functions successfully during planning, there must be agreement on the value of paid and integrated employment for individuals with severe disabilities. Once broad objectives have been defined, creative solutions can be developed. To a large extent, the later success of the employment option will depend on the ability of the planning group to investigate the feasibility of supported employment and select the particular approach, organizational structure, and work base for the program. It might be helpful for the group to visit model programs, read program descriptions, and contact other community groups as a means of building consensus on program goals.

COLLECTING PLANNING INFORMATION

Beginning the planning process by collecting information helps the planning group make informed decisions about the kind of program to be developed. Collecting information also provides the factual basis for a program proposal, and helps in defining strategies for accomplishing the start-up tasks described in Chapter 4. Figure 3.1 provides a preliminary list of questions to guide initial efforts to collect information. The list will be supplemented in most communities as the initial answers raise additional questions. Figure 3.1 is designed as a worksheet to help a planning group keep a written log of acquired information. The questions listed in Figure 3.1 are discussed in the following sections. The purpose of the investigation is to obtain enough relevant data on resources and barriers to permit informed decisions by the planning group.

Are There Individuals in the Community Who Could Benefit from a Supported Employment Program?

Once a planning group with a shared mission is formed, the group should determine more precisely the extent of the need for supported employment in its community. The number of individuals requiring services and the nature and severity of their disabilities will affect the type of option created. Many communities have lengthy waiting lists of people not currently served by existing adult programs. Secondary school students approaching the last years of their entitlement to education are being added to these waiting lists. Still others are being served in institutions or are underemployed in other day programs. The total service needs in communities are rapidly expanding as more service providers and states begin to target day programs for conversion to supported employment. The combined service needs

Information for decisions	Planning group record
Are there individuals who could benefit from supported employment in the community? How many?	
Would they be served adequately by simple expansion of existing services?	
What work opportunity exists in the community?	
What program approach best fits service need, work opportunity, and availability?	
How much money will the organization need to start up and operate?	
What funds are available for ongoing support?	
Are funds available for initial start-up costs for a new project?	
If not, is there volunteer commitment sufficient to start the organization?	
Is there sufficient community support for an active board of directors?	

Figure 3.1. Planning worksheet for initial information gathering.

within a community are thus likely to be indicative of a diverse group of individuals with extremely different levels of disability, and therefore, highly varied needs for support. During the initial phase of planning, therefore, it is important to identify the total service need. Data on the community's population of adults with disabilities will facilitate the decision on the best type of program for the community.

Finding the best program involves learning how many persons who would benefit from supported employment are not receiving services, how many will complete public school programs each year, and how many are served in segregated or nonvocational services who would be better off in a supported employment program. These individuals should be described as thoroughly as possible in terms of interests and abilities, previous programs, and work histories. Planning groups must be optimistic about individual abilities when deciding if supported employment is the best option for an individual. Historically, there has been a tendency to provide a more restrictive environment than is appropriate. The principle of providing the *least restrictive environment* must be considered when designing systems for providing employment support to individuals.

Good sources of relevant information include the local office that manages services for people with developmental disabilities, the local Association for Retarded Citizens, other parent and advocacy groups, existing day and employment programs, and local school districts. This information should include a count of individuals in each category of disability, information on their disabilities and anticipated support needs. If a substantial number of individuals have very severe disabilities that are expected to create social and work performance problems, the planning group will need to focus its attention on developing an employment option in which the continuous presence of a skilled trainer and supervisor may be provided. Alternatively, a less restrictive employment option must be designed if service priorities are indicated for individuals with milder disabilities.

How Well Do Existing Services Address the Need for Supported Employment?

A community must have a range of employment options that offer varying degrees of job support, different working conditions, and different types of work. Investigating the types of services already available will be helpful in designing programs that offer choices to individuals. Competition between service organizations may be created in some communities. Competition may be good for communities that have justified having only one service-providing organization on the basis of a disinclination to duplicate services. Broad objectives to create jobs for previously underemployed adults with severe disabilities may be more readily met when more than one organization is working to create an array of opportunities. Information on community services is usually readily available from the state or local office of developmental disabilities or rehabilitation. Other sources include associations such as the Association for Retarded Citizens, mental health agencies, and service providers. Planners should meet with local advocacy and consumer groups to gauge their concerns or support for the local development of supported employment.

It may be that a simple expansion of existing services would be the most effective and cost-beneficial means of employing those identified as requiring services. The planning group should evaluate the performance of organizations offering supported employment. If an organization is effectively providing supported employment, other questions, such as the following, should be discussed: How would expansion of an existing service be likely to affect the quality of the program? How might the intended innovation be different from current operations, or cause changes in the organization? Is the organization interested in expansion?

Is There Enough Community Backing to Sustain a Supported Employment Program?

A new program will need several things from the community to be successful, particularly qualified and active board members, job opportunities, referrals, and funding. The program developers must also be aware of regulatory and other obstacles that might reduce the likelihood of success, even within a supportive community.

The feasibility of beginning supported employment is also a matter of determining whether adequate funding is available. Two major components of funding require attention: the level of ongoing public support available from service fees or operating grants, and start-up or capital funding. Various supported employment approaches require differing levels of both funding and flexibility in the funding mechanism.

Entrepreneurial programs, such as a work crew or bakery, generally will require more start-up funding than personnel approaches. Entrepreneurial programs require capitalization to acquire needed equipment and to establish initial business operations. Ongoing funding levels may vary depending on how much ongoing support is provided and the success of the business. Personnel programs need start-up monies, for example, to purchase training to meet the high cost of individualized placement or to purchase adaptive equipment for use in an enclave setting. A personnel services program, such as supported jobs, requires greater funding flexibility. This allows sequential placement over time, and retraining when job duties change or jobs are lost.

Funding issues are among the most difficult to assess and resolve during this early planning stage. Planners should first determine the amount available for start-up and ongoing operations, and compare this with information gathered from other service providers on the costs of various supported employment approaches.

Identify Support in the Responsible Public Agency The first step in investigating public resources and constraints involves identifying the public agency that would have regulatory and financial responsibility for the program, should it be established. This is likely to be the state department of vocational rehabilitation, the department of mental health, or the developmental disabilities office. More than one agency may be involved in some situations.

For each agency, one should determine the extent to which the agency as a whole, or key individuals within the agency, have an interest in the objectives of the planning group. For example, ask if the agency has a priority to establish supported employment options for people with severe handicaps. Identify the individuals within the agency responsible for supported employment. Obtain and review any planning documents that the agency has developed relating to supported employment or services for people with severe disabilities. Hold discussions with representatives to determine how much interest, support, or opposition can be expected from these agencies during the planning and implementation of the supported employment option.

Identify Regulatory or Policy Constraints Supported employment is a relatively new priority for individuals with severe handicaps. Many public agencies still maintain policies and regulations concerning nonvocational day activity programs that interfere with the establishment of supported employment. Some states have policies or program guidelines limiting the time spent in vocational activity, or requiring specific nonvocational training or leisure activities. These prevent, or at least inhibit, supported employment. These issues must be identified early in the planning stage so that barriers to employment may be removed. Program developers must find out how willing the appropriate agencies are to change regulations or policies that block implementation of supported employment. At a minimum, program developers must gauge willingness of the agencies to waive the regulations in question.

Determine the Support of Key Individuals Opposition or support from key individuals or groups will affect the development of supported employment. Identify supporters from local businesses, advocacy groups, and others likely to be important to the success of the program. If possible, identify who opposes the program, and why. This will facilitate discussion, persuasion, and consensus-building. Some cases in point are provided by several programs that subcontract work from large companies. The program developers had expressed concerns that they might lose their subcontracts when the large companies initiated enclaves. Planning meetings between program developers and the companies stressed the importance of generating work for the enclaves that would be drawn from within the companies, rather than from subcontracts to organizations already employing persons with severe disabilities. As a result, the companies expressed their commitment to the subcontracted work, and the program developers agreed to support the enclave.

Determine the Potential for Getting Qualified Staff The success of a service program depends largely on the abilities of the management and staff, regardless of the resources available. Thus, for the supported employment option, assessing a community's potential to attract skilled personnel is an important aspect of the feasibility and planning stage. Factors affecting recruiting include salary levels and benefits, the size and attractiveness of the community, and the local economic climate.

Are Sufficient Business Opportunities Available?

A major part of determining the feasibility of supported employment in a community is identifying the business profile of the area. This includes the types of industries, company sizes, and the number of companies in the area. The business and industrial base of a community defines the possibilities for local employment opportunities. For example, establishing a subcontract assembly firm providing supported employment in electronics almost certainly requires a strong regional electronics industry. A mobile work crew may be set up in a rural area without a strong manufacturing base, unless existing competition in its business specialization has cornered all available work. Personnel approaches such as enclaves require one successful business large enough to support targeted work and integration outcomes for a small group of employees with disabilities.

Good business practice requires that the market need for a product or service be identified before embarkation on a new venture. The "market" is the set of all individuals and organizations who are actual and potential buyers of a product or service (Corthell & Boone, 1982). Frequently, developers of vocational services have first focused on designing the service program. Only after the developers have hired a staff, procured a building, and selected supported employment candidates, have they sought to provide work opportunities. Within supported employment the focus changes; opportunities for employment must be created before services can be delivered. Thus, it is important to identify employment opportunities during the planning phase, to

ensure that the support organization is organized to compete successfully for the available work opportunities.

To complete the process of identifying employment opportunities, the planning group should consider questions such as:

What are the alternative market opportunities?
How do these alternatives affect the supported employment objec-
tives of the company?
What are the needs of the potential customers (or, our current
customers)?
What is being done to address these needs at present?
Are changes in customer needs expected because of the economy of
the community?
Are changes anticipated in local industries?
What do labor market statistics and projections show?
What are the community economic trends?
What is the economic development focus of the community or region?
What do we know of the skills, preferences, and relevant experiences
of the people to be employed by this new venture?

Information on local and regional business and industry may come
from various sources, including state and local government offices,
personal knowledge of the area, and business associations. Two tac-
tics that have been used to gather this information are presented next.

Review Existing Economic Planning Documents Most communities, and the counties and states in which they are located, have conducted investigations that summarize relevant information on economic indicators and business needs. Community development
councils, chambers of commerce, business advisory boards, labor and
commerce offices, and economic development commissions often
have information on the number of jobs both currently available and
projected in particular industries, as well as information on specific
companies within the area and various market studies. These documents may provide the basis for selecting the type of business with
the most potential to generate jobs for individuals with severe
disabilities.

Conduct Market Surveys Market surveys may be conducted to
obtain more specific information on potential markets. A survey may
be sophisticated (and expensive), and performed by a professional organization that would determine the market for a specific product or
service. Or, it may be as simple as a review of the number of companies within an area that might use a particular product or service.
For example, an idea for a product that might be manufactured within
a small company and sold to the public would likely require a de-

tailed market analysis. In a small community without an industrial base, but with 400 motel beds and proximity to a major freeway, one would need little more than the yellow pages of the phone book to determine that a possible market exists for crews that contract to clean motel units, or for an agency that specializes in training and supporting persons with severe disabilities who work in motels. However, further information would be needed on how the motels currently had their units cleaned, whether they were satisfied with this service, and whether existing competition precluded entry into this potential market. Table 3.1 provides a list of typical questions a market survey would include, regardless of the approach being planned.

An instance of a community's use of a market survey occurred in Seattle, where a local resource developer employed by King County, working with an informal planning group, commissioned a market study. One member of the planning group had heard of a successful program in another part of the United States that employed a mobile crew of workers with and without disabilities to clean and maintain boats. Since the Seattle area is surrounded by many bodies of water—and boats—the planning group commissioned a study of the local market. A fairly brief and inexpensive market survey identified the marinas that would use such a service, the approximate number of boats requiring cleaning and maintenance, existing competition providing similar services, and other relevant information. An outline of that survey appears in Table 3.2.

Is a Supported Employment Program in This Community Feasible? The final question to be answered during the first planning

Table 3.1. Typical questions asked in market surveys

Who is the market?
 Who needs the service or product?
 What are the important characteristics of this market?
 Is its population in the vicinity?
 Is there potential to expand the market to other communities or regions?

What is the size of the market?
 How many potential customers (users of your services) are there?
 How many competitors have you for this market?
 What are the growth possibilities within this market?

What market strategy might you employ?
 How will you attract a share of the market?
 Can you reasonably compete at a price the market will bear?
 What considerations are customers using to select among competing products
  or services?
 What advantages do you offer customers?

Table 3.2. Sample contents of a boat-cleaning market survey adapted from a survey completed by Ketchum Investigations, Federal Way, King County, WA

Page

Purpose of the study...1
[Includes who conducted the survey. The purpose was to determine the feasibility of initiating a boat-cleaning service for boat owners in the Everett-Seattle-Tacoma area. This service would include employment of persons with developmental disabilities.]

Moorages..1
[Includes a count of the number of boat berths in the market area, the percentage of time these berths are being used, and areas where moorages had 100% utilization and a waiting list.]

Defining cleaning terms...1
[The types of jobs relating to boat-cleaning are defined, including bright-work cleaning, detailing, waxing, refinishing, and hull cleaning.]

Select boats and moorages for cleaning services....................2
[Defines which types of boats are primary customers for cleaning services. Also defines which moorages are most likely to generate customers.]

Statistical analysis...3
[Interviews with moorage owners and operators provide statistical information on the numbers of boats using services. Eight percent, or 600 berths, used a cleaning service.]

Cleaning services..4
[Information is provided on competition, current fees charged by competition, and dry dock facilities available.]

Marketing...5
[Marketing methods used by competition are briefly discussed, with the point that boat cleaning is not seriously marketed. Specific strategies for marketing are identified.]

Additional information..7
[People are identified who would be willing to provide technical services to help the business get started.]

Conclusion..7
[Report concludes market is sufficient to continue development of business plan. It suggests poor marketing techniques may be leading to underutilization of existing boat-cleaning services.]

Appendix...8
[Appendix lists moorages in area of survey, and companies providing cleaning services.]

phase requires a synthesis of the information collected by the planning group to this point. Perhaps more than any other planning element, the answer to the question of feasibility requires a subjective response. The planning group can gather data for informed decision-making, and in most large communities will easily identify a service need, local support, and a variety of adequate business opportunities. In these communities, a lack of public funding may be the only major factor making the program unfeasible. Conversely, the group may decide that with a relatively high unemployment rate, few service or manufacturing opportunities, and some community opposition, the availability of funding is not sufficient for them to consider the establishment of a program.

In a small, rural community, a planning group faces greater challenges in identifying qualified staff, job opportunities, and other resources required for a successful program. The problem of feasibility lies in part with the group's level of interest, effort, and creativity in finding a local solution. In recent years, the Alaska Vocational Rehabilitation and Developmental Disabilities Offices have joined efforts to address the state's problem of initiating supported employment in tiny rural communities. The purpose of these agencies' efforts is to train full- or part-time job coaches in communities where no service providers and few persons with developmental disabilities reside. The Alaskan program includes visits to job coaches from Vocational Rehabilitation counselors or the Developmental Disabilities case manager.

DEVELOPING A PROGRAM PROPOSAL

A proposal may take many different forms. It may be an internal memorandum, a formal application for funds, or a program description that precedes formal application. This section describes the decisions that need to be made to support the development of any proposal, as well as a brief overview of proposals. The focus is on the decisions that strengthen the planning effort, regardless of whether an elaborate proposal is required. Developing a proposal requires integrating information from several sources so that decisions about how the program will be structured and operated can be made.

Planning Decisions

At the end of the first planning phase, the type of work to be done and the type of supported employment structure to be created should be determined by the planning group. This involves a synthesis of the group's investigations into community service needs, public resources, and potential markets. The decisions will require integrating the information obtained from various sources to determine what type of supported employment option would best fit the community, given available resources and constraints, and given knowledge of the preferences of persons targeted for services. Each set of information provides only one piece of the puzzle to be solved by the planning group.

For example, identification of a market need only provides information on the product or service that will provide employment opportunities; planners also need to determine which organizational structure or approach to implement. For example, in California's Silicon Valley, numerous electronics firms provide evidence of opportunities for supported employment within that industry. Yet, planners still have many questions: Is an enclave feasible or warranted? Should a subcontracting business be established that will provide subassemblies to area industries? Is a personnel company that would place and train individuals with ongoing support with existing Silicon Valley manufacturers the right approach? The answers to questions like these cannot be based simply on the availability of work in the electronics industry. The decisions must consider information about existing personnel support and entrepreneurial businesses, the level of support required by the individuals for successful job performance, and constraints imposed by individual companies or the electronics industry.

The appendix to this chapter provides a detailed set of questions for the planning group and some decision-making guidelines. The actual decisions to be made in any community may require an even larger, more detailed set of information. Several of the more important planning decisions are briefly discussed next.

What Part of the Group of Potential Service Recipients Is Targeted? During the initial planning phase, information was collected by the planning group on the individuals in the community who might benefit from a supported employment program and their interests, abilities, and work histories. In most communities, the planning group may need to concentrate its efforts on only a portion of this total service need. Identification of the general group to be targeted for service is required in order to focus many of the decisions of the planning group. In one West Coast community, several parents formed a planning group to develop a vocational service for their adult children with severe autism. Although many of them had excellent manual dexterity, these individuals required intensive support to learn and maintain appropriate work behaviors, and were excluded by existing programs. Identification of this target group helped narrow the search for an appropriate employment vehicle by defining the needed support structure.

What Work Specialization Should Be Selected? During the initial planning phase, the planning group collected information on potential business and employment opportunities in the area. While developing a program proposal, the group needs to select the work specialization that will be pursued to develop employment options. This decision requires consideration of several factors. What work specialization is preferred by the target group of service recipients? Which market appears to offer the most stability or potential for expansion of work opportunities? Are sufficient capital and expertise available to enter that market? Is it reasonable to expect that the type of work targeted will provide access to tasks that may be performed by the target group?

The creation of choice within communities is also an important and often overlooked aspect of the opportunity development that should occur. For example, if a small community already has a bakery that is run by a cooperative that includes workers with severe disabilities, the value of creating choices would argue for developing a different option with different employment prospects. Similarly, a community whose only supported employment option is a company that provides individual job placements and ongoing support in food service industries should consider other types of support structures in other industry sectors (perhaps crews, manufacturing, or individual jobs outside of food service and related occupations).

What Kind of Supported Employment Approach Should Be Selected? There are many descriptions of supported employment models in print, including direct comparisons of the pros and cons of each. The most important consideration concerns the amount of support that will be required after initial skill acquisition to enable the employee to continue to meet the expectations of the workplace.

What Kind of Organization Is Required? The organizational structure should depend on the type of support the service provider is to give. A personnel organization that places individuals in competitive environments should be organized to do this effectively, with management and staff roles emphasizing identification of jobs, training and ongoing support for jobs, and necessary administrative functions. An entrepreneurial endeavor, such as a light manufacturing firm, must organize to produce its product as well as provide additional support to persons with severe disabilities. The organization will therefore include staff functions relating to production systems, such as quality assurance, marketing, and inventory management.

What Specific Goals Does the Planning Group Have for the Program? Based on previous planning information, the planning group should specify the goals it expects the program to achieve. How many individuals will be employed? How many hours per week will each be employed? What wages and benefits will employees earn? How much integration will be achieved by program participants? What support needs does the planning group intend to meet? By specifying goals for the program, the planning group will shape program direction, provide a basis for development of the program's proposal for funding, and set a standard against which to compare actual program outcomes.

What Is the Tentative Starting Date? Planning for a supported employment option requires that several diverse activities be completed about the same time. Public funding must be ready to support start-up and ongoing operations, work opportunities must be available, the individuals to be served must be selected, hiring logistics need to be completed, and a myriad of other organizational tasks must be accomplished to permit the smooth start-up of operations. When selecting a starting date, planners should be mindful of funding cycles, the amount of time needed to procure work, and the opportunity to complete other start-up tasks.

Where Should the Program Be Located? The location of the program will be determined by a variety of factors, the most important of which are the location of the identified work opportunity and factors associated with meeting the integration objectives of supported employment. In personnel support approaches, including supported jobs and enclaves, employees with disabilities will work at the actual job site of the employing or host company. *Work stations* within the company should be near where nonhandicapped employees are doing similar work, and should permit opportunities for social interaction with other employees. Location of the host company on public transportation routes and close to community facilities such as stores, restaurants, and banks will further facilitate achievement of integration objectives. Because workers with disabilities will be served at the host company's site, the offices for such personnel support organizations need not be selected with concern for integration objectives.

The planners of supported employment programs using entrepreneurial models, however, should select the program's location carefully. A central meeting place often is required for mobile crews, which may work out of a van. This meeting place should be close to public transportation, but away from other programs, to avoid the unnecessary congregation of individuals with disabilities.

Small manufacturing or retail businesses typically operate in a single location that should be selected to enhance the business image of the program and its employees. There are several strategies that are commonly used to accomplish this. For example, the program can be located away from other service providers and in an area with similar businesses. The location should offer opportunities for independent community access, to enhance on-site integration. Thus, a small electronics assembly firm may choose to locate on a bus line, in a business park that includes offices, other small manufacturing businesses, and services such as restaurants.

Developing a Program Proposal

Once the planning group has decided if it is feasible to start and operate a supported employment program, support a specific group of individuals (given funding levels), and compete in a particular market, the group may develop a program proposal.

Proposal Timelines Usually, community agencies award funds per a schedule of pre-established timelines, rather than "as proposals are received." Information relating to timelines for submitting proposals, notification of awards, and receipt of funding is critical to the timely development and submission of proposals. A group that has spent 10 months investigating and planning a new supported employment option would be devastated to discover that it missed the annual deadline for submission of proposals by 2 weeks. Thus, questions such as the following must be asked early in the planning process: Are start-up funds available? When are proposals due? Are awards made once a year, once a quarter, or on some other cycle? Does the funding agent have the flexibility to stagger funding? How long does it take to process applications? How long after notification will funds actually be released? The answer to each of these questions has drastically different implications for the planning and start-up phases of a new supported employment option.

Proposal Content The program proposal should provide information on service needs that have been addressed, organizational management structure, work specialization, types of support to be provided, integration opportunities, program goals and objectives, timelines, and a budget.

In most communities, funding agencies will request that proposals be developed in a standardized format to facilitate review. Specific proposals must meet local guidelines. However, most funding agencies will at least ask the questions included in Table 3.3.

The proposal should summarize much of the information gathered by the planning group and the decisions made by the group. A

Table 3.3. Questions typically included in requests for proposals

Introduction
Who is in the planning group that is proposing the program?
How did the group do its work?
Give a brief summary of the need, objectives, method, and request.

Problem and need
What group of individuals will benefit from the proposed program? What is their current situation?
What is the nature of these support needs?
What employment and integration outcomes are currently being achieved?
How will supported employment improve this?
Why is a new program needed (i.e., why not more of what the community already has)?
What is the rationale for the specific approach to supported employment that is proposed?

Objectives
What will happen to whom as a result of the proposed program?
Two objectives are normally important in establishing a supported employment program: The benefits to be received by service consumers, and the capacity of the community to offer supported employment to other individuals in the future.
How many people will be employed?
For how many hours?
What levels of wages and integration are expected?

Methods
What are the major steps in establishing the program?
How will the program operate during the first year?
What are the major features of this approach?
What will be the work specialization?
What types of support will be available? Provide timelines for major activities and outcomes.

Evaluation
What measures would you expect the funding agencies to use to evaluate the success of the supported employment program?

Budget
What funds will be needed, and on what timeline for start-up?
What level of funding will be required to maintain ongoing operations?
What other income sources will be used?

well-written proposal serves as a plan that guides the management of start-up activities and that provides a standard by which to evaluate the development of the supported employment option.

SUMMARY

This chapter focuses on the planning required to develop a funding proposal for starting a supported employment option. Recommendations are provided on the composition of a planning group and the questions that must be resolved before submission of a funding proposal. Guidelines for developing a program proposal are provided.

REFERENCES

Corthell, D. W., & Boone, L. (1982, June). *Marketing: An approach to placement.* Paper presented at the Ninth Institute on Rehabilitation Issues, University of Wisconsin, Stout, WI.

Mank, D. M. , Rhodes, L. E., & Bellamy, G. T. (1986). Four supported employment alternatives. In W. E. Kiernan & J. A. Stark (Eds.), *Pathways to employment for adults with developmental disabilities* (pp. 139–153). Paul H. Brookes Publishing Co.

APPENDIX

Planning group decisions: A questionnaire

A. Is it feasible to start a supported employment program in this community?

1.	Has a service need for supported employment been identified?	Yes	No
2.	Have adequate business opportunities been identified to establish a work option?	Yes	No
3.	Is expertise for planning and operating a supported employment program available?	Yes	No
4.	Have public funds to start and provide ongoing funding for a supported employment program been identified?	Yes	No

If you have answered NO to one or more of the above questions, additional investigation should be done before a proposal is developed and submitted.

B. What are the support needs of the targeted group of service recipients?

1. Will the potential service recipients require ongoing support to meet job requirements for behavior, quality, productivity, socialization or mobility?

Yes ___	No ___	Some ___
If yes, continue planning for a supported employment option.	If no, plan for the development of a transitional, competitive employment service.	If only some of the potential recipients require ongoing support, both supported employment and transitional employment services are needed.

2. What are the current and anticipated ongoing support needs of the individuals targeted for supported employment?

Support needs	Number or names of people
a. Skilled supervision and training	
continuous, intensive	_____
continuous	_____
intermittent	_____
b. Transportation support	
training to use public transportation	_____
special transportation service	_____
taxis	_____
transportation provided by the support organization	_____
other (list)	_____
_____	_____
_____	_____

c. Environmental and performance adaptation support
   to enhance mobility   _____
   to enhance accuracy or rate
     of job performance   _____
   to enhance integration   _____
   to enhance communication _____
   other (list)   _____
   _____   _____
   _____   _____

d. Individual services support
   self-management training _____
   procedures to decrease rates
    of targeted behaviors _____
   procedures to increase rates
    of targeted behaviors _____
   intrusive behavior management support to eliminate
    injurious behaviors _____
   counseling _____
   other (list) _____
   _____ _____
   _____ _____

e. Personal management support
   assistance with using
    bathrooms _____
   assistance with eating _____
   assistance with dressing _____
   assistance with menstrual
    care _____
   other (list) _____
   _____ _____
   _____ _____

f. Medical support (list)
   _____ _____
   _____ _____

g. Other (list)
   _____ _____
   _____ _____

C. What work specialization should be selected?
1. Have work specializations in supported employment options existing in the community been identified?
   Yes _____   No _____
   If yes, list:
2. Have other industries been identified that might provide opportunities for supported employment?
   Yes _____   No _____
   If yes, list:
3. What are the work interests of the targeted group of recipients?

List: _____   Number or names of people

     _____   _____

     _____   _____

     _____   _____

D. What kind of supported employment approach should be selected?
   1. Have existing approaches been identified in the community?
      Yes ____   No ____
      If yes, list:
   2. Are there alternative supported employment approaches that
      would be appropriate, given the target group and work specializa-
      tion selected?
      Yes ____   No ____
      If yes, list: If no, continue research or:
                                           1) consider expanding ex-
                                               isting service.
                                           2) consider starting an-
                                           other service using the
                                           same approach.

*Use the compiled information to select or design a personnel support or
entrepreneurial organizational approach that: 1) satisfies the identified
support needs, and 2) provides employment in the most integrated, least
restrictive alternative for each individual to be employed. Be creative and
resourceful in considering alternatives.*

E. What kind of organization is required?
   1. Is the selected approach a small business or mobile crew?
      Yes ____   No ____
      If yes, design an entrepreneurial organization.
   2. Is the selected approach supported jobs or an enclave?
      Yes ____   No ____
      If yes, design a personnel support organization.

F. What goals does the planning group have for the program?
   Has the group identified program goals in areas such as:
      number of individuals to be served?
      hours per week of employment?
      wages and benefits?
      level of integration?
      support needs to be met?

G. What is the tentative start date?
   1. Date start-up funds will be available   ____
   2. Date ongoing operational funds will be available   ____
   3. Anticipated date work opportunities will be available   ____
   4. Anticipated date individuals will be available to be hired   ____

H. Where should the program be located?
   1. Is the program a personnel-support type organization?
      Yes ____   No ____
      If yes, locate "work stations" within host company close
      to others who are performing similar work and in an area

that allows social interaction; and locate support organization office in a convenient place that projects an appropriate business image.

2. Is the program a mobile work crew?

   Yes ＿＿＿   No ＿＿＿

   If yes, locate a central meeting place/office close to public transportation.

3. Is the program a small business that will operate out of its own facility?

   Yes ＿＿＿   No ＿＿＿

   If yes, locate the program:

   a. distinctly separate from other service providers.
   b. close to public transportation.
   c. close to community resources such as stores, restaurants, and banks.
   d. in an area appropriate for that type of small business.
   e. in a building with an appropriate business image.

_____

Chapter 4

Initiating Supported Employment

This chapter is intended as a guide for community groups that have already developed a proposal for implementing a supported employment program and are in the process of getting that program started. Start-up requires coordinated timing of several tasks which program developers control only partially, at best. The process is particularly difficult because most of these tasks are one-time requirements with which few individuals have had extensive experience. Furthermore, facility at accomplishing start-up tasks may be completely unrelated to the ability to provide ongoing management of a supported employment program.

This chapter outlines the many tasks that may be required in starting a supported employment opportunity. Naturally, the great diversity among communities, funding agency requirements, procedures for case management, work specializations, and organizational approaches makes the start-up tasks for every program unique. The chapter provides a general guide to the most frequently required activities and a discussion of exceptions, where relevant.

The five major accomplishments of supported employment organizations described in Chapter 2 provide a framework for organizing the tasks required to start a program. The start-up task can best be viewed as an effort to complete the activities related to each supported employment accomplishment at about the same time. Successful start-up occurs when work opportunity, capacity to perform work, management systems and funding for the program, individuals needing ongoing service, and the opportunity for integration are all simultaneously present. The absence of any of these elements increases costs, delays program establishment, or compromises program goals.

This section lists major start-up tasks within the framework of the five accomplishments. Table 4.1 summarizes the most significant

Table 4.1. Summary of accomplishments and major start-up needs for supported employment

Accomplishments	Major start-up needs
I. Establish organizational capacity to deliver support.	A. Establish an organization to provide ongoing support. B. Obtain funding to establish and operate the program. C. Establish staffing and personnel systems. D. Establish management systems: a) financial policies and procedures b) organizational planning and evaluation.
II. Establish ongoing support services for employees with disabilities.	A. Establish selection and hiring process for individuals who will receive support. B. Complete selection of employees with disabilities. C. Complete individual service planning. D. Complete pre-employment logistics.
III. Obtain paid employment opportunities.	A. Identify prospective companies. B. Secure work commitment.
IV. Establish capacity to perform work to employer requirements.	A. Develop staff skills. B. Obtain equipment. C. Complete job design and analysis. D. Train employees.
V. Establish integration opportunities.	A. Establish opportunity for integration. B. Analyze physical and social integration opportunities.

start-up activities. Each of these is discussed briefly in the following sections.

ORGANIZATIONAL MANAGEMENT

Generally, the first activity that will be completed during the start-up phase is establishment of the organization that will deliver the support needed to sustain the employment of the targeted individuals. To establish the capacity to provide support, an organization must be developed and have funding, staff, and established operating policies and procedures. (See Table 4.2).

Establish an Organization to Operate the Program

The initial planning group should identify individuals who agree to take responsibility for forming the supported employment organization. Individuals forming the initial governing body need not have been part of the initial planning group, but must be committed to the values and goals of that first group. This governing body bears the ultimate responsibility for ensuring success in delivering paid employment within a maximally integrated setting. Many programs have started with a board of only three or four members that took on the start-up responsibilities and expanded as the organization stabilized.

Once a group with shared objectives and values has been established, it may file for incorporation and fulfill other legal requirements of a new organization. A purpose statement, articles of incorporation, and bylaws consistent with the values and objectives of supported employment must be drafted and formally approved by the board. An appropriate name must be selected that highlights the business image of the company rather than the disabilities of the people it has been organized to serve. Documents must be filed with the Internal Revenue Service to obtain an employer identification number and, if appropriate, to secure nonprofit status. Federal wage and hour certification must be obtained if any employees will be paid subminimum wages. Worker's compensation and organizational liability insurance must be obtained, as well as any required state or local licenses, permits, or certification. Specific procedures and requirements vary from community to community and state to state. A state's commerce division can help identify requirements.

Obtain Funding to Establish and Operate the Program

The typical funding agent for social service programs is the county or community government system. A thorough understanding of how this system interacts with current and potential serviceproviders is necessary in order to establish timelines and schedule activities that will ensure a smooth transition from planning through start-up of operations. During planning and proposal development, the planning group answers critical questions about the source, amount, and nature of funding available, the processes by which an organization gets access to those funds, and the timelines that must be observed. In some states and communities, existing funding mechanisms or regulations may provide barriers to implementing supported employ-

Table 4.2. Start-up checklist for establishing the organizational capacity to deliver support (Check off tasks as completed.)

Major start-up needs		Tasks	Notes
A. Establish an organization for providing ongoing support.	___1.	Complete planning activities, with resultant management commitment to program.	
	___2.	Establish board membership and size.	
	___3.	Provide orientation for new board members.	
	___4.	Select name with appropriate business image.	
	___5.	Establish formal operating procedures, including board notebooks and minutes.	
	___6.	File articles of incorporation and bylaws.	
	___7.	Meet applicable external legal requirements, e.g.:	
		—obtain employer identification number	
		—secure nonprofit status, if applicable	
		—complete applicable local and state business permit and tax requirements	
		—obtain worker's compensation and organizational liability insurance	
		—obtain wage and hour certification, if subminimum wages will be paid	
B. Obtain funding to establish and operate the program.	___1.	Identify relevant state and local funding agents, contracting procedures, timelines, and requirements.	
	___2.	Identify requirements or policies that may inhibit implementing supported employment.	
	___3.	Negotiate necessary changes in requirements or policies to facilitate the development of supported employment.	
	___4.	Develop budget for start-up and initial operations.	
	___5.	Project ongoing funding needs.	
	___6.	Submit program proposal.	
	___7.	Complete negotiations and sign contract with funding agencies.	

C. Establish staffing and personnel systems.

___ 1. Establish job descriptions and hiring procedures.
___ 2. Develop personnel policies.
___ 3. Recruit, select, and hire staff.
___ 4. Plan and provide initial staff training.
___ 5. Plan staff incentives for achieving defined job accomplishments.
___ 6. Establish staff evaluation and feedback system.

D. Establish management systems: financial policies and procedures.

___ 1. Establish financial policies and controls.
___ 2. Develop chart of accounts, books, and general ledger system.
___ 3. Arrange for bookkeeping assistance, if needed.
___ 4. Establish budgeting, financial reporting, and budget comparison system.
___ 5. Establish payroll system.
___ 6. Establish petty cash system.
___ 7. Establish bank accounts, including reserve accounts.
___ 8. Set up invoicing procedures, including billing procedures to funders.
___ 9. Develop specific cash flow projection and arrange to meet cash flow needs (including credit line if needed).

E. Establish management systems: organizational planning and evaluation.

___ 1. Develop business plan.
___ 2. Define format for reviewing annual and long-term objectives.
___ 3. Define organization's information system, feedback loops, and format for reporting organizational outcomes.
___ 4. Define format for meetings with staff.
___ 5. Define format for reporting to the board.

ment. The nature of supported employment—with its emphasis on paid employment, integration, and finding work opportunities before delivering service—requires flexible funding levels, timelines, and requirements to permit creative solutions to employment problems. The role of a planning group, therefore, may include identifying barriers to supported employment in public policy and procedures, and negotiating changes or exceptions to permit program development.

Before start-up, the organization must also find enough funds to meet both start-up and ongoing operational needs. New supported employment organizations require start-up funds for covering many of the one-time costs of beginning operations, such as those related to higher staffing levels when workers are first employed, office space renovations for a personnel support organization or mobile crew, renovations of a manufacturing space and for a facility-based small business, accounting or legal fees for establishing the organization, and furnishings and equipment. Start-up capital may be particularly important in establishing one of the entrepreneurial approaches to supported employment. Unfortunately, programs are initiated too often with little or none of the capital needed to make the business successful. When available, start-up funds are usually designated for initial funding of basic staff and operating costs, and a minimal amount of equipment. By contrast, few private sector enterprises start without enough capital to make success possible. Few private sector businesses assume that they will break even—much less make a profit— in their first years of operation. Yet, social service programs are frequently expected to do this. The result for programs without adequate start-up capital is often failure to reach objectives.

The amount of capital required should be related to the type of business being established. One would not start a restaurant with only several thousand dollars to furnish and equip the site. A personnel support business would not require as much start-up equipment as an injection-molding firm, but might have higher initial training and support costs. An enclave within a large company may have the advantage of access to company-furnished equipment, or, as a condition of establishing the enclave, may have to purchase additional equipment for use by enclave employees because of their lower productivity levels. Some host companies may choose to absorb these costs. However, extra equipment and personnel expenses resulting from low productivity can be justifiably considered part of the public costs for establishing an enclave. In planning for start-up funds, therefore, personnel support organizations such as enclaves must consider not only the obvious direct costs of start-up, but also the hidden costs borne by the company that might require payment from public funds.

Expecting business to assume all these costs may discourage business participation in supported employment.

Besides its needs for initial capital, the organization must identify sources of continuing funding. In some situations, such sources will not be the same ones that made start-up possible. In one state, vocational programs are often started with 12- to 18-month program development funding available through developmental disabilities regional centers. Before this start-up period ends, the organization must apply for ongoing support funds, which may be requested from the same office or from the vocational rehabilitation agency, depending on the nature of the program. Programs started with development funds but that do not meet the priorities or requirements for ongoing funding by either agency risk termination when the start-up funding period ends.

The amount of available start-up and ongoing operational funds varies greatly from state to state and community to community. Communities may award funds to service providers by predetermining an amount of money that will be paid per person receiving services during a time period. Levels may vary depending on the type of service provided (e.g., a work activity center service may be paid at a different rate from a supported employment service), the level of disabilities served (e.g., greater funding may be available for individuals who present seriously challenging behaviors or require significant personal assistance), or the "source" of the individuals employed (e.g., a community waiting list or institution). Requests from new service providers for funding must not exceed these predetermined levels. In this case, the question facing the governing board becomes: "Can we provide the level of support necessary, and compete in the targeted market, given this pre-determined level of funding?"

Other communities award funds based on the proposals received. A request for proposals is released that broadly defines the type of service needed and, often, the maximum funds available. Providers respond by submitting a proposal that includes objectives, a plan for how services will be provided, and a budget for implementing the plan. The funding agent's decision as to which proposals will be funded, and at what levels, is based on the quality and quantity of proposals received, costs, and availability of funds. This approach to dispersing public support funds permits wider flexibility in choosing types of organizations and support mechanisms. A sample of the questions asked in requests for proposals is included in Chapter 3. Funding agencies may respond to a proposal by suggesting changes in the start-up or operating plan, and, more likely, by offering less funding than requested. It is important that the board of directors or planning group clearly understand any changes requested or required by the funding agent, and consider the impact of these changes on organizational objectives. Significant differences between anticipated funding levels and the estimated minimum funds required must be negotiated before a contract is signed.

Establish Staffing and Personnel Systems

The challenge facing companies engaged in supported employment is to retain personnel with both the skills required for successful operation of the business providing the employment opportunity and the skills to provide support to the employees. The degree to which business and service roles are emphasized or combined within a single person's job responsibility depends on the type of supported employment option being created and the size of the company. In general, small, entrepreneurial approaches require development of an organization whose staff is selected, organized, and trained to provide all functions. The development of enclaves within industry allows a much greater specialization in the effective provision of job support to individuals with disabilities. In such an approach, many routine tasks are retained by the larger, for-profit business. Therefore, the range of staff skills and training required is less than in entrepreneurial approaches. Chapter 11 presents a set of staff competencies for implementing supported employment.

For a new organization, the first task in establishing staffing and personnel systems is to develop a job description and vacancy announcement for the organization's management position. The manager must have knowledge and skills across the full range of supported employment competencies, including the type of work to be performed. This breadth is required for three reasons: 1) during start-up, the manager must be able to complete a variety of tasks with few staff; 2) the manager must be able to train new staff, troubleshoot and evaluate staff performance for all supported employment competencies; and 3) knowledge of, and at least some involvement in, all aspects of operations ensure both a good model for other staff and quality control of staff performance.

Once the manager has been hired, the board of directors may delegate responsibility for developing job descriptions for other staff, establishing formal hiring procedures, drafting other personnel policies and procedures, and hiring. Personnel policies and procedures should describe both the benefits and conditions of employment. They should include hiring conditions, employee orientation provisions, grievance procedures, employee behavior policies, termination policies and procedures, sick leave, vacation benefits, and other topics typically covered by the personnel policies of a business. Policies and procedures must be developed that apply to both employees with disabilities and employees with no apparent handicaps. In most cases, one policy may apply to both types of employees. Supported employment programs using personnel support strategies may require personnel policies and procedures that recognize that some support organization "employees" actually may be employed directly by the host company.

When staff are hired, the organization should provide initial orientation and training to ensure that new staff support the mission and objectives of the organization and possess sufficient knowledge and skills to do their jobs. At this point, the organization may also establish an evaluation and feedback system for staff performance, and plan incentives to encourage staff members to achieve defined job objectives. Staff evaluation, feedback, and incentives are discussed further in Chapter 11.

Establish Other Management Systems

Once initial staff have been hired, other management systems can be developed. Policies and procedures must be established concerning the remaining traditional management functions of planning, budgeting, operating, and controlling. Many possible systems exist, but those actually chosen for implementation should meet the dual criteria that they be appropriate to the type of business to be operated and the support provided.

A new organization must give particularly careful attention to the establishment of financial policies and procedures. Controls must be designed to give adequate protection to the fiscal assets of the organization. In small business, both early survival and prosperity during developing stages depend on effective financial planning and control. For entrepreneurial firms, a chart of accounts and a bookkeeping system must be established that permit separation of commercial and habilitative costs, and provide adequate financial information for decision-making. The authors often recommend that new organizations hire an accountant as a consultant to review, if not develop, the company's accounting system. Entrepreneurial firms maintaining inventories for manufacturing goods or with substantial equipment assets must make sure that inventory, depreciation, and bad debt accounts are established and used properly so that financial reports will accurately reflect the business's true worth.

For proper business management, timely interim financial reports are needed in addition to those prepared at the end of each financial year. During program start-up, the board and management must define what financial reports will be needed and how often. An organization that has few funds to manage or little variability in expenses may require no more than a quarterly income statement and balance sheet. Organizations facing greater risks may require additional reports, such as a cash flow statement or statement of changes in financial position. These reports may be required on a monthly basis.

Other start-up tasks relating to financial management include establishing a payroll system, a petty cash system, bank accounts, and invoicing procedures. The organization must determine how funds will be transferred to the program from the funder. This may require, for example, monthly billing for reimbursement of actual costs, or arranging block grant payments at the start of each quarter. At start-up, management must also carefully review cash flow needs. When funding agencies provide funds only as a reimbursement of actual expenses, the organization must arrange for a line of credit or other means of meeting immediate cash needs. Start-up represents a critical time in the financial life of the organization. Careful attention must be given to financial systems to ensure that they will meet the needs of the developing organization.

Establishing management systems also includes developing organizational planning and evaluation. A business plan that presents the organization's strategies for achieving its mission and a mechanism for reviewing performance against that plan are needed. An information system for collecting data, organizing it for decision-making, and providing feedback must be established. Effective staff meetings to review responsibilities and accomplishments are needed, as well as formats for reporting organizational outcomes to the board, funders and others. Management systems for planning and evaluation are discussed more fully in Chapter 5.

ONGOING SUPPORT FOR EMPLOYEES

During start-up, the activities associated with meeting an individual's service needs involve establishing processes for selecting employees with disabilities, the actual selection of employees, individual planning, and completing the logistics required for the individual to begin work. Table 4.3 summarizes these activities. The most important initial consideration is to ensure that individual service needs will likely be met by the employment options and support that is to be provided by the program.

Establish the Hiring Process and Select Employees

Policies and procedures must be established to guide staff's selection of individuals with disabilities. The support organization must

Table 4.3. Start-up checklist for establishing ongoing support services for employees (Check off tasks as completed.)

Major start-up needs	Tasks	Notes
A. Establish selection and hiring process for individuals who will receive support.	___ 1. Develop written policies and procedures for hiring, including selection process and criteria. ___ 2. Develop application format. ___ 3. Develop checklist for selection and hiring process (including pre-employment logistics. ___ 4. Determine documentation requirements for screening, selecting, matching, and completing pre-employment tasks. ___ 5. Identify transition process for individuals still in school.	
B. Complete selection of employees with disabilities.	___ 1. Obtain and prescreen referrals of qualified applicants. ___ 2. Select individuals and match with work opportunities. ___ 3. Establish individual files, maintaining documentation of process and decisions.	
C. Complete individual service planning.	___ 1. Identify advocates, individual planning team; coordinate with team. ___ 2. Schedule first individual planning meetings. ___ 3. Assess potential needs. ___ 4. Conduct individual planning meetings and develop plans. ___ 5. Develop transition plans for individuals still in high school. ___ 6. Maintain file documentation of assessments and individual plans.	

(continued)

67

Table 4.3. *(continued)*

Major start-up needs	Tasks	Notes
D. Complete pre-employment logistics.	1. Determine logistical tasks, timelines, and responsibilities.	
	2. Provide orientation to prospective employee, family, advocates, and home provider.	
	3. Notify prospective employee of personnel policies and fringe benefits (e.g., worker's compensation, health benefits, vacation and holiday benefits.)	
	4. Complete case management tasks.	
	5. Complete Social Security forms, if necessary.	
	6. Complete tax withholding forms, if necessary.	
	7. Complete transportation plans; initiate training as needed.	
	8. Maintain documentation in individual files.	
	9. Establish start date.	

clearly understand whom the organization is intended to serve, in order to assist case managers in referring individuals for whom this long-term employment option is designed. It is important to determine which behavioral and training needs can be addressed adequately, and which cannot. Because not all supported employment options are appropriate for all persons with severe disabilities, it is important to establish and make public the policies, procedures, and criteria that the business will use in selecting employees. Selection criteria should be established that ensure that the selected individuals require the level of support that will be provided. Employment in a setting that is organized to provide more support than is needed by an individual is overly restrictive. It also precludes employing an individual in that position who does require the level of available support. Lengthy community waiting lists, anxious parents of students nearing the completion of school, and deinstitutionalization mandates may create pressures on new supported employment options to include individuals for whom a transitional employment service would be more appropriate.

The objective of developing a screening and selection process is to assure that the needs, skills, and preferences of each individual are noted and matched with the most appropriate, least restrictive alternative employment option. Specific start-up tasks in these areas include developing written hiring policies and procedures, an application format, a checklist for tracking progress through the hiring process for each individual considered, and documentation requirements for the screening process. The organization should also establish or identify a transition process for students who will enter the adult service program when they leave school. This process should begin well before students finish school, to ensure that all support needs will be met.

The question of who will be employed becomes even more complex for personnel approaches such as enclaves in industry settings and individual supported jobs. In these instances, the host company, whether or not it is legally the employer of the individuals, will also influence personnel selection. Too often, employers may seek to employ individuals with milder handicaps or those for whom fewer barriers must be overcome. It is the responsibility of the support organization, as it identifies the host company for an enclave or an individual job in the community, to work with the employer to ensure that individuals with more severe handicaps will have access to these more integrated employment options as well. In one enclave, the host company's original perception was that the enclave would be most beneficial if people were employed who could move through the enclave and become regular members of the company. During negotiations with the host company before the enclave was started, the support organization took care to ensure that the company understood the type of support needs the enclave approach was designed to meet. Three years of successful operations later, these discussions were continuing. As openings became available within the enclave, the host company was willing to consider for employment some individuals whom it would not have considered at the project's onset.

Complete Individual Service Plans

Once the supported employment organization has selected someone for possible employment, an individual planning team should be called together. This team comprises the individual, his or her advocate or family members, the case manager, and all involved service providers. Its role is to review the individual's needs and alternative employment opportunities, and determine if the supported employment program being developed is the most appropriate. If this setting is selected, the team should set initial goals and objectives and review the methods the support organization will use to achieve them.

Complete the Employment Logistics

The start-up tasks associated with selecting workers may take several months before all targeted individuals are fully employed. Obtaining referrals, conducting interviews, selecting employees, and informing applicants of hiring decisions will consume only part of the time. Like any business, supported employment programs should bring on additional employees only when the workload warrants. Therefore, although entrepreneurial programs such as mobile crews or assembly companies could control hiring timelines directly, these timelines should be established with consideration of the amount of work available. In personnel approaches, hiring timelines are likely to be controlled by the host company of an enclave or the employers in individual supported jobs, rather than by the timelines of the support organization or the funding agent. A host company in the midst of a hiring freeze can be expected to apply that freeze to the enclave or supported jobs as well.

Hiring timelines may also be affected by the particular training and support needs of the individuals employed. Initiating a company that places and supports people with disabilities in individual jobs will require a gradual, staggered start-up phase while jobs are developed and individuals are trained to perform those jobs. During the training phase, as one individual's support needs lessen, the trainer can assume responsibility for another. In entrepreneurial programs or enclaves, hiring one or two individuals at a time permits intensive training of new employees, to acclimate them to work routines and teach them initial tasks.

While screening and selection proceed, several related tasks must be completed. Individual employee records must be established that include such things as previous history, medical needs, emergency information, employee pay and benefit records, and hiring documents. An orientation should be provided to the prospective employee, his or her family, advocates, and home provider concerning the nature of the employment opportunity, the types of support provided, anticipated outcomes of the employment, and expectations of the prospective employee. Information provided at this time should concern appropriate work clothing, the starting date, hours, payroll procedures, fringe benefits, personnel policies, and any other relevant organizational policies. Additional start-up tasks may comprise individual pre-employment logistics such as completing case management forms, and completing Social Security and tax withholding forms. During this time, the organization usually must help employees determine how they will travel to and from work, and may provide training in the use of public transportation systems.

OBTAIN PAID EMPLOYMENT

Table 4.4 summarizes tasks that may need to be completed to develop work opportunities during start-up. These include identifying prospective work opportunities and reaching agreements with customers to perform work.

Identify Prospective Work Opportunities

In the previous chapter, the authors urged the development of market analyses that identify the best business opportunities available for the development of the supported employment program. The analyses should answer questions about the nature of the market, its size, how program developers might attract part of it, and whether it is profitable. Once the proposal has been developed and the organization established, activities to develop work opportunities shift to market planning, advertising, and sales. Regardless of the type of program being established, a specific marketing plan should be developed that establishes marketing objectives, timelines, strategies to achieve those objectives, and contingency plans to be implemented if objectives are not met. The marketing plan is an extension or part of the business plan already discussed.

Table 4.4. Start-up checklist for obtaining paid employment opportunities (Check off tasks as completed.)

Major start-up needs	Tasks	Notes
A. Identify prospective companies.	___ 1. Plan marketing strategies and resources for identifying prospective companies.	
	___ 2. Develop marketing materials.	
	___ 3. Establish, monitor, adjust information system for marketing outcomes.	
	___ 4. Establish marketing contingency plans.	
	___ 5. Establish and maintain relationships with business network.	
	___ 6. Make initial and follow-up contacts with key person(s) from prospective companies.	
B. Secure work commitment.	___ 1. Evaluate prospective company, e.g., size, stability, type of work, social and physical integration.	
	___ 2. Obtain requests for quotation (entrepreneurial firms).	
	___ 3. Develop and submit bids (entrepreneurial firms).	
	___ 4. Negotiate logistics and responsibilities.	
	___ 5. Reach agreement.	

The specific objectives and strategies developed will depend upon the type of supported employment approach, market conditions, and location. The strategies used to obtain janitorial contracts for a mobile work crew in a small town will be quite different from those used to identify one large firm to host an enclave. If located in a large urban area instead of a small town, that same work crew might need a very different set of strategies for obtaining contracts. Because of this variety of potential strategies, a marketing plan based on local factors will focus company efforts on an organized, unified approach to achieving the company's objectives.

Objectives set targets to be met by specified dates and therefore serve as guideposts for evaluating the implementation of selected strategies. When reasonable objectives are set, not meeting them should lead managers to ask a series of questions: Were the objectives really attainable? Were strategies implemented appropriately? Should other strategies be pursued instead of, or in addition to, those originally selected? How may resources be more effectively managed? What other resources may be applied to achieving the objectives? Contingency plans, included in the original marketing plan, may need to be elaborated and implemented when objectives are not met. Table 4.5 provides examples of marketing objectives, resources, strategies, and contingency plans that might be included in a marketing plan by supported employment organizations.

Once the plan is developed, the staff may then turn to developing presentations, presentation materials, business cards, and stationery, spending time implementing the strategies, and developing the network of contacts that will generate work. One organization on the East Coast that established a small manufacturing firm developed and marketed a proprietary product to businesses. Advertisements were placed in the newspaper and manufacturing journals; a direct mail campaign was also used to reach targeted firms. A West Coast organization for supporting enclaves formed a small group of high-level business executives to aid its marketing efforts. This business group directly contacted individuals in other firms, and provided information to these persons on the costs and benefits of the enclave approach. Whether making individual job placements, developing an enclave, or establishing a small business, potential customers must be identified, contacted, and convinced before supported employment will occur.

Reaching Agreements with Customers

The activities required to secure specific work commitments after the customer has expressed interest depend greatly on the type of sup-

Table 4.5. Sample marketing plan components

Marketing objectives: What will be accomplished and when?
Examples:
—Number of people to be employed each month with the assistance of the personnel support organization
—Planned timeline for start-up of an enclave to employ six persons
—Amount of commercial revenue generated, number of customers or contracts, or number of bids to be submitted by an entrepreneurial firm each month

Marketing resources: What resources will be devoted to achieving the objectives?
Examples:
—Amount of money available for marketing materials, travel, and other expenses
—Staff time to be allocated to marketing activities
—External resource development, such as the recruiting of a volunteer retired sales executive
—Materials and expertise available

Marketing strategies: What strategies will be devoted to achieving the objectives?
Examples:
—Develop and maintain a network of business contacts by joining business associations that bring together decision-makers from targeted companies.
—Establish a group of business executives to recruit and inform other firms about an enclave approach to supported employment.
—Place advertisements in the yellow pages, newspapers, magazines, business directories, or journals for a mobile work crew or other business.
—Conduct a direct mail marketing campaign to potential customers of a retail business.
—Identify the firms that will be contacted, the individuals within each firm to be contacted, and the manner in which they will be contacted.
—Specify shop rates, costs, or profitability factors to be included in bids submitted by a subcontract firm.

Contingency plans: What adjustments will be made to the plan if objectives are not met?
Examples:
—Revise monthly objectives and anticipated trends.
—Identify methods of obtaining additional resources to be applied to meeting marketing objectives.
—Select additional or alternative strategies that may be implemented.
—Identify decision points for implementing contingency plans.

---

ported employment being developed. When a potential host company or business customer is identified, the support organization will likely need to evaluate the size and stability of the company and the potential for obtaining appropriate work. Personnel support organizations should consider the potential to achieve desired physical and social integration outcomes. Supported jobs and enclaves may require the development of an agreement that specifies the roles and responsibilities of the employer and the organization providing placement and job support. A sample agreement used by a supported jobs program is included in Figure 4.1. Entrepreneurial approaches will have to include development of the opportunity to bid on services or products to obtain access to work. Agreements in all cases should include the basic points: 1) what will be done by whom, 2) when these activities will take place, 3) what compensation is included, and 4) the right to cancel the contract.

When a program is being established, careful consideration is given to such activities as identifying a market and obtaining customers for products or job placements. However, markets fluctuate as communities and consumer interests change. Generally speaking, the traditional plan of finding permanent, lucrative contracts must be cast aside as unrealistic. In the open market, today's products will likely not account for the majority of a business's products in 10 years. Companies attempting to maintain supported employment opportunities, therefore, need to prepare for changes and opportunities in markets. Regardless of the type of business, maintaining the source of work on which the job opportunities depend will be facilitated by an up-to-date market analysis. For entrepreneurial ventures, such as mobile crews performing janitorial services or small manufacturing plants operated by the support organization, all products must satisfy certain customer needs. Market analysis is an ongoing activity that should continually provide feedback on the product or service need that exists in the identified business area.

CAPACITY TO WORK TO EMPLOYER REQUIREMENTS

Regardless of the business or program approach being taken, the normal demands of the job must be met. For small businesses, this requires attention to the processes and activities that will ensure that a competitive product is delivered on time. For placement organizations or enclaves, additional demands might be created by the employer, such as minimum requirements for productivity or social behavior. Particularly important for developing the capacity to perform work when getting started are knowledge and skills in the type of work to be performed, job analysis and design, and employee training. Particularly for entrepreneurial firms, appropriate equipment for the work specialty must also be obtained. Table 4.6 summarizes the start-up tasks related to this accomplishment.

Ensure That Staff Are Skilled in the Work Specialization

Staff in organizations providing supported employment need a variety of skills (see Chapter 11) to perform competently. Human services

I. _____, the employer, agrees to employ an individual arranged for and supported by JKL Personnel Systems in the position of _____.

II. **Intent and responsibilities of the parties**
   A. **Intent**
      The intent of JKL Personnel Systems is to provide thorough training and smooth transition of the worker supported into _____, and to provide *long-term* support services (including training, skill maintenance, retraining as needed, and supervision as needed) to both _____ and the worker.

   B. **Responsibilities**
      JKL Personnel Systems will:
      1. Perform job analysis.
      2. Recruit an employee for the position.
      3. Provide comprehensive training at the work site in tasks listed in the attached job description.
      4. Guarantee quality control and completion.
      5. Provide orientation for employer's staff.
      6. Collect information on employee performance, productivity, and other job-related matters, and share the information with the employer.
      7. Provide ongoing support services to employer and employee.
      8. Assist the employer in acquiring subminimum wage permits, tax credits, or other benefits associated with this position.

      _____ will:
      1. Provide regular work schedule: _____

      2. Provide access to the workplace for JKL staff to accomplish job analysis, do training, and provide support services.
      3. Provide a company orientation, including personnel policy information, to JKL staff before the employee starts on the job.
      4. Provide equipment and supplies necessary to complete assigned responsibilities.
      5. Provide feedback on the performance of JKL staff and the employee.
      6. Notify JKL prior to changes in job duties, work schedule, or other job-related matters.
      7. Handle payment of the employee's wages, and other direct labor costs, including worker's compensation, Social Security, and unemployment insurance.

III. **Terms of remuneration**
   A. Base wage is set at _____ per hour.

(continued)

Figure 4.1. *(continued)*

    B. The *actual* rate of pay for work performed will be based on measured productivity under written authorization provided to the employer by JKL Personnel Systems. For example, if the employee is measured at 75% productivity, the actual rate of pay would be 75% of the base wage rate.

    C. The employee will be eligible for review and evaluation of performance and increases in the base wage rate as specified in the employer's personnel policies.

    D. The employee will be eligible for standard benefits as specified in the employer's personnel policies.

IV. **Terms of agreement**

    A. This agreement shall continue in full force and effect from the date of signing.

    B. In order to ensure proper training of the employee for this position, a JKL staff person shall begin the position _____ .

    C. An employee recruited by JKL will begin training _____ .

    D. This agreement can be terminated immediately by EITHER party with cause.

    E. Termination of this contract by either party without cause may occur with 10 working days written notice.

Representing _____

_____

Name and title   Date

_____

JKL Personnel Systems Representative   Date

Figure 4.1. Sample employment agreement for a supported jobs program.

skills relevant to the training and supervision of employees with disabilities are useless if staff do not know *how* to do the actual work required by the employer or customer. For example, staff may need to be skilled in normal industry practices for janitorial services, yard care, electronics assembly, or restaurant operation in order to develop a profitable, stable business, to establish an enclave in a large corporation, or to support individuals in community jobs. These skills are most critical for entrepreneurial firms where work performance relies totally on the knowledge and skills of employees. The staff of personnel support organizations may rely more on the host company for guidance on *how* to do work. In one situation, an electronics firm that

Table 4.6. Start-up checklist for establishing worker capacity to meet employer requirements (Check off tasks as completed.)

Major start-up needs	Tasks	Notes
A. Develop staff skills.	___ 1. Assess staff skills and training needs. ___ 2. Provide staff training.	
B. Obtain equipment.	___ 1. Establish equipment selection criteria. ___ 2. Review available equipment options. ___ 3. Select and purchase equipment needed for start-up. ___ 4. Negotiate equipment needs with host company (personnel support organizations).	
C. Complete job design and analysis.	___ 1. Complete detailed job analysis. ___ 2. Establish job design with consideration to work efficiency and training costs. ___ 3. Develop fixtures or other performance adaptations as necessary. ___ 4. Complete task analyses.	
D. Train employees.	___ 1. Assess performance. ___ 2. Provide training, using appropriate assistance, reinforcement, and correction methods. ___ 3. Collect training data. ___ 4. Analyze data and adjust training procedures. ___ 5. Design and implement procedures for maintaining performance over time.	

hosts an enclave provided specific electronics assembly training to the enclave supervisor, who was provided by the support organization and was already skilled at training and supervising individuals with severe handicaps. However, a support organization's familiarity with industry practices may be an important factor in a host company's decision to establish an enclave or to hire an individual into a supported job.

Obtain Equipment

Adequate equipment is essential to saving time and energy, completing work to specifications, and making the business successful. The particular type, amount, and features of equipment vary dramatically from one work specialization to another. For entrepreneurial firms, equipment must be selected by staff, based on their own knowledge and assessment of the industry. Selection factors may include initial purchase costs, ongoing costs, durability, maintenance requirements, safety, anticipated return on investment, availability of purchase versus lease arrangements, and ease of operation. Equipment to be operated by employees with disabilities should be selected with consideration of training requirements and necessary adaptations.

In personnel support approaches, equipment needed for completing work usually is provided by the host company. However, support organizations must be aware of the increased burden a company carries if equipment is not used to full capacity because of the lower productivity of employees with disabilities. It is reasonable to use public support funds to defray any excess costs that may be assumed by a company hiring individuals with severe disabilities. Therefore, personnel support organizations may offer to provide equipment or tools for low-productivity workers to avoid increasing host company costs.

Complete Job Design and Job Analysis

Whether individuals with severe handicaps are employed in entrepreneurial firms or through personnel support organizations, the jobs they will do must be designed and analyzed to facilitate training and the maintenance of performance. Approaches to job design should include consideration of both production efficiency and training costs. Alternative methods of doing jobs may be required if individuals with severe handicaps are to receive supported employment. Fixtures may be designed to help employees do tasks correctly, meet quality specifications, and improve productivity. For example, adaptations may be necessary for individuals with physical handicaps, or for individuals unable to read, count, or use other academic skills.

Fixtures are commonly used in industry settings to facilitate employee performance, and thus should not be avoided in supported employment. Care should be taken, however, to ensure that such fixtures do not present a negative image to others. For a more complete review of task design factors from the perspective of assembly tasks, see Bellamy, Horner, and Inman (1979).

Once trainers have established the general methods the employee will use to perform the job, a detailed job or task analysis should be completed. This analysis should identify the frequency, settings, and schedule for tasks, the specific task-related cues, the tasks or steps to be performed in response to those cues, and the criteria for each task or step. The range of variability in tasks, materials, and responses must be identified. In personnel support organizations providing individual supported jobs, job analysis begins with support organization staff performing the assigned job and assessing work and social demands of the job setting. Through a process that may require 1 to 2 weeks, staff complete a detailed analysis of the range of stimulus and response variation demanded by the job.

Supported employment's focus on integrated settings increases the complexity of job analysis. Variability in both work and social demands must be assessed to ensure that workers with disabilities will be trained to perform appropriately in all anticipated situations. Routine job events, and those expected to occur infrequently, must be analyzed. If all stimulus and response variation is identified, the analysis forms the basis for creating a data system to assess acquisition of the job. During training, the employee must demonstrate competence across the range of variation identified during the analysis. This general case analysis is an emerging technology that may be critically important to implementing supported employment successfully in community settings. For further information on general case analysis, see Albin, McDonnell, and Wilcox (1987), Engelmann and Carnine (1982), and Horner, Sprague, and Wilcox (1982).

Train Employees

Individuals with severe handicaps will require direct and systematic training to do jobs in integrated settings accurately and productively. Employment training specialists must be able to assess performance and provide assistance, reinforcement, and error correction as needed in a manner that will facilitate task acquisition, yet not intrude excessively upon the job setting. Data collected during training must be constantly reviewed to analyze errors and determine if any adjustments in the job analysis and training procedures are needed. Trainers must also design and implement procedures that will help individuals with severe handicaps sustain acceptable levels of performance. This responsibility is particularly important in individual jobs in community settings where trained supervisors may not be consistently present.

Detailed analysis of training skills and strategies is beyond the scope of this book. The reader is referred to several excellent sources for more complete discussions of training procedures relevant to supported employment: Bellamy et al. (1979); Gifford, Rusch, Martin, and White (1984); Horner, Meyer, and Fredericks (1986); Mank and Horner (1987); Sailor, Wilcox, and Brown (1980); and Wilcox and Bellamy (1982).

INTEGRATION

The start-up tasks related to achieving integration are summarized in Table 4.7.

The task with the greatest potential effect on the integration of most employment programs is selecting the location of the employment option. Whereas mobile crews have access to a larger community as they travel from one work site to the next, supported employment programs housed in one place (e.g., a bakery, electronics assembly firm, or a crab pot manufacturer) are limited by the integration options available on-site or in the community surrounding the work place. Thus, an assembly firm that is established specifically to provide supported employment must select the business site carefully. The firm must ensure that the building is suited to the type of work to be performed, that it is located where similar businesses might be found, and that it offers opportunities for integrated community access.

In personnel approaches, issues relating to the selection of the location of individual work stations, work routines, and applicable personnel policies of the host company must be negotiated to ensure that employees with disabilities are maximally integrated into the company's work force and work routines. An enclave located in a separate building on the grounds of a large company or otherwise separated from the work areas where nonhandicapped employees are congregated unnecessarily restricts the integration opportunities of employees with disabilities.

During start-up, the support organization should do an environmental analysis to assess the potential integration opportunities within and around the workplace. Integration is achieved when employees enjoy frequent contacts with persons who are not disabled and who are not paid caregivers—coworkers, supervisors, customers,

Table 4.7. Checklist for start-up tasks related to achieving integration (Check off tasks as completed.)

Major start-up needs		Tasks	Notes
A. Establish opportunity for integration.	—1.	Select location with consideration to opportunities for integration (entrepreneurial organization).	
	—2.	Negotiate with employer to include employees with disabilities within normal company personnel policies and routines (personnel support organizations).	
	—3.	Negotiate location of "work station," breaks, and lunch to enhance integration opportunities (personnel support organizations).	
B. Analyze physical and social integration opportunities.	—1.	Establish format for performing environmental analysis to identify physical integration opportunities.	
	—2.	Establish job analysis systems for assessing social integration demands and opportunities.	
	—3.	Identify normal company routines and social integration demands and opportunities on the job site.	
	—4.	Implement environmental analysis system.	
	—5.	Maintain data and documentation of job-site integration analysis and environmental analysis; update as needed.	

and others in the vicinity of the work place. Opportunities to develop friendships, participate in joint activities, and simply exchange greetings enhance the benefits of the employment setting. During the start-up phase, identification of the normal community activities of other employees, such as using local stores, restaurants, parks, and employee break areas, will facilitate later planning and training for integration.

SUMMARY

Instituting supported employment programs requires the commitment of a group of individuals to complete start-up activities. During the start-up phase, a governing board must be formed and funding obtained. Management systems, such as personnel policies and procedures, must be established. Staff must be hired, and employees with handicaps must be selected. Employment opportunities must be available before employees with disabilities are hired. When employment sites are selected, the integration possibilities both on and off the job site should be considered, in order to maximize the benefits received by individuals with severe handicaps who become employed. The start-up phase for supported employment programs is completed when all employees have been hired and trained to perform jobs.

REFERENCES

Albin, R., McDonnell, J., & Wilcox, B. (1987). Designing interventions to meet activity goals. In B. Wilcox & G. T. Bellamy (Eds.), A comprehensive guide to the activities catalog: An alternative curriculum for youth and adults with severe disabilities. Baltimore: Paul H. Brookes Publishing Co.

Bellamy, G. T., Horner, R. H., & Inman, D. (1979). Vocational habilitation of severely retarded adults: A direct service technology. Baltimore: University Park Press.

Engelmann, S., & Carnine, D. (1982). Theory of instruction: Principles and applications. New York: Irvington.

Gifford, J. L., Rusch, F. R., Martin, J. E., & White, D. M. (1984). Autonomy and adaptability: A proposed technology for the study of work behavior. In N. W. Ellis & N. R. Bray (Eds.), International review of research on mental retardation, 12, (pp. 285–318). New York: Academic Press.

Horner, R. H., Meyer, L. H., & Fredericks, H. D. (1986). Education of learners with severe handicaps: Exemplary service strategies. Baltimore: Paul H. Brookes Publishing Co.

Horner, R. H., Sprague, J., & Wilcox, B. (1982). General case programming for community activities. In B. Wilcox & G. T. Bellamy (Eds.), Design of high school programs for severely handicapped students (pp. 61–98). Baltimore: Paul H. Brookes Publishing Co.

Mank, D. M., & Horner, R. H. (1987). Self-recruited feedback: A cost-effective procedure for maintaining behavior. *Research in Developmental Disabilities, 8*(1), 91–112.

Sailor, W., Wilcox, B., & Brown, L. (1980). *Methods of instruction for severely handicapped students.* Baltimore: Paul H. Brookes Publishing Co.

Wilcox, B., & Bellamy, G. T. (1982). *Design of high school programs for severely handicapped students.* Baltimore: Paul H. Brookes Publishing Co.

Chapter 5

Management
From Plans
To Accomplishments

This chapter focuses on the ongoing management of a supported employment program from the perspective of its general manager and board of directors. Many management issues that should be anticipated in supported employment are typical of those faced by managers of other businesses. This chapter describes these issues and offers suggestions and tools for managing a supported employment operation. The authors view management as a continuous process of performing functions that are critical to an organization's long-term success. Although there are many useful definitions of management, the perspective here is on what must be done to direct an organization toward accomplishing its goals.

Historically, there has been a tendency to believe that public sector management—and by extension, management of private, non-profit organizations—poses challenges to managers that are fundamentally different from those faced by their private industry counterparts. This view has enjoyed less and less support among management professionals. All managers face the same kinds of tasks relating to giving the organization direction, setting objectives, and organizing resources to accomplish organizational objectives (Drucker, 1974, 1985).

SUPPORTED EMPLOYMENT
AND SMALL BUSINESS MANAGEMENT

At a fundamental level, managing supported employment programs will require the same skills and tools needed to manage any other small enterprise in either the public or private sector. The basic functions of managers remain unchanged, whether there is a single manager or several people sharing management roles. These functions have been variously categorized, but typically include elements from Gulick's list of management tasks—planning, organizing, staffing, directing, coordinating, reporting, and budgeting (Gulick, 1937). Inherent in these functions are the difficulties associated with managing a small business. Managers of supported employment organizations face the same challenges associated with cash flow, personnel management, government regulations, inadequate capital, and dozens of other factors that characterize so many small businesses. These factors enter into an equation that determines the success or failure of supported employment programs.

Whether the supported employment program is a small, nonprofit bakery, an assembly plant wholly owned by its employees with and without disabilities, or a personnel support organization, it will have more similarities than dissimilarities to other community businesses. It will need access to an accountant, a lawyer, and an insurance broker. It will find business and trade organizations valuable sources of information. Dozens of publications are available to assist the small business manager. A few of these are listed in the appendix to this book.

Perhaps the major dissimilarity between a for-profit small business and a supported employment organization is that business success is only a prerequisite for supported employment. Business success is necessary to ensure job stability and enough work to generate paid jobs, but it does not guarantee high-quality supported employment. The profitability of a company is a partial means to the end objectives of economic well-being and maximum integration for persons with severe disabilities. Success in delivering the support needed to maintain or enhance employment and integration outcomes is needed as well.

Supported employment is confined neither to public nor private sector organizations. It may be provided through for-profit businesses, nonprofit organizations, or government agencies. The variety of ways to provide employment with ongoing support to individuals with severe disabilities should grow exponentially in the near future, combining the prescribed features of well-known approaches such as enclaves and supported jobs with local innovation. In spite of this diversity, certain management features within supported employment remain constant. The size and specialization—both commercial and service—that define supported employment will help managers avoid the diverse markets, roles, and unmeasurable objectives that historically have plagued many social service organizations.

MANAGEMENT AND OPERATIONS

Careful planning will be of no value unless it is rigorously maintained after the program begins. In the previous chapters, the steps involved in planning and starting personnel and entrepreneurial approaches to supported enployment are discussed. Managing a program after it has been established involves continuing many of these same functions. For example, the availability of capital has to correspond with anticipated growth, staffing skills must be maintained and improved, and the program must keep in step with the business market that creates job opportunities. In this section, major issues and suggestions concerning ongoing operations and management of supported employment programs are described using the framework of the five major accomplishments discussed in previous chapters.

Developing Work Opportunities

Too often, planning processes are not continuous; planning often becomes no more than an annual event or a response to crises. However, there are many reasons why careful planning comes first on the list of activities performed by successful managers. Once a business has made a good start and the managers and staff are versed in the fundamentals of business administration, planning should become routine. By making a frequent and critical appraisal of the supported employment organization, managers can identify strengths and weaknesses, then formulate and revise plans accordingly. A written plan functions as a tool to guide the financing and management of the operation. The process of developing the plan should force the manager and board of directors to look carefully at the organization in its entirety.

Supported employment planning issues may be separated into two groups: 1) those encountered within the type of business being used to generate employment opportunities, and 2) those related solely to supported employment. For example, careful planning and market analysis led one individual placement organization to shift toward intensive job development in the retail industry. Market analysis indicated a large number of retail operations in the local areas, with a wide range of job types for possible employment development. Population growth figures and local economic plans also clearly suggested that the retail industry was an expanding market. This information enabled the organization to focus job development efforts more sharply. Planning for this company also had to include the unique tasks of focusing on the progress being made by each employee in supported employment and the degree to which jobs affect the quality of life of each person. Planning may be used in this area, for example, to review and adjust the allocation of training resources or to develop additional support mechanisms for individuals in jobs.

Planning guidelines for supported employment closely follow the conventional wisdom of many businesses. The authors' list includes the following:

Focus on Tangible Outcomes   Despite their similarities to other small businesses, nonprofit organizations face many unique challenges. The most frequently documented of these challenges are the unmeasurable, unclear, or conflicting objectives that characterize these organizations. In the absence of a profit motive, success has often been measured more by budget size or numbers of clients receiving services than by tangible program results. Whereas the for-profit sector must satisfy specific markets, social service organizations frequently have diverse constituencies. Rehabilitation facilities have not been immune to these classic problems. The historical development of workshops has further complicated difficult management issues by creating expectations that these programs provide preparatory training for future employment, comprehensive rehabilitative services, and sheltered employment for those individuals deemed incapable of competitive employment. These different service outcomes create conflicts among both service expectations and strategies to attain outcomes.

Supported employment, however, has the potential to avoid some of the historical pitfalls of service organizations. It has a very specific mission. Organizational performance is easily measured, through such indicators as how many hours people are at work, the nature of the environment where their jobs are located, and the wage rate they are paid. This shared mission helps alleviate the ambiguity and conflict generated by the multiple service roles so prevalent in current vocational and prevocational services. The goals of supported employment should provide a firm basis for establishing standards, influencing organizational strategies, and providing boundaries for decision-making.

Build Slowly, and on Strengths   Increasing the number of people an organization serves is senseless if that organization already serves many individuals who do not receive wages or employment within an integrated environment. The consequences of funding the expansion of programs that have not yet built the systems required to produce needed outcomes can be disastrous. Success must be established in a small way before the population served is expanded. Businesses rarely have minimum standards or economies of scale relating to the size of their work force. From "mom and pop" businesses to large corporations, the size of the work force is dictated by demand. Social service organizations frequently grow because service needs and funding have been identified. Supported employment creates a different challenge to these service organizations. The managers of supported employment, which is limited by definition to very small service units and requires the presence of work opportunities before service is provided, must emulate their industrial counterparts rather than cleave to their social service origins. Business demands that generate the job opportunities should control the size of the labor force, with requirements for integration being one of the factors determining whether persons without disabilities should be hired instead of additional persons receiving supported employment. For example, a small manufacturing company might hire nonhandicapped persons both to meet growing work requirements and to increase work force integration. A janitorial service might need to hire additional crew employees based on business needs for additional labor. The company may do this by employing five or six individuals with severe disabilities in each of several crews, but to meet the definition of supported employment these crews must work in physically separate locations and either include nonhandicapped crew members or work in integrated settings. For personnel organizations that place and train individuals in dispersed community jobs, the businesses in which these individuals are placed will also base hiring on identified labor needs.

The issue of size is discussed further in Chapter 7 in the context of change strategies for existing programs. Whether reorganization is occurring or a new, independent program is providing supported employment, the emphasis on social as well as physical integration will profoundly affect organizational structures and strategies.

Maintain a Clear Employment Strategy In their book, *In Search of Excellence*, Peters and Waterman (1982) list the features they believe have been crucial to the development of America's most successful companies. These include simplicity of organization and a tendency to stay close to the business in which a company has skills. Most business consultants have reached the conclusion that unchanneled diversification is a losing proposition (Peters & Waterman, 1982). The consistency with which business advice echoes the findings of Peters and Waterman should serve as a lesson for the managers of supported employment organizations. Supported employment will also be difficult to manage should organizations attempt simultaneously to operate placement programs, enclaves, and entrepreneurial models, or to work in a wide variety of businesses. Although theoretically possible, this task is difficult for many reasons. Perhaps the most important of these is that virtually all approaches that generate jobs require competition. To compete, supported employment managers must devote enormous resources to their business, often in an arena in which their competition has advantages of resources or market history. With each type of business or program, the support organization requires more complex knowledge and skills, accountability, public relations, and management. The support organization must be specialized so as to concentrate its resources, providing an effective service to business customers and simultaneously providing effective service to the supported employees.

Plan for Competition between Business and Service Needs If a supported employment program is to operate as a business, then business success must be a major concern. Even so, a focus on each individual with disabilities must not be lost. Unlike most businesses, supported employment programs focus on the needs of persons with severe disabilities, and decisions related to individual needs should be balanced against the business needs of the organization. Competition between business and service needs may be evidenced in a variety of ways. Business needs include competitive pricing of goods and services, quality that conforms to customer specifications, and timely performance. These must be balanced against the service needs of providing paid employment in integrated settings to individuals with even the most severe handicaps. Decisions concerning hiring, work scheduling, pay levels, and allocation of training resources provide potential sources of conflict between business and service. For example, in one enclave in a manufacturing firm, the company closely monitors the productivity of all employees, including enclave workers. The company's business needs require the enclave supervisor to focus on maintaining or increasing productivity. Productivity usually decreases for several weeks whenever a worker is taught a new assembly task. Therefore, the enclave supervisor must balance the business pressure for high productivity levels with the combined business and service need to expand the task repertoire of the work force.

An entrepreneurial firm that does not have enough work to employ eveyone full-time must consider many questions. Who will get first access to the limited available work? Will work be assigned to the most productive employee—to meet the business need—or to the worker with the greatest service needs? Will the most efficient work schedule be followed, or will the schedule be adjusted to maximize access to work for the individuals with the most severe disabilities?

Questions such as these will likely continue to plague supported employment providers just as they have plagued rehabilitation facility programs. Planning for this competition between business and service needs should include the development of clear guidelines for decision-making. For example, one mobile crew company that pays its workers on the basis of their productivity has established a work access policy that requires crew supervisors to allocate work first to the person with the fewest skills or lowest wages, selecting the task in which that person is most productive. The person with the next fewest skills is then allocated work, and so on, until all work for that site is assigned. This policy ensures that the most severely disabled person employed by the crew gets maximum access to work, while still providing work for other participants.

Guidelines such as these must allow for the dual role of a supported employment organization. Business and service needs must be balanced. Neither should rule the other in all circumstances. An entrepreneurial supported employment organization, or the host company assisted by a personnel support agency, must be sufficiently profitable to be able to provide employment opportunities at all. However, an employment opportunity that does not respond to the service needs of individuals is likely to be inappropriate for persons with severe handicaps.

Work Performance

A second major concern for managers in supported employment is to make certain that the available work is analyzed and done in a way that ensures customer satisfaction and organizational strength. Chapter 4 provides a discussion of the issues related to job analysis. This section considers management issues related to maintaining work performance at acceptable levels.

Two sets of issues in job settings affect the performance of employees with severe handicaps over time. First, whether in businesses run by the nonprofit support organization, or in job placements in competitive environments, the components of almost all jobs change over time. Even routine, minor job changes or changes in supervisors can significantly affect the ability of a person with severe disabilities to do the job. Second, although employees with severe handicaps can learn many complex skills, acquired behaviors may not be sustained, even when conditions remain constant. Particularly among more severely handicapped workers in competitive job settings, maintenance of acquired behaviors has proven the nemesis of successful, remunerative employment (see, for example, Greenspan, & Schoultz, 1981; Hill & Wehman, 1983.)

Horner and Albin (1986) suggest that three classes of variables affect the maintenance of new skills over time: training variables, transition variables and performance variables. Training is a process in which the worker learns how to make certain responses and recognize when the responses should be performed (i.e., the stimulus conditions that should elicit the behavior). The stimulus control developed during training will maintain over time as a function of the level or strength of the control acquired during training (Baer, 1981; Engelmann & Carnine, 1982; Haring, Liberty, & White, 1980). In other words, the better the employee learns the job, the more likely his or her performance will be to maintain over time. Transition variables that affect maintenance reflect the extent to which "training stimuli" are gradually transformed into "performance stimuli" after the worker begins performing correctly during training. All cues used during training should be gradually adjusted to match those that will be available in the performance setting. All positive consequences should be gradually modified to approximate the type, amount, and schedule of reinforcement experienced in the natural performance setting. Finally, the opportunity to perform the target response should gradually change from initial training levels to the levels naturally experienced in the performance setting.

The third class of variables affecting the maintenance of new skills over time reflects the nature of the performance setting. The support organization must ensure that the cues that controlled work behavior during training continue to be present in the performance setting. For example, a worker who learned to do a sequence of tasks in response to certain clock times cannot be expected to perform the same sequence if the clock is removed. Work behavior will also fail to be maintained unless it is reinforced. This is especially problematic in natural work settings if the job, coworkers, and supervisors do not provide enough reinforcement to maintain work skills. Alternatively, others in the environment may reinforce competing, inappropriate behaviors, further hindering maintenance of the desired work skills. Finally, the performance setting must provide sufficient opportunities to use skills. Without continous opportunities to perform, workers are less likely to maintain newly acquired skills over time.

Based on this analysis, the maintenance of work behaviors should involve: 1) carefully programmed training that builds strong, generalized stimulus control, 2) graduated transition, once employee competence is demonstrated, from training conditions to those experienced in the natural work setting, 3) ongoing access to the relevant work cues, 4) sufficient opportunities to perform the work; and 5) effective consequences for appropriate responses. Ongoing monitoring of individual performance and job changes, coupled with continued availability of training support, will further enhance job performance over time. For supported employment within more controlled environments that have specialized staff available at all times, these activities require a relatively straightforward set of tasks. Chapter 4 provides references for training and general case analysis.

For supported employment within fully integrated environments, three strategies may be followed to ensure maintenance of job skills. These include training workers with disabilities to use self-management strategies, transferring technical skills in training and behavior change to the natural environment, and providing follow-up activities that will enable the host company to get assistance when necessary.

Self-Management Self-management occurs when individuals monitor and manage conditions to change or maintain some aspect of their own behavior. Techniques of self-management have been applied to diverse behaviors and include techniques for self-assessment and monitoring, prearrangement of cues and consequences, self-determined reinforcers, self-determined criteria for reinforcement, self-determined punishment, and self-instruction. Self-management procedures have been applied extensively among nonhandicapped populations; in the last several years, some researchers have studied the use of self-management procedures by individuals with mental retardation in work settings. (See, for example, Mank & Horner, 1987; Rudrud, Rice, Robertson, & Tolson, 1984; Rusch, Morgan, Martin, Riva, & Agran, 1985; Sowers, Verdi, Bourbeau, & Sheehan, 1985; Wacker & Berg, 1986). Self-management strategies appear to provide effective methods that may be used by support organizations to help maintain performance over time in conventional job settings.

Transferring Technical Skills to the Natural Environment In personnel support organizations, the technology of training and supervising so frequently required for the job success of a person with severe disabilities must be transferred in part to the supervisors or coemployees of the company for which he or she works. This transfer of technology should occur before the presence of trained support staff is faded out. One organization in the state of Washington that supports an enclave in a manufacturing plant employing about 1,000 people holds small classes for workers and supervisors involved with employees with disabilities. In 15–20 hours of class time, 5–10 coworkers and supervisors get an opportunity to discuss concerns and participate in lectures and practice sessions in analyzing tasks for training, providing training in work tasks, and managing work behavior.

Providing Follow-Up Activities to Maintain Presence following Fading from the Job Site The support organization should negotiate a routine program or placement review process that will provide the opportunity to ensure both employer and employee satisfaction. Individual Program Planning is a partial strategy for doing this; however, this process takes place too seldom to ensure maintenance of job standards. Within one enclave, the support organization uses routine "visits" for casual appraisal of worker performance and employer satisfaction, but maintains a formal quarterly review with managers and supervisors of individual worker productivity, overall progress, and social issues concerning each worker. Training for supervisors and coworkers, plans for addressing inappropriate workplace behaviors, and methods for increasing pay and productivity are among the regular topics of this meeting.

Integration

Resources must continue to be allocated to monitor the progress of integration, and to support further integration activities where required. However, it is often believed that formal systems of categorizing integration opportunities, training individuals to perform the activities, and monitoring the extent of integration will be replaced by informal systems. There is the assumption that personal contacts will be made, friendships will develop, and other natural exchanges will occur routinely. Social integration cannot be assumed, however, and energy and resources must be devoted to integration if it does not occur naturally. Establishing the capacity for integration in a setting is insufficient. Attention must also focus on ensuring that integration occurs.

Ongoing Support

Virtually all landmark legislation from educational to rehabilitation services since the early 1970s has included provisions for the development of individual plans to guide program decisions for people with disabilities. As the structure of traditional services changes, it will be important to create or carry over systems to ensure that the needs for individual service coordination are met. O'Brien (1987) presents a guide to "personal futures planning" that results in a description of a desired future for the person with severe handicaps, a schedule of activities, and a list of supports needed to organize resources to move toward that future. In this process, a comprehensive, collective vision is developed by a group of people involved with—and including—the person with disabilities. This vision then guides the group in planning steps to be taken to overcome barriers, expand opportunities, and ensure ongoing support.

Such planning meetings, however, are best had outside the work setting and during nonwork hours. In supported employment, particularly in regular work settings, the support organization must take care not to disrupt normal work routines or unnecessarily call attention to the person with disabilities as somehow "different." In these settings, efforts should focus on including the worker in the usual employee evaluation system. By protecting the company from special meetings and extra paperwork, the support organization also emphasizes integration with the nonhandicapped workforce. Information from this performance evaluation may be used later in an individual planning meeting held in a nonwork setting.

Maintain Organizational Capacity

Despite renewed reliance on private, for-profit industry for the creation of employment opportunities, nonprofit organizations that provide support will remain a critical component of the service system. The support organization is both a service developer and an advocate for the people in supported employment. It must be managed to address the expectations of the purchasers of services, applicable external regulations, and consumers. In addition, maintaining the capacity to deliver support includes employing quality personnel, maintaining the business image, ensuring financial stability, and other traditional management functions. Difficulties that supported employment organizations have in maintaining management controls and functions may have two general sources (Bellamy & Boles, 1984). The first of these relates to external environmental changes, for example, changes in state-regulated standards or in funding levels for services. The second source of difficulty is internal to the support organization, and originates in the failure to establish clear, definable service outcomes, and in inadequate management controls. The remainder of this chapter describes several management tools or strategies for guiding decision-making within supported employment organizations.

TOOLS FOR DECISION-MAKING

The list of tools presented in this section is intended to provide ideas to program managers, but is not comprehensive. These tools have emerged from the experiences of supported employment programs participating in the authors' research and development efforts. These programs span the United States and encompass a variety of employment approaches. Despite their diversity, the programs share a commitment to assess their impact on benefits to consumers, and to focus on work and its direct benefits to working individuals. Their collective use of management tools to aid in planning and management has been useful in measuring and correcting performance of activities to assure that program objectives and plans are being accomplished.

Effective direction of supported employment programs requires the use of such management tools to facilitate decisions linked to the benefits received by service consumers. To be used effectively, these tools must be seen as part of a system in which plans are made and documented, performance follows planning, and measures of actual outcomes are compared against initially projected outcomes. Versions of these basic steps are frequently presented as "decision loops" (see Figure 5.1).

Decision Loops

The decision loop illustrates the cyclical nature of planning. This cycle begins before initiation of the program (Chapter 3), when program developers first select from among alternative missions and objectives. During start-up (Chapter 4), the board of directors selects or develops the policies, strategies, and procedures for achieving the planned mission. This process is generally described as *annual* planning: 1) establishing desired accomplishments, 2) examining alternative strategies to achieve those accomplishments, 3) evaluating alternatives based on the best information available, 4) selecting an alternative, and 5) documenting the objectives and alternatives selected. Many types of plans use the same basic planning process,

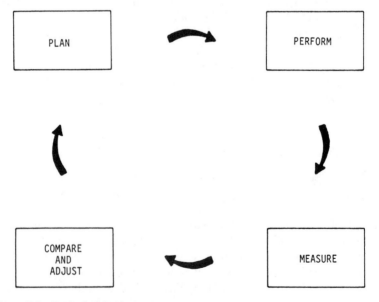

Figure 5.1. Basic decision loop.

among them monthly organizational plans, staff utilization, marketing plans, and procedural plans. All, to be effective, require an accurate data system that supplies necessary, timely information for every level of decision-making.

Organizations providing supported employment can take advantage of the clear outcomes expected of supported employment in designing such an information system. Supported employment organizations are intended to have an impact on people's lives. Defining service outcomes is a process of specifying the valued outcomes of supported employment in terms of the direct benefits that accrue to individuals with disabilities. The measure of these benefits define which accomplishments are to be expected from the program. The consumer benefits in question are much the same as those used to evaluate the quality of life of anyone in contemporary society: income level, social life, participation in chosen activities, presence of intimate relationships, and other common quality of life indicators. The organization must develop a system that routinely tracks outcome data and continuously monitors progress toward its goals. The efficient system will generate measures that will support decisions at all levels of program operation. Decision loops may be used to conceptualize the steps taken in all parts of the supported employment program, such as policy decisions made by the managers and board of directors, operating decisions to execute policies, and individual daily decisions by support staff to help each consumer attain his or her goals.

Policy Decisions Generally, decision loops are most useful when policymakers are conceptualizing the organizational framework for broad planning and controlling functions. The board of directors and management staff decide on the program outcomes that are consistent with the mission, they establish measures to determine if outcomes are met, and they generate a planning document to reflect the decisions made. Figure 5.2 presents an example of an annual management plan that is consistent with the organization's broad business plan, and that provides a specific "roadmap" of activities and measures for the ensuing year.

Backing up this annual plan are several documents generated from the organization's information system. One of the most important is the analysis of the financial impact of the plan. A "budget worksheet," whose format is presented in Figure 5.3 with instructions for its use, has proven helpful to the manager in developing this annual plan.

Formulated as needed throughout the year by the board of directors, policies are often used to support the mission of the organization

XYZ Crews 1987 Management Plan

XYZ Crews is a non-profit corporation organized to provide supported employment to individuals with severe handicaps through the successful operation of small service industry businesses. XYZ Crews currently employs 15 crew workers (including 13 individuals with severe handicaps), three crew supervisors, a general manager, and a half-time administrative assistant. Since its inception in November 1983, XYZ Crews has focused business efforts in two major areas: general cleaning of offices and groundskeeping. In calendar year 1986, these markets have supported 25 hours per week employment for all crew workers, an average monthly worker wage of $180 for productivity-based employees, and contributed $57,270 to overhead and retained earnings. Total commercial revenues for the same period were $106,070, representing a 120% increase over those of the 14–month start-up period (11/83–12/84), and about a 20% increase over 1985.

The focus of activities in 1987 will be to expand business efforts into additional markets in order to increase the amount of work available to XYZ Crews. This work expansion will facilitate meeting two objectives of the organization: to increase the number of individuals with disabilities who are provided supported employment through the company, and to increase the integration level of each crew by hiring additional workers without disabilities. The specific objectives are provided below, with five targeted accomplishments.

Accomplishment Area: Paid Employment Opportunities Provided

A. Current status:

	1984	1985	1986
Total commercial revenue	$48,000	$88,390	$106,070
Number of crew workers			
1. Productivity-based	1–13 (ave. 7.3/ mo.)	13	13
2. Hourly	1	1	2
Average hours/week			
1. Productivity-based	15	21	25
2. Hourly	35	30	25

B. Objective: Expand total commercial revenue (TCR) in 1987 to $132,300.
   1. Strategy: Expand marketing efforts to target post-construction clean-up in addition to general office cleaning and groundskeeping. Based on a market analysis completed 12/86, there are several major construction projects in process or planned to begin over the next few years as part of the development of the Western Industrial Park and for housing subdivisions. Construction

(continued)

Figure 5.2. *(continued)*

firms contacted indicated they have a need and interest in contracting with a cleaning business to do this work.
2. Financial implications
   a. Monthly commercial revenue projections
January–March	$8,840/month
April–September	$11,200/month
October–December	$12,900/month
   b. Personnel needs
      1. By April 1, 1987, add one new crew focused on post–construction clean-up. This is expected to require reorganizing current crews as well as hiring one hourly and two productivity-based crew workers, and one crew supervisor.
      2. By October 1, 1987, hire one hourly and one productivity-based crew worker.
   c. Equipment needs
      1. One van $9,000 ($1,500 down payment, 3-year loan, monthly payments, including insurance, approximately $400)
      2. Cleaning equipment for one crew, $2,000
   d. Source of funds
      1. Personnel costs for all crew workers will be paid through increased commercial revenue.
      2. Personnel costs for crew supervisor:
         i. 75% to be paid through public funds (21 worker-months @ $425/month/worker = $8,945)
         ii. 25% of salary to be paid from commercial revenue.
      3. Start-up funds from Developmental Disabilities Office @ $1,750/worker = $5,250.

Figure 5.2. Sample annual management plan.

by ensuring that resources are properly distributed to reinforce the objectives of supported employment. The work allocation policy described earlier in this chapter and presented in Table 5.1 is one example of such a policy.

Program Operating-Level Decisions Program stategies that are defined by the board of directors and the policies that guide the implementation of plans are necessarily broad. Policy-level decisions must still be translated into the activities required for daily program operations. The process for making daily decisions is similar to the planning process already described, and requires making performance decisions, implementing the decisions, measuring actual performance against desired performance, identifying problems, and making adjustments when needed. The monthly tracking form presented in Figure 5.4 provides a framework for managers to summarize

1. Chart of accounts	2. Last year	3. Current year to date (# of months)	4. Percent of income	5. Budget draft #1	6. Notes ref.	7. New income/ expenses	8. Notes ref. for #7	9. Budget draft #2 (5 + 7)	10. Board revisions

Explanation of columns:

1. Enter the Chart of Accounts in this column.
2. Enter the total funds received/spent for the last full financial year (e.g., Jan. 1, 1986–Dec. 31, 1986)
3. Enter the funds received/spent for the current year to date, and the number of months included in this period (e.g., Jan. 1, 1987–Oct. 31, 1987; 10 months).
4. Enter the percent of income represented by each account. This percentage may be compared with anticipated percentages of budget drafts.
5. Project the 12–month period (e.g., January 1, 1988–December 31, 1988) based on the current experience recorded in columns 2 through 4, increasing according to rate of inflation or by more accurately identified means when possible. Decrease any amount by any significant one-time expenses (e.g., program start-up costs).
6. Reference or note the rationale and/or source of any changes made from previous experience (e.g., "10%" representing a general inflationary increase; "5% June employee raise" representing a cost-of-living increase for employees; or itemizing percentages and categories of payroll taxes).
7. New income/expense projections that are the financial impact of objectives listed on the annual plan (e.g., a new staff position at $18,000 or anticipated equipment purchase added to the anticipated depreciation costs).
8. Reference the plan objective and/or the rationale of new income or expenses.
9. Add columns 5 and 7 for a new budget draft.
10. Revise figures based on the discrepancy between projected income and expense, subsequent budget reviews by committee and board and any new information. These revisions will continue for several more drafts.

The final budget should include columns 1, 2, 3, the final projected budget approved by the board, and a narrative giving significant details of columns 6 and 8.

Figure 5.3. Sample budget worksheet.

Table 5.1. Sample work allocation policy

XYZ Crews, consistent with its company mission and goals, seeks to provide long-term supported employment opportunities for its employees. The intention of this policy is to ensure access to work for employees with disabilities. However, it is expected that crew organizations will maintain a sufficient volume of work that requires employment of workers without identified disabilities. Based on this, first access to work will always be given to workers with disabilities, with work then assigned to nonhandicapped crew members and supervisors. Among crew members with disabilities, work will be allocated first to the employees who know the fewest tasks or have the lowest monthly wages.

the policy-level planning documents in a format that tracks activities toward annual objectives.

The basic process of controlling the organization's progress toward accomplishment of its intended objectives is the same regardless of the topic. Staff must establish some form of expectations or standards, measure performance against these, and make any required adjustments. With personnel, for example, staff job descriptions can be useful in establishing the "standards" for personnel, with performance-based evaluations employing these documents. Chapter 7 provides further discussion and examples.

Individual-Level Decisions The same process for controlling progress towards accomplishments also applies to individual decisions. In individual planning, objectives are set and performance plans developed. Measuring performance against those objectives, and making adjustments in strategies when performance does not match objectives, complete the decision loop. The decision loop for decisions at the individual level is maintained both by the individual planning team that sets objectives and strategies, and by the "implementers" who provide training and other support to meet those objectives. At both levels, performance must be measured and plans or strategies adjusted to achieve objectives.

Analysis of Discrepancies

The final phase of the decision loop involves comparing what is reportedly occurring in the supported employment setting to the outcomes specified in the organization planning document. When discrepancies exist between planned and actual performance, the reasons must be determined so that corrections can be made. A good information system may supply the obvious reasons for performance problems; however, analysis must frequently go further than permitted by the data reports. The three tools described below vary widely in utility, but have proven useful in diverse programs.

Objective/activity		Jan.	Feb.	March	April	May	June	July	Aug.	Sept.	Oct.	Nov.	Dec.	Status
Total commercial revenue = $132,300	Target	$8,840	$8,840	$8,840	$11,200	$11,200	$11,200	$11,200	$11,200	$11,200	$12,900	$12,900	$12,900	
	Actual	$9,107	$8,650	$9,342										
	Cumulative Total	$9,107	$17,757	$27,099										
Number of productivity-based crew workers	Target	—	—	—	—	—	—	—	—	—	—	—	—	—
	Actual	—	—	—										
Number of hourly crew workers	Target	13	13	13	15	15	15	15	15	15	16	16	16	
	Actual	13	13	13										
Purchase van and equipment for 1 crew	Target	2	2	2	3	3	3	3	3	3	4	4	4	
	Actual	2	2	2										

Figure 5.4. Sample annual plan monthly tracking form.

Process Control Charts Successful employment is influenced by an individual's job performance, whether in entrepreneurial approaches or with individual jobs in competitive environments. Job performance depends partially on the quality of task analysis and training. It also depends on the ability of supervisors or support staff to identify performance problems. The *pareto diagram* is a powerful information tool for processing inspection data (Ishikawa, 1976). The pareto diagram simply indicates which problem should be solved first in eliminating defects and improving an operation. The usefulness of the pareto diagram was a fundamental part of International Telephone and Telegraph's eight-step recovery plan and was used to assure that areas of maximum return were dealt with first (McRobb, 1984). These benefits can extend to supported employment situations, regardless of the approach being taken. The value of the pareto diagram is that it is value free, can be easily made by anyone with experience with bar graphs, is very inexpensive to institute, and fosters a team approach to correcting failures.

Figure 5.5 represents a pareto diagram which depicts the manufacturing performance of a small number of disabled employees within an enclave in an electronics industry manufacturer. In this figure, workmanship problems are evident in four areas. The pareto diagram notes these areas, employs a bar graph to depict the number of occurrences, and records the percent of total errors that each type of error represents. For example, incorrect strip length and damaged wire were the two most common errors. These accounted for 68% of the errors. Improvement efforts are directed first to these two problem areas. On the second day, as shown in Figure 5.6, these problems were either remedied or diminished. The pareto diagrams in Figure 5.5 also demonstrate a rising material problem labeled "internal contacts," which grew from two to four instances during the two-day reporting period. These become the focus of concern for the supervisor and support staff during the second day.

Troubleshooting Tree The identified accomplishments or outcomes at each level of the organizational accomplishment model, as described in Chapter 2, appropriately focus management attention on outcomes first, rather than on employee behaviors. When targeted accomplishments are not attained, the organizational model can be used to pinpoint the area of concern in order to focus management attention in the right place before procedures or behavior are looked at. Interventions can then be designed to improve performance relating to the specific behaviors required. This is achieved by reorganizing the organizational accomplishment model into a "troubleshooting tree" format, as presented in Figure 5.7.

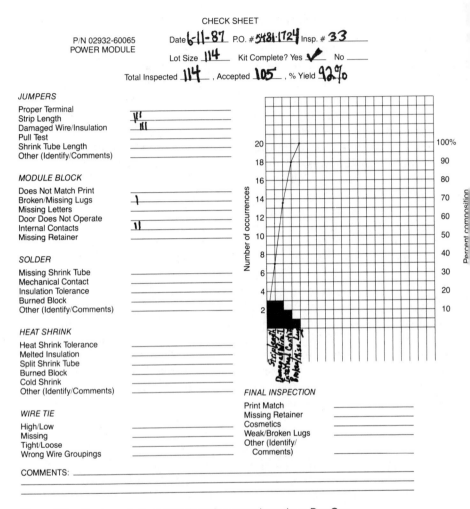

Figure 5.5. Pareto analysis of manufacturing errors in enclave: Day One.

Using a troubleshooting tree permits rapid identification of the area with the greatest potential for improved performance. To use the troubleshooting tree, obtain measures of actual performance and compare those against a set standard for each of the accomplishments at the top level of the tree. Select for initial attention the measure with the greatest potential for improvement against the standard, or with the greatest potential economic value to the organization if the improvement is realized. Continue in the same way down the tree, always selecting the branch with the greatest potential for improvement. In this manner, by asking the fewest number of questions, the

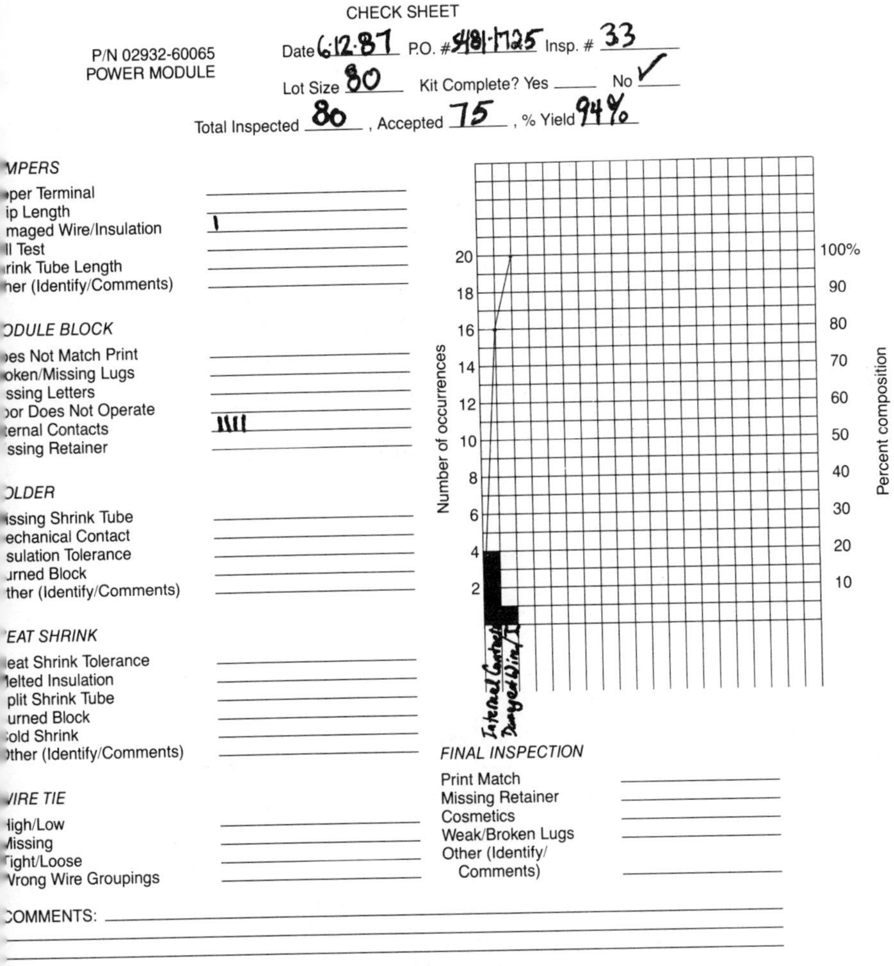

CHECK SHEET

P/N 02932-60065
POWER MODULE

Date 6·12·87 P.O. # 5481·1725 Insp. # 33

Lot Size 80 Kit Complete? Yes _____ No ✓

Total Inspected 80 , Accepted 75 , % Yield 94%

MPERS
- ⸱per Terminal
- ip Length
- maged Wire/Insulation |
- ll Test
- ⸱rink Tube Length
- ⸱her (Identify/Comments)

⸱DDULE BLOCK
- ⸱es Not Match Print
- ⸱oken/Missing Lugs
- ⸱ssing Letters
- ⸱or Does Not Operate
- ⸱ternal Contacts ‖‖
- ⸱ssing Retainer

⸱DLDER
- ⸱ssing Shrink Tube
- ⸱echanical Contact
- ⸱sulation Tolerance
- ⸱urned Block
- ⸱ther (Identify/Comments)

⸱EAT SHRINK
- ⸱eat Shrink Tolerance
- ⸱lelted Insulation
- ⸱plit Shrink Tube
- ⸱urned Block
- ⸱old Shrink
- ⸱ther (Identify/Comments)

⸱IRE TIE
- ⸱igh/Low
- ⸱lissing
- ⸱ight/Loose
- ⸱rong Wire Groupings

FINAL INSPECTION
- Print Match
- Missing Retainer
- Cosmetics
- Weak/Broken Lugs
- Other (Identify/ Comments)

COMMENTS: _____

Figure 5.6. Pareto analysis of manufacturing errors in enclave: Day Two.

manager can identify the duties or logistics that will have the greatest positive impact on performance of the selected major accomplishment. Only after one traces through levels of the troubleshooting tree from the most general to the most specific, should attention shift from accomplishments or outcomes to behavior. At this point, it is worthwhile to look at the information, incentives, facilities, and tools provided to staff to do the identified duty; at the individual's knowledge, capacity, and motivation to perform the duty well; and at the management system, including standards, organization, and resources.

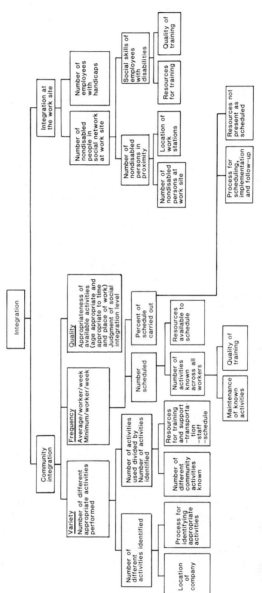

Figure 5.7. Sample troubleshooting tree for the accomplishment, "Achieve Integration."

External Evaluations   External evaluations are frequently useful for the boards of directors and others involved in program administration. These reviews compare the practices of a program with the policies and standards established by the governing board, purchaser of services, or regulatory agencies. The Association of Supported Work Organizations provides an excellent example. All member organizations have a policy requiring at least a yearly external review. The review employs a combination of outcome measures and probes of program policies and procedures to determine to what extent a program is maintaining the standards and outcomes required of members. The process helps boards and staff by providing technical assistance and verification that model procedures are being followed; the process similarly is helpful to funding agencies. Member organizations meet annually to update standards.

The association's review process is designed for use on a regular basis, rather than for "one-shot" evaluation. In each case, the review provides objective information about the progress of employees and the use of systematic procedures by staff. The review is designed to produce substantive reinforcers for staff as well as useful guidelines for change. Its primary purposes are: 1) to index the quality of procedures being used in an organization, 2) to identify functional tasks to improve implementation of procedures, 3) to record program accomplishments, including the employment and integration outcomes that occurred during the review period, 4) to determine the financial status of the company, and 5) to assist in the development of the organization's management plan. Figure 5.8 provides a demonstration of the features and standards of the checklist for a supported jobs approach.

SUMMARY

The basic management functions within supported employment programs are the same as in other businesses. The focus on specific, tangible consumer benefits has advantages for developing effective management systems. This chapter presented general issues that managers of supported employment programs are likely to face regardless of the approach these organizations take, and strategies for addressing some of those issues.

REFERENCES

Baer, D. M. (1981). *How to plan for generalization*. Lawrence, KS: H & H Enterprises, Inc.

Company _____
Address _____

Date of model implementation: _____
Number of staff: _____

_____ (Name)   _____ (Title)

Date: _____
Data reviewed from _____ to _____
Review team: _____

Type of review: _____

Level of model implementation: Total
Paid employment opportunities ___ %
Work requirements ___ %
Integration ___ %
Service coordination ___ %
Management ___ %

Number of current paid placements: _____

ACCOMPLISHMENT I: Paid employment opportunities available

Level of implementation _____

Responsibilities	Duties	+/-	Tactics
A. Jobs arranged and agreements signed MEASURES: Number of jobs filled during review period: ___ Number of employers contacted: ___ Number of new signed agreements: ___ Number of qualified employers: ___	1. Prospective employers identified		1. Complete market analysis. 2. Complete marketing plan. 3. Develop marketing materials and plan approach for phone and personal contacts with potential employers. 4. Establish and maintain employer files, documentation system for marketing contacts, information system for marketing outcomes, and system for managing recontact dates. 5. Implement marketing plan. 6. Develop networking strategy for identifying potential employers (e.g., establish job development committee, join local business associations.)

7. Evaluate and adjust marketing strategies as needed.
COMMENTS:

1. Establish format and decision rules for qualifying prospective employers.
2. Select qualified employers and notify unqualified prospects.
3. Maintain contact with qualified prospective employers and document contacts and status.
COMMENTS:

2. Prospective employers reviewed and qualified

ACCOMPLISHMENT II: Work requirements met

Responsibilities	Duties	+/−	Level of implementation — Tactics
A. **Work organized for performance** MEASURES: Number/percentage of jobs with completed job analysis: Number/percentage of jobs with completed task analysis:	1. Job analysis for individual performance completed.		1. Develop job analysis content, format, and procedures (e.g., layout, workflow, schedule, variable duties, productivity standards, social skill needs, quality standards). 2. Implement job analysis procedures. 3. Maintain job analysis documentation and update job analysis as needed.

Figure 5.8. Sample external review: Excerpt from supported jobs implementation checklist. Note: Plus sign (+) indicates "implemented," minus sign (−) indicates "unimplemented."

(continued)

Figure 5.8. *(continued)*

Responsibilities	Duties	+/-	Tactics
Number/percentage of jobs with maintenance plans: _____	2. Task design and analysis completed.		COMMENTS: 1. Complete task design for each job duty. 2. Develop needed performance alternatives. 3. Complete individual or general case task analysis. 4. Revise task designs and task analyses as indicated. COMMENTS:
	3. Develop strategies for maintaining performance.		1. Assess maintenance needs. 2. Develop plan for maintaining performance 3. Establish maintenance evaluation/information system. COMMENTS:
IIA: _____			
B. Work performed MEASURES: Number/percentage of workers in training: _____ Number/percentage of workers in maintenance: _____	1. Workers trained to perform jobs		1. Train worker to perform each job to specifications under supervision of the employer. 2. Maintain performance data during training and fading. 3. Assess productivity for payroll calculations.

110

4. Analyze data and adjust job analysis, training, and fading procedures as indicated.

COMMENTS:

2. Job performance maintained

1. Implement plan for maintaining performance, including periodic productivity measures.
2. Train workers in self-management strategies, as indicated.
3. Design and implement work-rate programs as needed.
4. Maintain worker performance data.
5. Analyze worker performance data, providing retraining, or adjusting maintenance strategies as indicated.

COMMENTS:

IIB: _____

111

Bellamy, G. T., & Boles, S. M. (1984, November). *Crisis prevention through management controls: Illustrations from community services for persons with severe mental retardation*. Paper presented at the Texas Department of Mental Health and Mental Retardation Symposium on Crisis Treatment and Prevention in the Mentally Ill and Retarded, Houston.

Drucker, P. F. (1974). *Management: Tasks, responsibilities, practices*. New York: Harper & Row.

Drucker, P. F. (1985). *Innovation and entrepreneurship*. New York: Harper & Row.

Engelmann, S. E., & Carnine, D. W. (1982). *Theory of instruction: Principles and applications*. New York: Irvington.

Greenspan, S., & Shoultz, B. (1981). Why mentally retarded adults lose their jobs: Social competence as a factor in work adjustment. *Applied Research in Mental Retardation, 2*, 23–28.

Gulick, L., & Urwick, L. (1937). *Papers on the Science of Administration*. New York: Institute of Public Administration.

Haring, N. G., Liberty, K. A., & White, O. R. (1980). Rules for data-based strategy decisions in instructional programs: Current research and instructional implications. In W. Sailor, B. Wilcox, & L. Brown (Eds.), *Methods of instructions for severely handicapped students*, pp. 159–194. Baltimore: Paul H. Brookes Publishing Co.

Hill, M., & Wehman, P. (1983). Cost-benefit analysis of placing moderately and severely handicapped individuals into competitive employment. *Journal of the Association for Persons with Severe Handicaps, 8*(1), 30–39.

Horner, R. H., & Albin, R. W. (1986). Toward lifestyle change in community settings: An applied technology of maintenance. Unpublished manuscript, Specialized Training Program, University of Oregon, Eugene.

Ishikawa, K. (1976). *Guide to quality control*. Tokyo: Asian Productivity Organization.

Mank, D. M., & Horner, R. H. (1987). Self-recruited feedback: A cost-effective procedure for maintaining behavior. *Analysis and Intervention in Developmental Disabilities*.

McRobb, R. (1984, May). Industry's lost costs. *Management Today*, pp. 56–59.

O'Brien, J. (1987). A guide to personal future planning. In G. T. Bellamy & B. Wilcox (Eds.), *A comprehensive guide to the Activities Catalog: An alternative curriculum for youth and adults with severe disabilities*. Baltimore: Paul H. Brookes Publishing Co.

Peters, T. J., & Waterman, Jr., R. H. (1982). *In Search of Excellence*. New York: Harper & Row.

Rudrud, E. H., Rice, J. M., Robertson, J. M., & Tolson, N. M. (1984). The use of self-monitoring to increase and maintain production rates. *Vocational Evaluation and Work Adjustment, 17*(1), 14–17.

Rusch, F. R., Morgan, T. K., Martin, J. E., Riva, M., & Agran, M. (1985). Competitive employment: Teaching mentally retarded employees self-instructional strategies. *Applied Research in Mental Retardation, 6*(4), 389–407.

Sowers, J., Verdi, M., Bourbeau, P., & Sheehan, M. (1985). Teaching job independence and flexibility to mentally retarded students through the use of a self-control package. *Journal of Applied Behavior Analysis, 18*, 81–86.

Wacker, D. P., & Berg, W. K. (1986). Generalizing and maintaining work behavior. In F. R. Rusch (Ed.), *Competitive employment: Service delivery models, methods, and issues* (pp. 129–140). Baltimore: Paul H. Brookes Publishing Co.

Chapter 6

Choosing Quality in Supported Employment

Choices about program quality are an integral part of any service system. For supported employment, these choices are made by legislators, who must decide if supported employment provides a greater return on public investment than competing services. Choices about quality are also made by public agencies, which implicitly endorse particular approaches in deciding which programs will get public financial support. Quality choices are made by service providers who wish to improve existing services, and by service consumers and advocates who select programs that best fit individual interests, needs, and values.

What these choices about quality have in common is an assessment of a supported employment program, and a consequent decision about participation in the program. These choices therefore fall within the framework of quality assurance (Wray, 1985) and decision-oriented program evaluation (Stuffelbeam & Webster, 1980). The purpose of this chapter is to provide a guide for considering quality during decision-making about developing, funding, operating, and participating in supported employment options.

The chapter examines four opportunities to choose quality in supported employment: 1) program development decisions concerning how to plan and organize supported employment efforts, 2) investment decisions related to deciding which programs to fund or support, 3) administrative decisions concerning how to improve existing services, and 4) participation decisions concerning which program is best suited to a particular individual. First, to provide a context for these decisions, the concept of quality itself is explored.

QUALITY IN SUPPORTED EMPLOYMENT

What Is Quality?

In business and human service discussions of quality assurance, quality is commonly defined as conformance to standards (Crosby, 1979; Wray, 1985). This definition raises questions about what the standards are, who determines their importance, and what values they reflect. In supported employment, quality is clearly an issue of judgements about what employment should provide to any working person. Consequently, a good way to start defining quality in supported employment is to look at the conditions and outcomes that workers in general consider important.

The job features each individual seeks are numerous and diverse. Compensation, quality of the social and physical work environment, security, job mobility, community characteristics, and level of interest in the work itself may be considered when one decides whether to accept, retain, or leave a job. The same considerations must apply to jobs held by persons with severe disabilities. Any effort to simplify these choices by reducing quality to a single job dimension makes a caricature of the working lives of persons with disabilities.

The concept of quality in supported employment is even more complex because supported employment is both a job and a service. The quality of services is indicated by such measures as public accountability, the extent to which the service reflects individual choice and dignity, and its effectiveness at creating successful outcomes for service users. Quality in supported employment is reflected in how well a job creates choices for the individual with a disability, structures his or her time, provides opportunities for advancement, creates social opportunities, and influences where and how he or she lives. At the same time, quality in supported employment reflects the effectiveness of publicly funded service programs in securing and maintaining jobs that actually create benefits for persons with severe disabilities.

Choosing Quality Is Important

Decisions made during the current period of rapid development of supported employment will structure the work opportunities available to adults with severe disabilities for the foreseeable future. Program planning and development decisions commit communities to particular approaches and build lasting expectations among employers, advocates, and service providers. Investment and administrative decisions determine how limited capital will be spent to develop and influence services, thereby creating self-perpetuating program structures and professional constituencies. Participation decisions have similarly enduring effects for the individual—once a program placement is made, funding constraints, personal relationships, and the skills one develops may all argue against transfer to a different program or job. Because the programs developed now can be expected to persist, the effort expended in decisions that influence quality will have lasting effects.

Choosing Quality Is Difficult

There is always pressure to base program decisions on considerations other than quality. For example, deinstitutionalization plans impel rapid program development. Consequently, it is often availability, rather than quality, that determines which programs are funded. The fear of having no service may lead parents and advocates to accept whatever is offered regardless of appropriateness or quality. Financial considerations prompt service agencies to prefer certain program approaches, and pressure to increase the population served often leads to unsatisfactory options for everyone.

Basing program decisions on considerations of quality is also difficult because there is no single optimal approach to providing supported employment. Unique strategies are needed for program planning and development to reflect local differences in the economy, service needs, and resources. Diversity also provides flexibility in creating job opportunities, and expands service consumers' choices. Since there is no single best way to provide supported employment, choices concerning quality must be made by identifying a few important features which can be used to compare different programs.

Indicators of Quality

Choices concerning supported employment will always involve compromises among a variety of desirable features of the service and employment situation. To base the decision to fund, recommend, or participate in a supported employment program on considerations of quality, one must either implicitly or explicitly combine information about several program features.

A useful way to integrate the many aspects of quality in supported employment is to return to the five accomplishments described in Chapter 2 as necessary components of any supported employment program. Quality in supported employment can be indexed by the extent to which each of these five tasks is done well and generates the intended benefits for employees with disabilities. For example, quality in the creation of work opportunities could be reflected in the number and variety of jobs available to an individual, the kinds of job development strategies used, the extent to which jobs are created in areas where potential workers prefer to live, and the income potential of those jobs. Each of the five accomplishments of supported employment programs has a similar array of possible quality features. These can be organized by distinguishing between *inputs, processes,* and *outcomes* as dimensions of quality in service programs.

The *input dimension* of quality consists of the resources and constraints with which a program begins the service delivery process. As such, inputs are often said to reflect the capacity of the program to offer high-quality services. Examples of inputs include the level of funding, staff characteristics, features of the community, and the needs of the individuals who will be served. Each of these inputs is required, but does not guarantee high quality.

The *process dimension* of quality refers to the actual performance of the organization—the interaction between the organization and the individual receiving services, and the management activities required to sustain that interaction. Processes evaluated as indicators of quality might include the training and behavior change procedures used by a program, recordkeeping systems, and management characteristics.

The *outcome dimension* of quality reflects the benefits which service recipients enjoy as a result of participating in the program. Outcomes are the aspects of one's life that change as a result of service, and could include measures such as income level achieved, skills developed, and level of community participation.

Whether something is considered an input, process, or outcome of service sometimes depends on one's perspective. An individual receiving services, a provider of those services, and a funder of services begin their involvement with different inputs, and influence somewhat different processes. The distinction is most useful when a single perspective is maintained. For this discussion, inputs, processes, and outcomes are defined from the perspective of the service program.

Together, the five accomplishments of any supported employment program and the three quality dimensions of inputs, processes, and outcomes provide a useful framework for analyzing quality features in supported employment. The Quality Features Matrix in Figure 6.1 uses this framework to describe the primary quality indicators for supported employment.

For the accomplishment of creating work opportunities, the critical input-related quality feature consists of the job opportunities available in the general community. These might be measured using the unemployment rate, the rate at which jobs are created in the community, or other general labor market indicators. The important pro-

	Create opportunity	Perform work	Ensure integration	Provide support	Manage organization
Inputs	Nature of local economy and labor market	Staff skills and organizational experience in teaching and performing work	Characteristics of job sites, including presence of people without disabilities	Level of disability of employees	Cost of startup and operations Management resources
Processes	Marketing procedures	Engineering and training procedures	Opportunity analysis, training, and support procedures	Individual planning and support procedures	Management systems and procedures
Outcomes	Number, type, and earning potential of jobs	Total compensation received by employees with disabilities	Social network Range of settings	Job retention Job promotion	Efficiency ratios (e.g., wages to public cost by disability levels)

Figure 6.1. The Quality Features Matrix: Quality features for supported employment.

cess-related quality feature is the program's procedures for developing job opportunities. This feature could be assessed by comparing procedures to a checklist of accepted practices, by asking what image of disability was created by the marketing effort, or by counting the occurrences of critical job development activities. The outcome quality feature consists of the number, type, and variety of jobs developed, together with the earning potential of these jobs. Earning potential might be indexed by the standard wage rate on which earnings would be computed, if productivity and pay were below minimum wage.

Other possible measures of this outcome include the average number of jobs developed each month, the average number of jobs from which each employee was able to choose, and the average commuting distance between an individual's home and job. These indicators are used somewhat differently for different quality choices. For example, an individual choosing among supported employment programs would be more likely to use information about job development outcomes in his or her neighborhood and area of interest, whereas funders of programs would be more likely to use aggregate measures of job development outcomes such as rate of job development and average income potential.

For the accomplishment of performing work to specifications, the input dimension of quality comprises the skills and experiences of the program and its staff in teaching and doing the available work. Previous experience, training, and certification are traditional ways of assessing these inputs. The process-related dimension of quality encompasses the range of procedures used to analyze and teach jobs, to supervise performance, and to arrange or adapt work flow, process controls, work stations, or other production systems to accomplish work output. Process measures might include the number of new jobs learned, product quality records, and the extent to which productivity improvement programs are implemented. The outcome quality dimension is reflected in the compensation earned by employees with disabilities. Employee wages and the value of benefits are useful outcome measures.

For the accomplishment of integrating workers, the input dimension of quality consists of characteristics of the program and potential job sites. Measures of inputs could include the proximity of businesses to community environments and resources, and the number of other persons with and without disabilities working in the vicinity. The process dimension encompasses the program's efforts to enhance integration through such means as training, support, schedule adaptations, and the provision of coworker information. The outcome-related quality dimension consists of the results of these efforts in terms of actual interactions, joint activities, and friendships with persons without disabilities, in conjunction with the use of typical environments. For the accomplishment of providing ongoing support, the input dimension of quality reflects the characteristics of the individuals served. For example, the anticipated difficulty in providing supported employment might be estimated with a combined measure of skill level, behavioral adaptations, health status, and difficulty of movement. The process dimension again consists of the program's procedures, in this case those related to ongoing diagnosis and remediation of difficulties associated with maintaining employment. The critical outcome feature is the maintenance of employment by persons with disabilities. This could be indexed by measures such as job tenure and advancement.

For the accomplishment of maintaining an effective organization, the primary input dimension is the level of funding received for providing services. This normally includes service fees, capitalization grants, and nongovernmental funding. It could also include attention to the adequacy of available management resources, including board and staff qualifications. Process-related quality features consist of the management procedures used in the program, including staffing approaches, recordkeeping systems, staff training, budgeting, and organizational decision-making. Management processes are a central concern of many widely used program accreditation and evaluation instruments. The primary output dimension of quality for this accomplishment consists of the efficiency with which the organization reaches its goals. This can be indexed by any of several efficiency ratios, such as the level of employee earnings divided by public costs (the public costs of generating income for service consumers), the ratio of earnings to disability level, or a measure incorporating all three indices. Most decisions about quality in supported employment are made with information on only some of these quality features. At times, program developers, funders, and consumers must all use objective information on inputs and processes to predict the outcomes of a service. On the other hand, administrative decisions at the state level may involve using outcome measures to diagnose possible problems with inputs and processes. In effect, informed choices about quality would be those based on consideration of all the components of the Quality Features Matrix. Missing information is filled in with the best guesses, based on the limits and possibilities implied by the inputs, the evidence on what can be expected from various processes, and the problems reflected in different outcomes. Just how this information can be useful is making quality choices is the focus of the remainder of this chapter.

PROGRAM DEVELOPMENT DECISIONS ABOUT QUALITY

The program development process described in Chapter 3 provides several opportunities for decisions about quality in supported employment. Whether the developers are staffmembers of existing service organizations or planning groups for new organizations, they necessarily make choices about the type of program to establish, where to locate it, and whom to employ. Each choice has lasting consequences for the quality of the resulting employment opportunities experienced by persons with disabilities.

Program development decisions largely involve selecting among alternative program inputs or negotiating for optimum inputs. The goal is to develop a combination of inputs that makes possible effective processes which will probably achieve valued outcomes. Inputs are often described in terms of values, for example, in relation to the type of work done or the proximity to people without disabilities. Inputs can also be viewed as factors that make the valued outcomes more or less possible.

Development decisions involve trade-offs. No supported employment program or opportunity is perfect in all respects. In addition, there are fewer jobs with the most desired features than there are persons with severe disabilities needing support in employment. Consequently, making quality choices when developing supported employment simultaneously requires both sensitivity to the situation and attention to several quality features. The objective is to create a pattern of inputs that makes the desired outcomes of supported employment possible.

The input dimensions that affect quality form a useful negotiation guide for program developers. Table 6.1 provides such a guide for developing a plan for establishing an enclave in a manufacturing company. The characteristics presented are examples and do not represent a comprehensive list of input dimensions. Any set of minimum standards would also serve as an example. Actual minimum standards should refer to local conditions and fit within state and federal guidelines.

PROGRAM INVESTMENT DECISIONS ABOUT QUALITY

Assume for a moment that you have been asked to serve on a grant review panel to select a new supported employment service for your county. The county's request for proposals specified that one new program would be funded to serve seven young adults who were leaving schools and a state institution. Proposals were expected to show how these individuals would be provided supported employment. Four grant proposals were received. One described the purchase of a successful local bakery. In this bakery, three of the incumbent employees would be retained, and seven individuals with disabilities would make up the remainder of the work force. The second proposal described the start of a new agency to place and support persons with disabilities in service occupations in the county. The third proposal involved funding an existing workshop program, which planned to return an accessory kit subcontract to a company so that the work could be performed in the company's plant by seven individuals from the workshop. The fourth proposed an enclave in the city parks department, which had agreed to pay on the basis of productivity for a parks maintenance crew that would receive ongoing support from a nonprofit corporation. What criteria would one use to make a selec-

Table 6.1. Sample input features for consideration when developing an enclave

Accomplishment	Input dimension	Less desirable	More desirable	Minimum standard
Ensure integration	1. Physical space	Physically separated from coworkers	Physical proximity to coworkers (e.g., same production line)	Employees NOT in separate segregated building
	2. Number of enclave employees (and/or ratio of enclave employees to coworkers)	More than 8 supported employees and fewer than 100 coworkers	1% or less of total work force	More than 8 supported employees in same work area
	3. Transportation	Segregated bus for people with disabilities	Ride share, public or company transportation	None defined
Obtain work	1. Type of work	Work not typically done by coworkers	Work typical of that done by the host company	None defined
	2. Work routines (hours worked, break and lunch times, and days worked)	20 hours paid work per week (different from coworkers)	40 hours paid work per week (same as coworkers)	20 hours paid work per week

(continued)

Table 6.1. (continued)

Accomplishment	Input dimension	Less desirable	More desirable	Minimum standard
Perform work	1. Personnel status	Legally employed by support organization	Legally employed by host company	Persons employed
	2. Pay and benefits			Based upon productivity, commensurate with wages and benefits received by coworkers
Provide support	1. Available support	Amount of available support is rigid.	Amount of available support is flexible.	Support adequate to maintain employment
	2. Disabilities of enclave employees	Limited service coordination exists; person may not require level of supervision afforded.	Service coordination mechanism determines appropriateness of placement.	Person considered to be in appropriate and least-restrictive environment
Manage organization	1. Enclave staff	Employed by support organization	Employed by company	Skilled supervisor/ trainer available

tion? What would one need to know to select the best of these programs?

Each of these investment decisions must be made before outcomes are available. One must rely on information about similar programs elsewhere, knowledge of the local economy, and the capacity of the respective service organizations to provide the required support. Quality decisions concerning program investment necessarily rely on indicators of an organization's capacity that are believed to be related to desired employment and integration outcomes, and to a description of the processes that will be used by the proposed program. Figure 6.2 presents a sample grant reviewer's guide that could be used to assess quality features of programs in making selection and funding decisions. Communities may weigh each section differently, or may establish minimum scores or requirements for each section.

CHOOSING QUALITY IN ADMINISTRATIVE DECISIONS

The administrator of a state's supported employment is required to rank-order many decisions affecting the quality of services. The administrators can provide technical assistance for programs needing help, expand the size of successful programs, discontinue or reduce the size of less successful programs, recommend that program developers or advocates visit a particular program to learn model practices, or develop performance contracts with service organizations to improve the quality of the supported employment they offer.

Administrative decisions need not be based on guesses about the relationship between input or process measures and the actual outcomes of services. As useful as these measures are in investment decisions, they can only provide an index of the capacity of a program to deliver quality services. Their presence does not guarantee quality. Actual economic benefits to employees and the levels of integration achieved provide an index of service quality. Once again, minimum standards are not adequate measures of quality. Is a wage of $2.50 per hour an example of quality? Yes, if the recipient had no prior earnings or job history and if disruptive behaviors challenge the skill of those providing on-the-job support. But such wages do not signify quality if the worker's performance matches that expected of nondisabled employees earning full wages. Like the input and process features discussed earlier, outcomes of supported employment options must be compared to the exemplary performance of other, similar employment opportunities.

Summary of scores	Reviewer's score	Possible score	Summary comments:
WORK OPPORTUNITY		20	
WORK PERFORMANCE		20	
INTEGRATION		20	
ONGOING SUPPORT		20	
MANAGEMENT		20	
Total		100	

I. WORK OPPORTUNITIES
How likely is it that the program will generate sufficient jobs of a desired type, earnings potential, and longevity to permit full employment to targeted service recipients?
Comments:

Note to reviewer: In answering this question, consider job commitments the program has obtained before submitting the proposal; the projected employment opportunities in the targeted job area and community; the likelihood of success of the sales and marketing procedures; existing contacts with and support from employers.
Score
1 2 3 4 5 6 7 8 9 10 11 12 13 14 15 16 17 18 19 20

II. WORK PERFORMANCE
How likely is it that employees with disabilities will earn significant wages by performing the available work at an acceptable quality and rate?
Comments:

Note to reviewer: Consider the technical skills of the program staff in performing the work; the skills of staff in teaching model work skills to targeted employees; procedures for job analysis, training, supervision, quality assurance, and the systems that improve or assure adequate performance.
Score
1 2 3 4 5 6 7 8 9 10 11 12 13 14 15 16 17 18 19 20

III. INTEGRATION
How likely is it that the program will result in use of normal community environments and resources and sustained social skills with persons without disabilities during the work day?
Comments:

(continued)

Figure 6.2. Sample grant reviewer's guide.

Figure 6.2. *(continued)*

Note to reviewer: Consider the presence of people without disabilities in the workplace and immediate vicinity; proportion of people with disabilities to those without disabilities; opportunities for normal community use during the work day; proposed procedures for identifying integration opportunities and helping workers take advantage of those opportunities; analysis of program measure to monitor integration.

Score
1 2 3 4 5 6 7 8 9 10 11 12 13 14 15 16 17 18 19 20

IV. ONGOING SUPPORT
How likely is it that individuals with disabilities will enjoy sustained employment, given the support procedures established?
Comments:

Note to reviewer: Consider level and type of disability of individuals to be served and employed. Do procedures and resources match likely support needs? What procedures are proposed to identify and remediate problems on the job? How will ongoing support be documented?

Score
1 2 3 4 5 6 7 8 9 10 11 12 13 14 15 16 17 18 19 20

V. PROGRAM MANAGEMENT
How likely is it that program resources will be used efficiently to create a stable support organization that produces employment outcomes for people with disabilities?
Comments:

Note to reviewer: Consider adequacy of program investment in direct service and elimination of unnecessary layers of management procedures used by the program to track its efficiency and success, level of involvement of board of directors in monitoring program outcomes.

Score
1 2 3 4 5 6 7 8 9 10 11 12 13 14 15 16 17 18 19 20

Information Systems to Support Decision-Making

Monitoring outcomes has become increasingly important in the administration of a variety of human services (Carter, 1984; Ciarlo, 1982). Choosing quality in those services involves at least five steps: 1) identifying the potential users of the information and the decisions they need to make, 2) defining the important or valued features of a program's outcomes, 3) developing a measurement tool and method, 4) establishing a process for data aggregation, and 5) distributing summary reports to all affected groups. Initial efforts to monitor outcomes for supported employment programs occurred in conjunction with program development in the state of Washington (Boles, Bellamy, &

Stern, 1984), and as a part of the national supported employment demonstration projects funded by the U.S. Department of Education (Employment Network, 1986). Table 6.2 presents the kinds of information these systems might offer providers, consumers, legislators, and other groups to monitor supported employment programs. This sample report addresses the performance on several key elements of a few programs within a region or state.

The design of an information system for monitoring outcomes begins with identification of who will use the information and what decisions will be based on it. Different user groups need different levels of information. To improve efficiency, service providers need information about the outcomes achieved by each individual and the amount and nature of the training and support delivered. An advocate or family member may focus on information about one individual's wages, the impact of those wages on Supplemental Security Income (SSI), and the nature of relationships that are forming on the job. For the purposes of resource planning, a state agency might focus on the percentage of individuals with severe disabilities who have access to supported employment, and on the costs of providing that service. The raw data summaries may provide the bases for graphic presentations, such as the one depicted in Figure 6.3, which reports data from Connecticut.

Reports such as those illustrated in Table 6.2 and Figure 6.3 are useful to many groups and for many decisions, yet they address integration only indirectly. Though integration is difficult to measure, more and more attempts are being made. Connecticut's government, for example, augments reports on wages and hours with information on community presence and community participation for persons moving into supported employment, based on Galloway and O'Brien's (1981) format for mapping the accomplishments of vocational services (Figure 6.4). Such state information systems can provide important data on the quality and impact of supported employment, including data on wages, costs, person characteristics, and integration.

Benefit-Cost Analysis

Declining resources, fiscal restraint in public budgeting, and the rising demand for adult services have given new importance to the allocation of service dollars. Agencies responsible for allocating funds may not be able to support all desired service options, regardless of the perceived needs for these services. These economic pressures are influencing the choices made among service alternatives.

Benefit-cost analysis involves procedures used to measure quality in terms of the total costs and benefits of a project or decision.

These analyses are frequently used in conjunction with more traditional measures of cost-effectiveness that compare cost of a program or decision with specific outcomes. The public costs of each placement made by a supported jobs organization, or the ratio of dollars in supported employment wages paid for each dollar invested by the public, are examples of measures of cost effectiveness.

Detailed discussions of benefit-cost theory and procedures are presented by Stokey and Zeckhauser (1978) and Thompson (1980). Benefit-cost analysis traditionally has been viewed from the standpoint of society, with all benefits and all costs identified and assessed for value. This net value represents the present and future impact on all individuals and interests involved with the program. There are difficult conceptual and empirical problems in this analysis that are described by Conley (1975), Noble (1977), and others.

Increasingly, however, simple benefit-cost procedures are being used to compare alternative programs within a well-defined context and from the perspectives of the different groups affected by the program, rather than in light of the total net effect on all of society (Cho, 1980; Noble, 1977; Rhodes, 1982). These applications permit greater technical accuracy, and are more practical for service providers and other decision-makers. Thornton (1985) provides an excellent framework for benefit-cost analysis applications in social programs. Hill, Hill, Wehman, & Banks (in press) use Thornton's benefit-cost accounting model to analyze longitudinal data from a supported work model of competitive employment, with results demonstrating substantial economic benefits to consumers and taxpayers alike. The following paragraphs provide a brief outline for conducting an economic evaluation of a program.

Determine the Decision to Be Made   Analysis of a supported employment program should focus on how it has affected individuals employed as a result of the program. Effects on the governmental unit and the company providing employment should also be analyzed. There are many possible decisions to be supported by the analysis— company managers may decide to continue or suspend the program, the local government may decide to continue funding, and consumers may decide on continued participation. These and other decision-makers can use the analysis to compare the program with alternatives. In making this comparison, the general rule is to choose the alternative that produces the greatest net benefit, although many other factors must be considered before a decision is made.

Consider the Effects of Time   Someone doing benefit-cost analysis must select a time period to analyze. There is little professional agreement as to how to estimate the future value of current services or

Table 6.2. Sample outcome report for supported employment programs (SEMP) in a region

State: XX Region: 7	Number in service	Average monthly cost per person ($)	Number in SEMP	Average monthly cost for persons in SEMP ($)	Number not in SEMP	Average monthly cost for persons not in SEMP ($)	Of those not in SEMP, number working 0–19 hours/week in groups<8
ANS	20	325.00	10	325.00	10	325.00	1
QLN	20	310.00	2	400.00	18	300.00	0
BRS	45	238.40	21	200.00	24	272.06	0
MLA	62	290.00	2	290.00	60	290.00	5
BMS	12	365.00	12	365.00	0	—	—
TRA	37	342.00	0	—	37	342.00	5
PLA	41	242.00	41	242.00	0	—	—
TOTALS	237	68,364.00	88	21,032.06	149	45,232.00	12
AVERAGES		288.46		239.00		303.57	

Of those not in SEMP, number working 20–40 hours/week in groups > 8	Average monthly wage all in service ($)	Average monthly wage all not in SEMP ($)	Average monthly wage all in SEMP ($)	Of those in supported employment: type of work				Of those in SEMP, wages earned for every public dollar spent	Of those not in SEMP, wages earned for every public dollar spent
				Individual job	Enclave	Crew	Small business		
4	195.00	40.00	350.00	6	4	0	0	$1.07	$0.12
18	83.80	52.00	280.00	2	4	0	0	$0.70	$0.21
12	164.40	37.00	310.00	10	7	4	0	$1.55	$0.14
20	62.58	51.00	410.00	2	0	0	7	$1.41	$0.18
—	198.00	—	198.00	0	0	5	7	$0.54	—
10	71.00	71.00	—	—	—	—	—	—	$0.21
—	476.00	—	476.00	41	0	0	0	$1.97	—
64	41,373.00	8,091.00	30,906.00	61	11	9	7	$1.46	$0.18
	174.57	54.30	351.20						

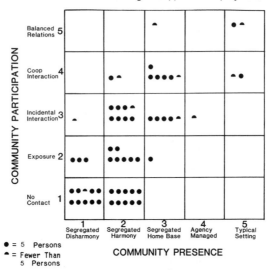

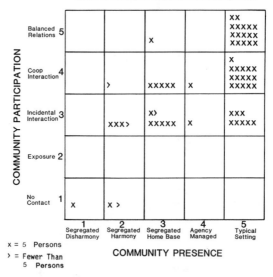

Figure 6.3. Sample supported employment report (Connecticut Department of Mental Retardation, July 1–September 30, 1986).

(a) Number of Participants by Program Model

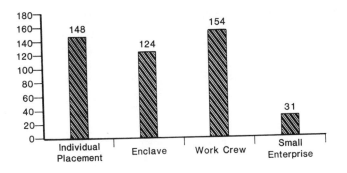

(b) Mean Per Person Annual Cost by Program Model

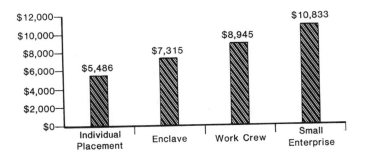

(c) Mean Hourly Wages by Program Model

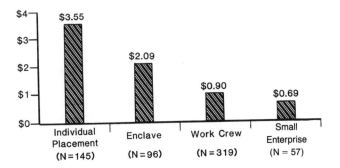

Figure 6.4. Chart depicting community presence and participation (Connecticut Department of Mental Retardation, July 1–September 30, 1986).

training received, unless the individual is being trained for a specific job for which near-term future benefits may be estimated. The authors therefore suggest that the aggregated effects of the program to date be used for analysis, without consideration of the impact of estimated future benefits and costs. With supported employment, there will be a stream of benefits and costs as long as the service is maintained. The most functional assessment will be based on verifiable information rather than on methodologies for predicting future effects of the program.

Analyze the Effects of the Program   A listing of benefits should be made for each of the groups being considered in an analysis. Benefits to one group may represent a cost to another. For example, payroll taxes paid by an individual will be a cost to that person and a benefit to the government. Determine and include the *opportunity costs* in the analysis. In the context of supported employment, an opportunity cost is the amount of benefits lost by not engaging in an alternative program. For example, an individual who earns $60 per day in Program "A" may lose the opportunity to participate in Program "B," which offers estimated earnings of $20 per day. Twenty dollars represents the opportunity cost. Figure 6.5 provides a sample worksheet that identifies some common benefits and costs of supported employment. Benefit-cost analysis provides a tool that may be used by program managers and funders to make administrative decisions based on quality and program impact.

PARTICIPATION CHOICES ABOUT PROGRAM QUALITY

The fourth critical choice concerning the quality of supported employment programs is made by and on behalf of persons with severe disabilities who use those services. These decisions more appropriately reflect individuals' unique values and interests, in contrast to investment and administration decisions, whose focus is necessarily on shared values about what constitutes quality in services. Which supported employment option is best suited to a person's interests, goals, and needs? Traditional diagnosis or vocational evaluations are not sufficient to answer this question. One must know far more than test results and other indications of individual needs and abilities. The choice also depends on the values and interests of the individual and his or her family and friends.

A possible tool for supporting such individual decisions is provided in Figure 6.6. The table, which would be made more elaborate for individual use, asks first what features of a program are important to the individual, and then the extent to which these features are

	Benefits		Costs	
Service recipient	Gross wages	_____	Federal taxes	_____
	Employment		State taxes	_____
	benefits		Lost opportunities	_____
	Paid vacation	_____	(e.g., wages from	
	Paid sick leave	_____	work activity center)	
	_____	_____	Reduced transfer payments	
	_____	_____	(e.g., medical benefits,	
		_____	welfare, Social Security	
			benefits)	_____
	Effects on health and safety, consumer satisfaction, functional behaviors, independence, and integration.			
Company	Tax credits	_____	Costs of service, including	
	Public subsidies	_____	extra costs of	
	Other identified		production	_____
	benefits	_____		
Government	Taxes received		Program subsidies	
	on labor	_____	(fees for services)	_____
	Transfer reduc-		Tax credits	_____
	tions	_____		

Many effects may be a benefit or a cost under different circumstances. For example, some jobs may increase a person's independence (viewed as a benefit), while others may decrease independence (viewed as a cost). These effects are typically difficult to quantify monetarily.

Figure 6.5. Sample worksheet for benefits and costs by sector.

present in any given program. A summary of the desirability of available choices can then be derived from the two sets of information.

CONSTRAINTS ON QUALITY CHOICES

Development, investment, administration, and participation decisions are not always based on quality considerations alone. The purpose of this chapter has been to bring quality considerations into focus so that they may be used more consistently in decision-making.

Although individuals and advocates must be concerned about choosing quality, it is important to recognize the constraints and limits of quality-focused decision-making. In few situations in any part of the United States can a choice be made among a number of excellent supported employment programs. In all cases, some trade-offs will be required. This underscores the need to set priorities among quality functions. Factors that limit quality-focused decision-making include constraints on opportunity, capitalization, and choice.

Accomplishment	Potentially desired job features	Presence of job features (0–3)	Importance of job feature to individual (0–3)	Overall rating (Presence multiplied by importance)
Work opportunity	1. Access to particular type of work 2. Variety of tasks 3. Outdoor work 4. Detail work 5. Proximity to current residence 6. Other _____ 7. Other _____			
Work performance	1. Quality demands 2. Rate demands 3. Strength demands 4. Presence of close supervision 5. Other _____ 6. Other _____			
Integration	1. Regular contact with coworkers 2. Regular customer contact 3. Cooperative work tasks 4. Proximity to community resources 5. Other _____ 6. Other _____			

(continued)

Figure 6.6. Job desirability summary. (Key: 0 equals low, 3 equals high.)

Figure 6.6. *(continued)*

On-going support	1. Continuous social service supervision 2. Parent participation in individual planning 3. Other ____ 4. Other ____			
Program management	1. Responsiveness to family interests 2. Image of disability projected by organization activities 3. Stability of the organization 4. Other ____ 5. Other ____			

Opportunity Constraints

In many communities, access to jobs may be an issue. High unemployment rates for the general community may result in an insufficient number of jobs to meet all service needs. Alternatively, all available job opportunities may be in a single industry (e.g., service jobs). Consumers and advocates are then faced with choosing what is available versus having no employment.

Capitalization Constraints Another common constraint is the lack of sufficient capitalization to start and maintain a program. Few regular businesses enter markets without adquate capital or expect commercial income to support significant noncommercial costs. Insufficient funding can mean low staff salaries, and therefore an inability to attract and maintain highly skilled staff, which results in a program of less quality. Insufficient funding can also lead to constraints on the intensity of training and support, thereby limiting access to a variety of work opportunities for persons with the most severe handicaps.

Lack of sufficient capitalization may also constrain equipment purchases, limiting a program's ability to penetrate a specific market that may offer remunerative work opportunities, or the program's ability to negotiate equipment costs with a prospective host company for an enclave. Whether the supported employment option is an entrepreneurial company or personnel-support organization, public funds should cover the habilitative costs of operating the program. Excess supervision costs, specialized trainers, and uniquely adapted equipment are some of the habilitative costs that are rightfully borne by government. Using commercial income to support such costs may be inappropriate, particularly when it reduces an entrepreneurial firm's ability to compete. Expecting companies to pay additional costs may limit the involvement of these companies in supported employment. *Commercial* costs are rightfully covered by commercial income, and should not be subsidized with public funds. *Habilitative* costs are rightfully paid from public funds. Retained earnings from the commercial activity of an entrepreneurial firm engaged in supported employment should be used at least in part to reinvest in the firm with the purpose of enhancing its position in the market. Remaining retained earnings may be used to reduce public costs. Capitalization constraints may have serious implications for the quality and long-term effectiveness of a supported employment program.

Choice Constraints

Several factors may constrain choices made for program development, investment, administration, and participation. A region's economy may limit the types of work from which program developers and investors may choose when establishing a program. A limited number of existing service providers may restrict an individual's choice of program support structures. Lack of transportation alternatives may limit a person's access to some options, and thereby limit choice. Choices may also be restricted by the home environment, which may be unable to support participation in jobs that require nonstandard work hours. In addition, although several opportunities may be available to an individual with severe disabilities, they are unlikely to be of equal quality. As a result, choices must be based on the values of the individual and significant others, and the relative importance of various quality features.

These constraints should not be accepted as limitations on the strategies to select quality. Some constraints will probably always exist. Seldom will a community be able to support all types of opportunities, with full capitalization, and permit absolute choice without constraints. Yet, it seems clear that an important aspect of the development of supported employment will be advocacy that insists on the development of high-quality options.

SUMMARY

Choosing quality in supported employment is as difficult as it is important. Compromises on quality made solely in the interest of cost or availability can be expected to hamper supported employment for years to come. The dimensions for quality decisions are now being framed. As consensus grows concerning these dimensions, the context will be set for choosing and building supported employment programs with high-quality outcomes for persons with severe disabilities.

REFERENCES

Boles, S. M., Bellamy, G. T., & Stern, J. A. (1984). *A decision support system for managing work programs serving developmentally disabled adults.* Final Report, U.S. Department of Education, Office of Human Development Services, Contract No. 90DDD0041/01. University of Oregon, Specialized Training Program, Eugene.

Carter, R., (1984). Measuring the success of public agencies. *New England Journal of Human Services, 4*(4), 11–18.

Cho, D. (1980). *An economic evaluation of the Japanese model factory employment of handicapped persons.* Wichita, KS: Wichita State University.

Ciarlo, J. A. (1982). Accountability revisited: The arrival of client outcome evaluation. *Evaluation and Program Planning, 5,* 31–36.

Conley, R. W. (1975). Benefit-cost analysis and vocational rehabilitation. In M. Wersinger, I. P. Robinault, & E. C. Bennett (Eds.), *Program evaluation: Selected Readings.* New York: ICD Rehabilitation and Research Center.

Crosby, P. (1979). *Quality is free: The art of making quality certain.* New York: McGraw-Hill.

Employment Network (1986). *Supported employment information system.* Unpublished manuscript, University of Oregon, Specialized Training Program, Eugene.

Galloway, C., & O'Brien, J. (1981). *Mapping vocational services accomplishments.* Decatur, GA: Responsive Systems Associates.

Hill, M., Hill, J. W., Wehman, P., & Banks, P.D. (in press). An analysis of monetary and nonmonetary outcomes associated with competitive employment of mentally retarded persons. *Research in Developmental Disabilities.*

Noble, J. H., Jr. (1977). The limits of cost-benefit analysis as a guide to priority setting in rehabilitation. *Evaluation Quarterly, 1*(3), 347–379.

Rhodes, L. E. (1982). *Alternative investment analysis of services for severely handicapped people.* Unpublished dissertation, University of Oregon, Eugene.

Stokey, E. & Zeckhauser, R. (1978). *A primer for policy analysis.* New York: Norton.

Stuffelbeam, D. L., & Webster, W. S. (1980). An analysis of alternative approaches for evaluation. *Educational Evaluation and Policy Analysis, 3*(2), 5–19.

Thompson, M. S. (1980). *Benefit-cost analysis for program evaluation.* Beverly Hills: Sage Publications.

Thornton, C. (1985). Benefit-cost analysis of social programs: Deinstitutionalization and education programs. In R. H. Bruininks & K. C. Lakin (Eds.), *Living and learning in the least restrictive environment.* Baltimore: Paul H. Brookes Publishing Co.

Wray, L. D. (1985). *Issues in quality assurance working paper number 1: Quality assurance—A framework for human service agencies.* St. Paul: Minnesota Department of Human Services.

_ Chapter 7

Strategies for Change for Facility-Based Programs

Although change is complex, human services experience constant change and development impelled by needs, new ideas, and emerging innovations. Brager and Holloway (1978) describe change within human service organizations as resulting from "problems" or a "frustrated system of strongly held beliefs" (p. 11). Often this process of change begins with a few isolated instances of innovation that eventually affect an entire system. Supported employment, for example, has risen from its beginnings in demonstration programs to a position of influence on the entire service delivery system for adults with severe disabilities. Literature on organizational change refers to this process as the *Spontaneous Contagion Model,* in which change spreads from a small number of practitioners to an entire delivery system (Rothman, Erlich, & Teresa, 1981). This concept of spontaneous contagion applies within an organization as well, where innovation often begins with a single individual trying out a new idea.

Perhaps most fundamental to achieving change is the adjustment required in an organization's goals to make them consistent with solving identified problems in service quality (Rothman et al., 1981). However, at least three additional variables must be addressed for change to occur. These variables include the impact of the change on people, on technology, and on the organization's structure (Brager and Holloway, 1978). Presently, many service provider organizations are vigorously developing supported employment. For this change process to be successful, it must address issues related to implementers (people-focused change), the procedures and strategies for delivering supported employment (technological change), and the organization itself (structural change).

Structuring an organization to develop and maintain supported employment opportunities presents complex issues for existing service providers. Sheltered workshops and rehabilitation facilities have long championed employment for persons with disabilities, and have operated services that frequently contain elements of supported employment. Yet, supported employment's focus on who is served, program size, immediate (rather than future) employment gains, and integration will almost certainly necessitate fundamental changes in many organizations. To complete the changes needed to meet the accomplishments presented in Chapter 2, support and understanding will be required at all levels of the organization. Supported employment planners must address many of the start-up issues discussed in Chapter 3, while also attending to existing organizational features that are incompatible with supported employment and thus obstruct successful implementation. Therefore, the process for achieving organizational change necessarily differs from the development process for new organizations, even though the objectives are the same.

Private providers of developmental, prevocational, and vocational services have been the primary source of community services for people with severe disabilities. These nonprofit organizations have been the heart of the service delivery system, and have a history of responding to the growing demand for community-based care. The late 1950s and early 1960s saw a vast expansion in vocational programs. This was followed by the rapid development of day services for persons with severe intellectual and physical disabilities during the late 1960s and early 1970s, as communities responded to nationwide deinstitutionalization policies. A similar flexibility and innovation is required to expand supported employment opportunities. This chapter presents strategies that service providers can use to restructure their current operations to provide supported employment. It begins with a brief discussion of the development of present services, and describes obstacles to implementing supported employment faced by many existing facilities. Finally, strategies that can be applied by existing nonvocational day programs as well as by organizations that have been providing facility-based employment are presented as examples of the planning and implementation of change.

DEVELOPMENT OF PRESENT SERVICES

Services for persons with disabilities have developed in response to changing service needs and policy initiatives. Most early programs were initiated by residential institutions, charities, and parents' organizations. Programs were provided in a sheltered setting in which some work was possible, with the implicit assumption that work in competitive environments was impossible. Society's investment in vocational rehabilitation has been gradually extended from industrially injured workers to other disability groups, with the realization that it is better to help a person overcome a disability and benefit from work than to have the individual subsist on welfare (Dart, Dart, & Nosek, 1980). This logic was applied to persons with intellectual disabilities by the Vocational Rehabilitation Act of 1954, which provided incentives to prepare individuals for competitive jobs. The services created by this act focused on preparation for job placement. Evaluation for work readiness was stressed, as well as adjustment services designed to help individuals overcome specific, disability-related barriers to employment.

As vocational services emphasized placement and preparation for placement in competitive jobs, growing numbers of persons leaving institutions were considered unsuited for placement in sheltered workshops, and were consequently denied access to these services. Once again, communities and parent groups responded, creating day programs that were often considered prework programs. These day services were generally intended as stepping stones to the more vocationally oriented programs. Growth of these day services was phenomenal during the 1970s (Bellamy, Sheehan, Horner, & Boles, 1980; Buckley & Bellamy, 1986).

A byproduct of the continuum of day services developed under governmental policies since the 1940s has been the creation of conflicting program objectives for service providers. For example, vocational service providers typically have been expected to provide ongoing sheltered employment while simultaneously placing individuals within local businesses, including those in direct competition with the service provider. Logically, it may be assumed that the organizational structure, staffing, and expected results would be very different for these two types of objectives. A program that *prepares* a person for a future job is different from a program that *provides* a good job. Many organizations, seeking to fill the full range of their communities' service delivery needs, have tried to meet these conflicting objectives at the same time. Not surprisingly, few have been successful (Bellamy, Rhodes, Bourbeau, & Mank, 1986). However, in trying to satisfy these community pressures, many organizations have invested in program structures and strategies that must now be reconsidered to meet supported employment outcomes.

IMPLEMENTATION OBSTACLES

Many service providers, in measuring their agencies against the expectations of supported employment, have discovered significant obstacles to implementation. These include the size and structure of the organization, the wide range of needs of the individuals served, existing personnel roles, the program's location, and insufficient access to work. Each of these is discussed next.

Size and Organizational Structure

The definition of supported employment emphasizes the value of integration. To encourage innovation, the minimum expectations for integration are deliberately kept imprecise. The "natural" work site and the "competitive environment" are stressed. Social interaction beyond mere physical presence is necessary but, at present, meaningful measures are lacking. At the very least, however, consensus should be possible on what constitutes the extremes. There is no doubt that the average workshop or work activity center, with 50 employees working in a segregated facility, does not qualify as integrated supported employment. Because the smaller the group, the easier it is to see people as individuals and assimilate them into the work force, federal guidelines suggest that no more than eight persons with disabilities should be grouped together. To provide employment to individuals with disabilities in groups limited to eight or less, traditional programs are often faced with the necessity to split large programs into smaller units of operation in dispersed locations. This implies that a single, large organization may find it necessary and desirable to reorganize into small organizational units or divisions, each with its own specialization, program identity, assigned resources, and accountability mechanisms. Staffing patterns, facility use, organizational structure, and business specialization may all require modification to permit development of these units. In some cases, reorganization may even result in program "spinoffs" that create several independent, single-purpose corporations.

Individuals Served

Many programs serve people who require ongoing support, as well as those who require time-limited support or transitional services. Transitional employment programs may be the most appropriate for the latter. Transitional programs may rely on strategies that overlap with some types of supported employment but provide only short-term training and follow-up. Accomplishments in transitional programs are measured by conventional criteria, such as the number of persons placed in competitive jobs, entry level earnings, and the job retention rate. Transitional programs vary in structure and approach, but many include a period of unpaid training at a central site before placement in an employment setting.

It is inappropriate for persons to be placed indefinitely in transitional programs that are not designed to provide ongoing support in paid employment settings if long-term support is needed. Thus, in converting a large, traditional program to supported employment, it will probably be necessary to establish both transitional training programs for those people for whom time-limited support can be expected to result in competitive employment, and small supported employment programs for those people who may be expected to require ongoing support to maintain employment. The proportion of individuals served who require transitional services, as opposed to those who require ongoing services, will, of course, vary from one program to the next. Indeed, in many existing organizations there are individuals for whom significant, intensive, and ongoing support will be required for successful long-term employment.

The question that must be raised during planning for implementing supported employment is, "With whom shall we begin?" The answers are both important and difficult, and generally have taken two forms. In many situations, organizations and advocates have begun by developing small supported employment projects for those in the agency with the most severe disabilities. The argument in favor of this position points out that the individuals with the most severe disabilities have always been the last in line for improved services, and that a shift to supported employment must begin with success for these individuals. Others have argued for first developing options for those served by the agency who are considered the most capable and who require the least intensive training support in community jobs. This strategy for initial development has been viewed as an opportunity for agencies and staff to experience more immediate success, improve confidence, and create a stronger commitment.

The nature of the response to the question of where to begin will have a significant impact on those served by an agency and the direction the agency takes. Will (1986), in a presentation to state projects engaged in systems change to supported employment, proposed a nonexclusive approach. That is, states and agencies should begin by creating community options for a range of persons needing jobs, from those considered to have the most severe disabilities to those considered to have milder disabilities. This approach, *heterogeneous staging*, has several advantages. First, it makes a clear statement that supported employment is needed and possible for all persons requiring long-term support for employment success. Second, it allows states and agencies to develop competence in meeting a range of needs from the outset. Third, it makes a clear statement that access to employment will not be determined by severity of disability. In this way, access to integrated and supported employment will be determined by the collective ability to develop viable community jobs for individuals, rather than according to the perceived "difficulty" of serving a person.

Personnel Roles

An organization's staffing structure develops in response to internal and external factors such as service demands, availability of resources, staff competence, and management style. An organization's goals, strategies to achieve those goals, and size are perhaps the most signficant determinants of personnel structure. The varied objectives of many services create the need for specialized staff who have few, if any, direct service functions. Evaluators, for example, are likely to be among the best-trained staff, yet are not likely to provide ongoing, direct training and support to persons requiring services on an ongoing basis to maintain employment. The result of reliance on such specialized staff is a "tall" organizational structure, such as that depicted in Figure 7.1, in which many organizational levels—from direct service staff to the board of directors—are required to carry out the organization's mission.

An interesting question to ask of all staff in any agency is, "What do you do that *directly affects* getting people jobs and keeping them in those jobs?" For supported employment to work, staff dollars must be reinvested in direct service staff, rather than in many traditional rehabilitation facility positions. Job roles will have to be restructured in most organizations to accommodate the smaller size of supported employment services, reflect the business specialization of the unit, and increase expertise in direct service. Restructuring job descriptions to include direct service will:

1. Increase the resources available for developing work opportunities and training individuals with disabilities
2. Decrease the level of start-up funds required to meet the increased direct service requirements of supported employment
3. Produce faster results in achieving supported employment outcomes
4. Give persons with disabilities access to those staff who rose through the organizational hierarchy in part because they were the most skilled trainers

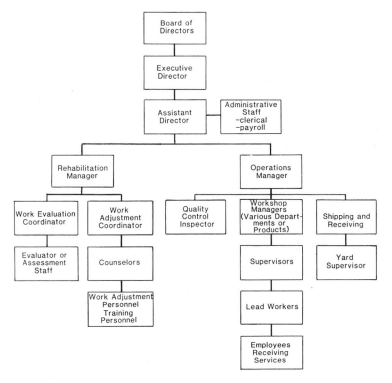

Figure 7.1. A sample "tall" organizational structure.

5. Keep all staff clearly focused on the employment outcomes actually being obtained by persons with severe disabilities

Many personnel will be challenged to develop new skills that blend a specialized business technology with the training technology now required of direct service staff. Chapter 11 provides a discussion of the range of personnel skills needed to implement supported employment.

Facility and Location

The focus on small, integrated settings will make most current facilities obsolete. Organizations that have invested substantial capital in physical facilities, or that have received government grants to build facilities that they are now obligated to use, many face major implementation problems. Facilities designed to meet the service needs of a large number of individuals; those located on the edge of town, or away from public transportation, other regular businesses, and community services; or those that portray a social service image rather than a business image, all face significant obstacles in attempting to implement supported employment. The capital investment made in these facilities may reduce the flexibility organizations have in relocating, and must therefore be carefully considered in any plan to initiate supported employment. Creative strategies may be required to overcome the barriers presented by an existing physical facility. Selling the building, leasing it to another firm, or remodeling it to create smaller spaces that may be leased to several regular businesses (in addition to one supported employment unit) may be required to implement supported employment.

Access to Work

There are several issues concerning access to work that many organizations must address. The first is the impact of the local economy on the organization's ability to provide employment. Opportunities may be limited in some communities, particularly in areas experiencing high unemployment rates for the general population. The types of job opportunities that will be developed must come from a realistic yet creative appraisal of possibilities within the community. The second access-to-work issue is how work is allocated to employees once it is obtained. In many organizations, much of the paid work is allocated to the most capable persons, in part as a means of job preparation and in part as a forced response to past Department of Labor policies that required that a guaranteed wage be paid to the more capable employees working under regular subminimum wage permits, but not to other employees under work activity center permits (U.S. Department of Labor, 1978). A related problem exists when persons are retained in the facility-based program because they are highly productive and are needed to meet production demands.

Although transitional training for competitive employment may be provided for a short time without access to *paid* work opportunities, supported employment cannot be. Thus, long-range plans should include attention to gaining access to paid work for program units that are established to provide supported employment. This may require opening new job markets or initiating new service strategies, as well as thinking differently about how and by whom available jobs are completed. The success of efforts to provide supported employment to people with severe disabilities depends largely on communities, and the individuals and organizations in those communities. If employment objectives are to become reality for the majority of citizens with severe disabilities, resources must be organized to overcome the barriers they currently face. Every community and organization has a variety of resources and opportunities; once identified, they may be used as a basis for change. Plans should be developed only after careful review of these resources. The authors view both the assets and the obstacles as opportunities on which to build, but only when the organization has generated a vision to guide its planning process and its emerging supported employment services. An organization faced with determining its role in the movement toward supported employment must plan carefully long before initiating specific steps for change.

Planning for change requires attention to the support needs and work preferences of the individuals being served. Establishing several mobile work crews to replace facility-based services may be an expedient answer for the organization facing external pressures to change. However, such a strategy is inappropriate if the individuals served do not require that level of support, if they have no interest in crew work, or if opportunities for individual placement are available and needed. Therefore, early in planning, an informal review of the support needs and work preferences of each individual to be served will help the organization when it selects alternative employment strategies.

The resources available to the organization to implement and maintain change also require preliminary consideration. Both internal and external resources should be considered. For example, having a staff person with experience running a print shop may present an opportunity to establish a small business in that specialty. The availability of start-up or changeover funding may permit an organization to consider ventures with higher initial capitalization requirements. A network of contacts in the construction industry may suggest a postconstruction cleanup operation as an option. The position and image of the organization within its community, the physical and financial assets of the organization, the support of neighbors and funding agencies, and similar resources should all be considered at this stage as factors that might help effect change.

With both an understanding of the needs and preferences of the individuals currently served and an awareness of the potential resources available to encourage and maintain change, the organization may begin to establish its goals and objectives for change.

One of the first questions the organization must answer at this time is, "What is the intended scope of change?" Is the organization committed to a total changeover in operations to community-based competitive and supported employment? Is it interested only in substituting supported employment for a portion of its operations? These questions will probably lead to a review—and renewal—of the organization's mission, and, perhaps, a commitment to providing integrated employment outcomes for all individuals with disabilities who are served by the organization.

Objectives for change may be developed by the board of directors, management staff, all staff, or a group composed of staff, funders, and consumers or their advocates. A single, clear goal or mission for the change should be determined as soon as possible, however, and be used to guide the remaining planning and implementation process. Often, this statement will need to be developed by the board and management of the organization. Representatives of all the groups that will be affected by change in the planning process should be involved as soon as possible. Including all groups in planning is one strategy to ensure that the organization obtains the commitment of all concerned to the objectives that are established.

The fears, attitudes, and expectations of incumbent staff, parents, and other concerned persons may be some of the greatest barriers to change faced by an organization. Therefore, they must be addressed early in planning. At one level, humans have a natural fear of new things, and announcing a change to community-based supported employment may trigger such a reaction. More specific fears may be raised for the physical and emotional safety of individuals employed in community settings. Planning for changeover must clearly and directly address those concerns. Partially because of the history of, and their experience with, the development of nonvocational, facility-based services for individuals with severe disabilities, many incumbent staff and family members may have low expectations for the employment abilities of these individuals. The history of such services may also lower expectations. Information can be made available to staff and parents on how supported employment is working in other organizations. Research and demonstration projects can be contacted for videotapes, slide shows, articles and other materials that demonstrate the capabilities of persons with severe disabilities. Brief presentations at staff, parent, or board meetings by individuals who are knowledgeable about supported employment can be arranged. Staff, family members, and others can visit other organizations that have already begun to implement supported employment. A combination of these and other strategies may be required to overcome initial uncertainty and conflicts and to create expectations for successful integrated employment for all persons served by an agency.

STRATEGIES FOR AGENCY CHANGE

Too often, organizations attempt to effect change by simply adding personnel. Little regard is given to the characteristics that influence organizational accomplishments. It has been said that zeal and good ideas may change the actions of persons, but are rarely, if ever, effective in bringing major change to organizations with traditions, long-standing goals, and organizational dynamics.

An organization planning to address the issues involved in changing to supported employment will undoubtedly encounter difficulties brought on by traditions, dynamics, and goals that run counter to new approaches for delivering supported employment. These conflicts must be addressed by policy decisions of the board of directors and management staff, and with support from direct service staff, funding agencies, employees with disabilities, families, and advocates. As already indicated, in setting the stage for change, planners must form a collective vision to guide planning. In particular, decisions must be made regarding the pace and scope of planned changes. The process of changing facilities is, of course, much more than a collection of tasks. Nonetheless, many tasks must be accomplished to achieve change. Table 7.1 and the subsequent text provides one way of grouping the major accomplishments and activities involved in changeover.

Accomplishment 1: Generate Employment Opportunities

Supported employment begins with employment. Once the overall plan has been developed, the first substantial issue facing many programs (as noted in Chapter 2, for any supported employment organization) relates to how to gain access to employment opportunities that will allow each individual to work at least 20 hours a week in settings with no more than seven other individuals with disabilities. Selecting the business or businesses that will be successful in promoting these jobs will be one of the toughest tasks faced by the organization. Final decisions about organizational structure, staff rules, and operating procedures will not be possible before the type of employment opportunity is identified.

Various strategies will be required to obtain work for persons without violating the requirements for individual or small group placement, particularly during the change process. Work may be reallocated immediately to one or more supported employment units if a program has already been involved in business ventures with the local community. This may involve establishing several small, separate enterprises to absorb the different types of work currently done within one large workshop. It might be possible to perform jobs at the customer's location in cases in which the work was previously contracted to the workshop. Such a plan would allow a program to build on its strengths. For example, Diversified Assembly is a sheltered

Table 7.1. Organizational change to supported employment

Generate employment opportunities	Reallocate available work Conduct market analysis Complete marketing plan Obtain job commitments
Create small operating units	Define program focus and transition plan Establish organizational structure for operating units Obtain start-up dollars Select program location
Staff small program units	Re-define roles for staff in present structure Select personnel Provide training opportunities for role changes Create staff incentives Provide tools and materials
Employ individuals with disabilities in each operational unit	Identify individual interests and needs Identify job demands Identify support levels and constraints Select employees with disabilities
Manage each operational unit	Define outcomes Develop operating policies and procedures Develop business planning and monitoring process Invest and monitor financial resources

workshop that manufactures patio blocks and pool tiles, and assembles subcontracted parts for a local motorcycle manufacturer. The volume of work available through these businesses would be sufficient to start two small operations, one in each of these very different industries. For example, the motorcycle parts subcontract could be converted into a small enclave at the manufacturer's site, while the patio blocks and pool tiles could be manufactured by a separate small business with its own identity.

Diversified Assembly may also need to establish new enterprises to provide adequate employment to all persons currently receiving services from the program. To do so, it may need to establish a transitional program to help individuals who do not require ongoing support get jobs, and may plan for another personnel support unit to provide placement, training, and ongoing support within industry. A market analysis will help the organization identify potential specializations. A marketing plan may be developed to guide activities to obtain work commitments.

Accomplishment 2: Create Small Operating Units

Once the type of job opportunity has been determined, small operating units can be created around the projects being established. These units are developed into individual operational entities during the transition of the organization. This accomplishment is fully achieved when all the persons served by the organization are employed in community jobs or small entrepreneurial setups. This will require innovation—purposeful and organized changes that will lead to employment opportunities. The creation of the small operating unit will require a plan that defines the goals, nurtures a structure that permits innovation, and defines the basic businesses that will be developed to initiate employment opportunities. The plan may be used as a basis for obtaining start-up or changeover funding. These plans will be significantly influenced by the skills and interests of existing staff and workers with disabilities, as well as the work opportunities available in the community.

The existing organization must create a structure that allows the innovative program units to be organized separately from existing programs. Drucker (1985), writing about establishing entrepreneurial units, said:

> Whenever we have tried to make an existing unit the carrier of the entrepreneurial project, we have failed. One reason is that . . . the business always requires time and effort on the part of the people responsible for it, and deserves the priority they give it. The new always looks so puny—so unpromising—next to the reality of the massive, ongoing business. The existing business, after all, has to nourish the struggling innovation. But the 'crisis' in today's business has to be attended to as well. The people responsible for an existing business will therefore always be tempted to postpone action on anything new, entrepreneurial, or innovative until it is too late . . . [E]xisting units have been found to be capable mainly of extending, modifying, and adapting what already is in existence. The new belongs elsewhere. (p. 22)

Drucker adds that the best way to avoid killing off the new by sheer neglect is to start the innovative unit as a separate business. This does not mean, however, that a newly incorporated company must be established for each operating unit. Planners must decide if units will be established as separate, freestanding corporations, or if some will be established as major divisions of an umbrella agency with a single board of directors. Either way, programmatic autonomy and accounting must be established as early as possible. Staff should not be assigned broad responsibilities outside the operating unit. A single focus is essential. If maintained as a part of the larger organization, each operating unit should be given the prestige of a demonstration project, and be carefully protected during early development and implementation.

Units with a similar market focus and strategy, but operated in different locations, are perhaps the best candidates for a common board. For example, South County Maintenance Corporation is a nonprofit organization providing supported employment to 15 individuals, organized into five-person mobile crews doing interior and exterior maintenance in different locations in an Oregon county. There is little reason for each crew to have its own board. However, should the organization attempt to develop and maintain a set of enclaves in the electronics industry, the organizational structure and strategies for these are sufficiently different from crew operations that effective oversight of each operating unit could be difficult. Therefore, the authors advise against one organization attempting to develop and operate on an ongoing basis a number of diverse operations. The authors' bias is toward single-purpose operations that focus the development of staff and board expertise, encourage "short" organizational structures with an emphasis on direct service at each level, and facilitate management and accountability. Although a transitional period may be required in which a single organization establishes multiple businesses for changeover of its operations, the long-term plan should include eventual spinoff of those components that differ substantially from others. One organization may be structured as a personnel support business which supports several enclaves as well as individual supported jobs. One company with expertise and contacts related to the electronics industry might reasonably operate a small electronics assembly entrepreneurial business, as well as support one or more enclaves in regular electronics companies. Another company might focus on service industries, supporting individuals in jobs, and perhaps operating mobile crews. A single organization should not attempt to operate both small businesses and personnel support organizations *and* encompass several types of business specializations at the same time.

Creating small program units permits gradual changeover of a large organization. One or two small units may be developed and stabilized at a time until, ultimately, the entire organization has been converted into small organizational units providing either competitive employment training and placement or supported employment opportunities. The sequence of program development and timelines for each unit should be specified in the changeover plan.

Figure 7.1 presented a typical structure of an organization providing sheltered employment and rehabilitation services. This same organization is presented in Figure 7.2 in the transition process, and again in Figure 7.3, after the change process has been completed.

Accomplishment 3: Staff Small Program Units

The staffing of small program units will be attained when each program unit is staffed by personnel skilled in meeting the specific business needs and direct service needs of employees with disabilities. This critical accomplishment defines personnel roles in a different manner from those of most traditional day activity, work activity, and sheltered workshop programs. Staff must have job expertise in the business specialization of the program unit as well as training and other service-related skills. To ensure staff support and success in changing job roles, staff should be involved in planning processes, particularly with respect to their own role changes and timelines. Staff preference and previous experience and expertise may be used as bases for developing and staffing the small individual program units.

For an existing rehabilitation organization, ensuring competent staff performance in the conversion of some of its operations to supported employment will require careful consideration. Five guidelines for ensuring competent staff performance are drawn from Gilbert (1978); these are applied to supported employment in the following paragraphs.

1. Select staff for program units who appear interested in and committed to the success of supported employment. The success of agency efforts depends on staff. Staff who *want* to do the job well and who *believe* in the organization's objectives will be more likely to succeed than those who are ambivalent or who disagree with the organization's direction. Because it is difficult to change employee inner motivation, according to Gilbert (1978), a motivated staff is best achieved through employee selection. Therefore, when staffing new program units, rehabilitation agencies should select from current personnel those staff who are most committed to making agency efforts in supported employment successful.

2. Give staff clear descriptions of what is expected of them, relevant and frequent feedback on their performance, and access to information on effective performance. Develop clear job descriptions for new staff roles and establish measurable performance objectives for each staff person. Consider the sample performance ob-

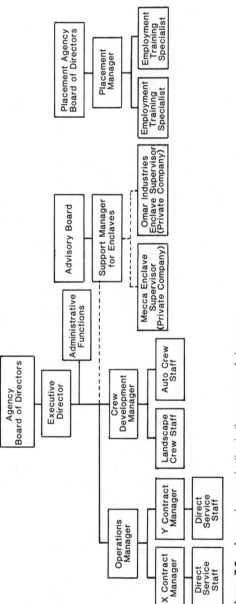

Figure 7.2. A sample organization in the process of change.

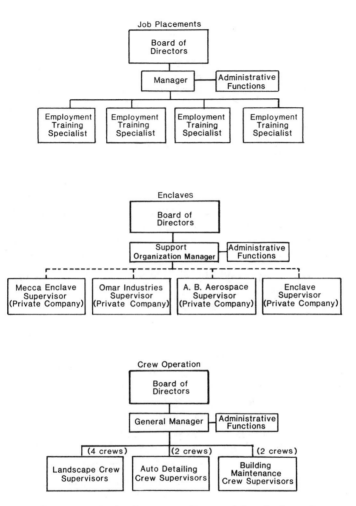

Figure 7.3. Sample organizational structures after completion of a change to community-based supported employment.

jectives for an employment training specialist in an organization providing individual jobs in community settings presented in Table 7.2. These provide a clear description of expectations and facilitate objective and relevant feedback on performance. Manuals and other guides on *how* to fulfill assigned responsibilities will further help staff to perform competently.

3. Provide the tools and materials needed by staff to do their jobs well. Staff cannot be expected to perform in an exemplary manner if their instruments are not designed to match their job performance needs. Adequate tools, equipment, and other resources are

Table 7.2. Sample performance objectives for an employment training specialist in a personnel support organization

1. Identify six potential jobs by February 1.
2. Train five employees in new jobs by April 1.
3. Maintain completed task analyses for 90% of identified job tasks.
4. Maintain weekly probe data on task analyses for 90% of tasks with task analyses.
5. Maintain 60% of employees in jobs for at least 6 months.
6. Submit 100% complete documentation packet each week by noon Monday.

essential for operating a mobile crew, bakery, or print shop. Staff doing marketing for personnel ventures need marketing materials to attract customers, or sufficient resources to develop those materials. Managers of any unit require an information management system for assessing performance in the pursuit of objectives. The most highly motivated and skilled staff will be handicapped by the lack of adequate resources, and their ability to achieve the desired outcomes will be significantly reduced.

4. Provide incentives based on staff performance. Both financial and nonmonetary incentives should be used to reward staff who do their jobs well. Raises should be contingent on achieving specified standards according to the established performance objectives. Other incentives available to rehabilitation agencies might include recognition programs, extra time off from work, promotions, or opportunities to gain new skills. Too often, organizations misapply incentives, such as when *all* staff receive an equal raise regardless of performance. Many organizations also lack imagination when identifying nonmonetary incentives. Staff training cannot be expected to change performance if incentives are not adjusted as well.

5. Provide training that increases staff knowledge and skills. Although staff may have information on what they are expected to do, feedback on how they are performing, appropriate tools and materials, and incentives that are contingent on defined performance standards, rehabilitation agencies should arrange for training suited to staff needs. Supported employment is a relatively new approach to vocational services that encompasses concepts and skills that may be new to incumbent staff. Training designed to provide necessary knowledge and skills will be needed by many of the incumbent staff of rehabilitation organizations.

The simplest method existing rehabilitation organizations may use to ensure that staff have the skills needed to implement supported employment is to select staff members for supported employment units who already possess those needed skills. However, if new skills are needed, a training program must be designed or identified that provides opportunities to practice the desired skills and obtain regular feedback on performance. An effective staff training program that results in the development of enduring, generalized skills must contain these features. Chapter 11 focuses on the staff knowledge and skill competencies required for providing supported employment and strategies for providing training to achieve desired outcomes.

Accomplishment 4: Employ Individuals with Disabilities

When work is available in integrated settings and plans are made for organizational and staff roles, final decisions can be made concerning which employment option will be provided to each employee with disabilities. While setting the stage for change, planners should have made a preliminary estimate. This accomplishment will result in the actual employment of individuals with disabilities through the various operating units. Assignment to individual operations should be less a matter of formal vocational evaluation than a mutual decision based on such factors as individual interests, values, skills, support needs, logistics (e.g., location and availability of transportation), and objectives.

The individual planning process provides the logical basis for determining the employment option for each individual served by an existing traditional agency. This process provides a forum for the individual, advocates, home providers, employment staff, and others where information and preferences can be shared. Individual barriers to employment may be addressed in this meeting, with plans developed to provide the types of support required for the demands of the employment setting selected. By matching each individual's objectives, preferences, and support needs with the available employment options and support systems, the planning group may set priorities among the various developed employment options. It is important that individuals be placed in options that provide the minimum support to maintain them in supported employment. Placement in a job setup that provides more support than is needed both restricts the individual and unnecessarily increases individual costs. Once specific individuals have been selected for program units, the support capacity of operating units can be tailored to meet needs as well. For units offering individual supported jobs, actual job development might be undertaken after the individuals have been selected. In this approach, staff may target specific jobs for development that match individual interests, abilities, constraints, and support needs.

Accomplishment 5: Manage Program Units

Once the organizational structure is established, qualified staff are assigned, work opportunities are developed, and individuals with disabilities are employed through each program unit, the next task is managing those units to achieve the work and integration outcomes defined by supported employment. Chapter 5 presents information on managing supported employment programs, including strategies for organizing to meet the five accomplishments of supported employment. After an organization implements a changeover plan, the management issues are similar to those relevant to the operation of any supported employment program.

SUMMARY

Existing programs face a difficult challenge in transforming operations to supported employment for individuals who have severe disabilities and require ongoing support. The process of change may begin with an individual or collection of individuals, but must be guided by a shared mission and values. Creation of small, separate program units, each with its own business specialization and staff, provides a strategy for completing the changeover of a traditional facility-based program to one that provides supported employment in integrated settings. Quality employment opportunities and major improvements in the overall quality of life of consumers are unlikely to be immediate, just as not all new businesses will be successful. However, some action must begin; ideas and actions that do not contribute to the desired accomplishments can be abandoned, while those that succeed can be pursued.

REFERENCES

Bellamy, G. T., Rhodes, L. E., Bourbeau, P., & Mank, D. (1986). Mental retardation services in sheltered workshops and day activity programs: Consumer outcomes and policy alternatives. In F. R. Rusch (Ed.), *Competitive employment issues and strategies* (pp. 257–271). Baltimore: Paul H. Brookes Publishing Co.

Bellamy, G. T., Sheehan, M. R., Horner, R. H., & Boles, S. M. (1980). Community programs for severely handicapped adults: An analysis of vocational opportunities. *The Journal of The Association for Persons with Severe Handicaps, 5*(4), 307–324.

Brager, G., & Holloway, S. (1978). *Changing human service organizations: Politics and practice.* New York: The Free Press.

Buckley, J., & Bellamy, G. T. (1986). National survey of day and vocational programs for adults with severe disabilities: A 1984 profile. In P. Ferguson (Ed.),

Issues in transition research: Economics and social outcomes (pp. 1–12). Eugene, OR: Specialized Training Program.

Dart, J., Dart, Y., & Nosek, P. (1980). A philosophical foundation for the independent living movement. Rehabilitation Gazette, 23, 16–18.

Drucker, P. F. (1985). Innovation and entrepreneurship. New York: Harper & Row.

Gilbert, T. F. (1978). Human competence: Engineering worthy performance. New York: McGraw–Hill.

Rothman, J., Erlich, J. L., & Teresa, J. G. (1981). Changing organizations and community programs. Beverly Hills: Sage Publications.

U.S. Department of Labor (1978). A guide to sheltered workshop certification. U.S. Department of Labor, Employment Standards Administration Wage and Hour Division.

Will, M. (1986, December). Presentation to semi-annual meeting of state supported employment projects, Washington, DC.

Chapter 8

Strategies for State Leadership in Supported Employment

Many supported employment programs now provide clear demonstrations of the productive capacity of persons with severe disabilities. Preceding chapters have focused on these local programs, identifying the accomplishments and tasks that allow organizations to provide paid work and meaningful integration to persons requiring ongoing support. In this chapter, the focus shifts from local programs to the state activities that support those community efforts. The extent to which the states assume leadership roles will determine, to a great extent, whether supported employment becomes widely available or remains a demonstrated possibility limited to exceptional local programs.

This chapter addresses the broad question of what state agencies can do to promote the development of supported employment as an alternative to day activity and extended sheltered work programs. The chapter is not a cookbook for change. Rather, it is intended as a resource for the development of comprehensive plans for implementation of supported employment. The chapter offers a conceptualization of the change process and illustrates a variety of strategies that may contribute to state leadership efforts. While different strategies will be appropriate in different states, the authors' intent is to provide a sampling of emerging ideas that will facilitate development and implementation of state plans. Although the chapter is primarily for staff within state agencies, it may also be useful to county or regional agencies that administer employment or day services, and to advocates interested in influencing state action.

IMPORTANCE OF STATE LEADERSHIP

The growing responsibilities of states in planning and managing social services is reflected in the critical role state agencies play in the
implementation of supported employment. States may depend on
federal agencies for assistance and cooperation in the shift toward
supported employment, but federal agencies cannot supply a substitute for state leadership. Indeed, the federal government provides
funds that are used by states to support ongoing services, but these are
fragmented among several federal agencies. As a result, there is no
single home in the federal government for ongoing day services, and
no clear responsibility for policymaking, goal-setting, or evaluation.
Not surprisingly, the efforts of federal agencies consequently often
conflict, with the result that program improvement efforts get little
effective guidance. Even if federal efforts were more coordinated,
state-to-state variations in responsible agencies, funding mechanisms, program goals, and delivery systems would make federal leadership insufficient. No matter how broad a federal consensus develops for supported employment, states will have to provide the
critical leadership needed to make this concept a widespread reality
among local communities.

The importance of state functions in no way diminishes the contributions of local programs. Local service delivery agencies have
been the primary source of the innovations necessary to shift from
day activity to supported employment, and they remain the delivery
system on which supported employment depends. Nevertheless, the
preconditions and context for broadly based change to supported employment must be determined by the states. Without state efforts to
develop supported employment through funding, regulations, incentives, and evaluation, even exemplary local efforts will result in no
more than isolated employment opportunities. The movement from
demonstration to implementation of supported employment requires
systematic planning and assistance from state government.

State leadership is also important because of the nature of supported employment itself. By defining supported employment in
terms of the three criteria described in earlier chapters—paid employment, integration, and ongoing support—federal policymakers
shifted critical eligibility decisions to the states. Because, by means of
their budgeting and legislative processes, only states determine who
receives ongoing services, only states can determine who will participate in supported employment. This is particularly important as
states respond to growing pressure from the parents of students with

severe disabilities who are completing public education. Since the passage of the Education for All Handicapped Children Act of 1975 (Public Law 94-142), many of these individuals have grown up in their home communities attending public school. As they have grown past the age of eligibility for the education entitlement, their parents and advocates have effectively lobbied for state appropriations for postschool services. The result is that many state agencies now have the opportunity to expand their ongoing services. That expansion may be directed toward increasing the size of the existing system of day activity and sheltered work programs, or toward promoting the development of supported employment alternatives. The choice lies largely with decision-makers in each state.

CHALLENGES FOR STATE LEADERSHIP

Four primary obstacles must be overcome by most states before effective development becomes likely. These are the uncertainties inherent in generalizing from program demonstrations to widespread practice, the barriers within the current structure of employment and day services, the lack of public control over employment opportunities, and the complexity of the system of service affecting employment.

Uncertainties in Generalizing to Widespread Practice

The great variety of supported employment demonstrations provides encouragement for efforts to implement the approach as a statewide alternative to day activity programs. Successful in both rural and urban areas, among a variety of business types, and with persons having several different characteristics, supported employment does not appear necessarily limited to any one group or setting. Nevertheless, no study or demonstration to date has attempted to include a representative sample of the persons who receive day services in an area or state. None has served all the individuals in a geographic area, so there is little information on possible saturation of the labor market. Also, too few studies and demonstrations have reported enough data on local economic circumstances for an estimate to be made of the potential influence of opportunity restrictions on statewide implementation. Nor is it clear to what extent the skills of staff in model programs can be replicated in statewide services. Even if potential staff were as skilled as those in demonstration programs, the professional recognition and personal accomplishment of initial developers are no doubt different from what will be experienced when model procedures are expected to become standard practice. Consequently, whereas supported employment's utility is quite clear for local programs, it remains to be determined exactly how much of a state's ongoing service need can be addressed with this approach.

Barriers within Day Services

Although day service management has evolved quite differently in different states, most programs' development and current operations share critical features. Major state and federal employment services have traditionally used eligibility criteria that have focused services on persons who could begin independent employment after a relatively brief period of training or rehabilitation. Alternative services and funding streams were developed for persons considered to be unlikely candidates for employment after such temporary services. These services were conceptualized and funded as extended sheltered workshop services in some states, and as day activity, day treatment, or prevocational training in others. In many states, responsibility for managing these ongoing day services was assigned to agencies different from those responsible for vocational services. This split was reinforced by federal programs that created opportunities to finance nonvocational services through the Social Service Block Grant, Medicaid, and the Developmental Disabilities program. In the states, growth of these ongoing day services has been spurred by service pressures related to deinstitutionalization and transition from school to adult services for persons with severe disabilities. The result of these developments is that a distinction developed in many states between the agency responsible for ongoing services and the one responsible for vocational services. This split in state administrative structures has hindered the development of work opportunities for persons with severe disabilities. Effective state leadership requires reconsideration of this traditional separation of agency responsibilities.

Not only does this pattern of agency responsibility tend to institutionalize a nonvocational emphasis in ongoing services, but it also complicates the process of organizing state efforts after a decision to promote supported employment has been made. Two, or often more, agencies can make a legitimate claim to primary leadership in a state's implementation efforts. The vocational rehabilitation agency may see supported employment as an extension of services to another population, and argue that experience with employment as a service goal qualifies the agency for leadership. Conversely, the state mental retardation or mental health agency may argue with equal validity that its experience in managing day programs, and its responsibility for other ongoing services that often complement employment, uniquely qualify the agency for leadership. Which agency provides the necessary leadership is not as important as meeting the challenge to develop new patterns of interagency coordination that produce supported employment opportunities. The danger is that competition among agencies will delay or hinder the coordination needed to implement supported employment.

Lack of Control over Employment Opportunities

Supported employment challenges states in ways that the implementation of educational and residential services does not. This is true because public agencies exercise less direct control over the elements that services require to be successful. Public money can be spent to create local services, but services alone are insufficient to make supported employment successful. Work opportunities in integrated settings are also needed. Consequently, efforts to create jobs will be necessary to supplement strategies that have been used to implement other service programs. Whereas the overall state of the labor market has long been considered largely a result of the macroeconomic policies of federal agencies, increasing attention is being focused on activities that states might use to improve economic conditions (O'Neill, 1985). Statewide implementation of supported employment will no doubt require a combination of service and strategies for stimulating economic opportunities.

Complexity of Relevant Services

The likelihood that an individual with a severe disability will be offered, accept, and be able to perform a job with support is affected by the actions of the person and his or her family, employers, service delivery agencies, and schools. When the many state programs that influence the activities of these parties are identified, a complex picture emerges. Figure 8.1 shows the primary programs in one state. The center of the figure represents the different state agencies that directly influence employment outcomes for persons with disabilities. Lines show which of the four parties feel the influence. Even casual inspection of the figure demonstrates that a change in one or even a few state programs may be insufficient to provide clear state leadership that promotes employment. Disincentives in individual income support programs, scant incentives for business, lack of support for integration in state set-aside programs, and nonvocational curriculum emphasis in public schools could all counteract the best efforts of vocational rehabilitation and mental retardation agencies. Implementing

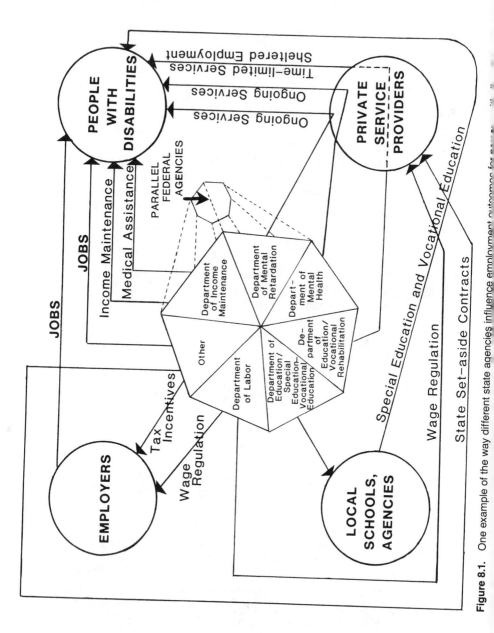

Figure 8.1. One example of the way different state agencies influence employment outcomes for people with disabilities.

supported employment requires an extraordinarily clear state policy goal and an unusual degree of interagency coordination to achieve that goal.

Supported employment initiatives create opportunities that are best managed at the state level if they are to result in widespread, enduring change. But what can state agencies do to take advantage of these opportunities presented by supported employment, while realistically addressing the complexity and barriers that exist in most states? The challenge facing states is to reshape the delivery system of day services into one in which integrated employment opportunities are available to all persons with severe disabilities who want to work and need ongoing support.

AN APPROACH TO STATE CHANGE

The task of shifting an entire state system from one form of service delivery to another is formidable. The gap between a few model programs and large-scale implementation has been widely discussed (Noble, Conley, & Elder, 1986). There is little reason to believe that a statewide move to supported employment can be made quickly or easily. Success across states implies a complicated process that necessarily involves a series of accomplishments. These must include redefinition of state agencies' roles and relationships with the present system, establishment of clear policies and funding techniques, and development of local services.

To make supported employment a genuine opportunity for all persons with severe disabilities, leaders need to accomplish four main tasks: gain access to work, develop and support the system for local services, address key factors in state management systems, and remain mindful of the importance of building consensus among the many important and involved groups present in any state. Accomplishing each of these tasks is essential to lasting statewide change in the availability of supported employment. Together, these accomplishments provide a framework for organizing the many strategies and activities that may be used to achieve change. Even though different strategies will be needed in different states, the objectives of state action can be considered across these areas. Each of these accomplishments is considered in greater depth in the following sections. Critical features of each accomplishment are provided, as well as a brief discussion of strategies to support each accomplishment, and measures of success. Figure 8.2 provides an overview of these accomplishments.

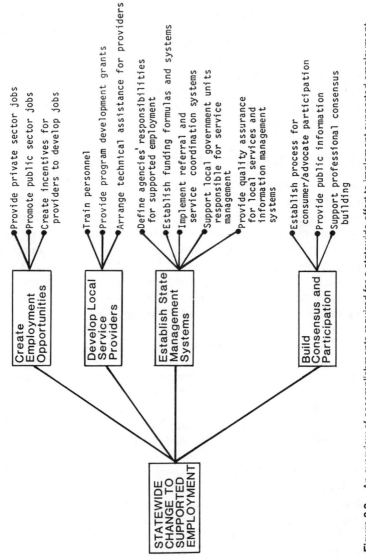

Figure 8.2. An overview of accomplishments required for a statewide effort to implement supported employment.

Create Employment Opportunities

Supported employment cannot exist unless jobs are created in employment markets. Therefore, perhaps the most critical accomplishment for supported employment is gaining access to jobs. However, creating employment opportunities has not often been part of state government responsibilities, because vocational services, rather than employment, have been the focus. The nature of possible work opportunities varies from community to community and from state to state; even so, without well-planned strategies aimed at gaining access to valued work, supported employment will not occur. Creating jobs is a complex task that is not completely controlled by state agencies.

A state's success at creating the job opportunities necessary for supported employment could be indexed by measures such as the number of persons with disabilities statewide who are employed and paid 20 hours or more per week in settings of no more than eight persons with disabilities, or the number of persons in supported employment compared to the number requiring supported employment. Such measures can provide a benchmark that yields information about success in gaining access to employment opportunities.

At least three major thrusts can be identified as important for creating employment options. These include promoting private sector jobs, promoting public sector jobs, and providing incentives to local businesses and organizations to generate access to employment in local communities.

Promote Private Sector Jobs Because the private enterprise sector in any state provides important opportunities for job development, creating a positive image and gaining the support of the business community are essential. Several strategies can be useful at state levels to increase access to private sector jobs.

One of the first strategies used in many states is to involve employers in planning for supported employment. Once aware of the personnel advantages of supported employment to the business community, private sector employers have become important contributors to planning. Some states have formed employer advisory groups and task forces to initiate employer-to-employer contacts concerning supported employment. This strategy can be combined with a state-level marketing approach to business leaders and major employers. Seeking corporate-level involvement is a strategy that creates a broad positive image and should result in job opportunities in local communities.

Another opportunity to promote private sector jobs can be created through involvement in state-level business and trade associations. Participation in such groups facilitates understanding of employer issues and opportunities and involvement in the business community.

The outcome of value is gaining access to jobs for people with severe disabilities on a statewide basis. The task at the state level is to work with the business community to make local job opportunities more likely. This state strategy can be combined with local job development to increase the availability of employment opportunities.

Promote Public Sector Jobs   In many parts of the country, government and related agencies are the source of significant employment opportunities. Although the public sector may not provide as many job opportunities as the private sector, governments are major employers in every part of the country. A focus on statewide and local employment options omits important opportunities if it does not include consideration of public sector employment. Several strategies might be included in promoting access to public sector employment.

One strategy is to review and adjust the set-aside programs that exist in many states. These state programs direct state procurement agencies to give facilities that employ or train individuals with handicaps priority consideration when they bid to provide commodities, services, or both (Cawood, 1979). In past years, state set-aside programs have consisted largely of contract work performed in segregated settings. Recently, however, several states have begun to consider set-aside programs in terms of access to integrated jobs. Considering set-aside programs in terms of jobs rather than contracts keeps a focus on the performance of work in natural and integrated settings. Initiated at a state level, restructuring of set-aside programs can create significant local job opportunities in the public sector.

A second public sector strategy calls for review of public personnel systems and barriers. One approach includes first exploring the development of supported employment with public service unions. Pay scales and procedures might also be reconsidered to allow payment based on productivity. Leadership from state agencies aimed at public service jobs can be expected to have an impact in many local communities.

Provide Incentives   The role of state agencies in the creation of employment opportunities is to make it easier for local service providers to secure jobs, rather than to secure individual jobs directly. Therefore, it is important to create incentives that promote local success. Incentives can be made available to local communities to develop supported employment options. Important incentives can be built into program development grant systems through requirements that applicants demonstrate that commitments from employers exist prior to funding. In this way, dollars create incentives for ongoing job development efforts. Incentives can also be established in a state through collecting and publicizing data on the number of jobs gained by local community programs. Such a system highlights success and provides momentum to progress as it is made.

Other strategies developed in a few states include making equipment and start-up funding available to businesses that choose to get involved in supported employment or providing tax incentives to employers to hire persons with disabilities. The appropriateness of these business incentives has been subject to debate. However, they offer strategies that some states may wish to consider to encourage employer participation.

These strategies are only a few that can be offered and managed by state-level decision-makers. Some states have developed such incentives with encouraging results. Which strategies a state chooses will depend on the strategies already in place, the nature of the state's economy and industry, and the presence of financial resources. No single strategy can be expected to generate a large volume of employment opportunities. However, offered in combination, strategies such as these can have a significant impact in local communities.

Develop Local Service Providers

Local nonprofit service providers make employment with support possible in local communities. Over the years, local service providers in many states have created opportunities and responded to the service needs of people with disabilities. Furthermore, developing the capacity and expertise of local service providers is critical to widespread creation of supported employment outcomes. In many cases, states have an important role in supporting the changeover of existing agencies from day activities to supported employment outcomes. In addition, new supported employment organizatons may have to be developed in many communities.

A state's measure of success in building local capacity can be indexed by the number of local programs that provide supported employment opportunities of 20 hours or more of paid work each week in groups of no more than eight persons with disabilities, or by the percentage of all day programs that provide supported employment and the success of each, with data on service to people with the most severe disabilities included. Such measures provide an indication of both new development and changeovers in existing agencies, such as the development by a new service provider of an enclave of four persons with severe disabilities, or the development by an organization of a mobile crew of three persons with disabilities.

Several state activities can support the development of local capacity, including training, development grants, and the provision of technical assistance.

Arrange Personnel Training As discussed in more detail in Chapter 11, supported employment creates new professional roles for which incumbent program staff may not be fully prepared. Supported employment represents a departure from services provided historically to individuals with severe disabilities. Personnel cannot be expected to shift roles intuitively and create and provide supported employment without specific training and support.

Personnel training that focuses on several needs is necessary in many states. Short-term inservice training options are needed that provide opportunities for personnel in existing agencies to gain skills related to generating employment, analyzing job demands, providing training in community settings, supporting persons in integrated jobs, working with employers, and managing supported employment programs. Training opportunities are needed that will produce skilled personnel capable of addressing a variety of supported employment options, so as to meet the range of needs in local communities. Furthermore, personnel in roles outside supported employment organizations also have training needs, if they are to facilitate the development and maintenance of supported employment. Personnel such as service coordinators, vocational rehabilitation counselors, residential providers, parents, administrative staff, and school staff can all make important contributions if trained in issues related to supported employment. Finally, inservice training events should be scheduled in several locations statewide, to encourage broad participation.

In addition to short-term training strategies, preservice training programs are needed in colleges and universities that produce skilled individuals capable of creating and managing quality supported employment programs. While short-term personnel preparation can help address present needs, long-term personnel preparation will provide competence and leadership in the years to come.

State government's role in developing a cadre of trained personnel to meet local needs may take any of several forms. First, state agencies familiar with current and future personnel preparation needs related to supported employment can encourage colleges and universities in the state to offer courses and practica that focus on the knowledge and skills required for implementing supported employment as a part of their regular curricula. Colleges and universities may have an interest in offering both career-focused preservice training sequences and shorter-term inservice training opportunities to help meet the state's needs.

Some states already include a personnel training function as a part of the role of the agency responsible for ongoing services to persons with severe handicaps. States may develop or expand this role to sponsor directly inservice training events related to supported employment. Alternatively, the state may provide funds to a private organization involved in personnel preparation or to a college to support the provision of a sequence of training opportunities in many locations around the state. Finally, if several organizations already provide personnel preparation related to services for persons with severe handicaps, the state should lead the development of a training consortium. Its function would be to coordinate the development and scheduling of inservice training events to maximize the effectiveness of existing resources.

Provide Program Development Grants   Program development grants are the basis of another powerful strategy that states may use to encourage implementation of supported employment. Just as personnel are needed who have a new set of competencies, organizations have needs in the development of systems for providing supported employment to people with severe disabilities. Neither existing nor new organizations can be expected to provide supported employment instantly without financial resources for development and start-up. The allocation of program development grants can be an important strategy for states to promote both supported employment and important opportunities for local service providers to produce local change.

One method available to state decision-makers is the use of request for proposal (RFP) processes aimed at encouraging innovative supported employment by local providers. Existing agencies and new organizations can respond with proposals that fit state direction, take advantage of local business opportunities, and encourage local innovation. Such a mechanism is flexible enough to provide financial incentives to existing agencies, as well as to groups in local communities interested in creating new supported employment options. It is important that development grants be offered in a way that encourages development of supported employment by traditional agencies, as well as by new, small organizations that focus on a specific employment opportunity.

Arrange Technical Assistance for Providers   A third strategy that states may use to develop local service providers is to offer specific technical assistance. Although training personnel and providing development grants are two important aspects of supporting local change, it is also true that local providers will face issues and development problems that call for specific, timely assistance. Consequently, a system for providing technical assistance becomes another way a state can support local providers and encourage development. Personnel from both within and outside a state can help solve specific local problems if a technical assistance project is available. For example, a community may be faced with attempting to generate employment options in economically depressed areas. Another community with similar economic conditions may have faced similar problems and successfully located jobs in service-related industries. Personnel working in the latter may be able to provide valuable, specific information. In other areas, individuals with specific skills might be brought from out of state to help solve specific local or statewide problems.

Several steps are important to consider in providing for technical assistance. A statewide technical assistance project can be set up to serve as a provider and broker of consultation and technical assistance. Such a project would maintain lists of local and other available consultants with particular areas of expertise. With state funds supporting the project, local service providers can gain access to timely and specific assistance, further promoting innovation in supported employment.

Local service providers in many places have demonstrated the ability to create innovative approaches to supported employment. Such organizations are the mainstay of employment opportunities. State-level efforts to provide training, development funds, and technical assistance can be important components of efforts to create incentives and provide needed support to the local provider network. As has been stated before, no single strategy is the best in any given state. Rather, a combination of contextually appropriate strategies must be chosen to build local capacity for supported employment.

Establish State Management Systems

Local employment opportunities and community organizations providing supported employment are required in any state. However, it will be much more difficult to effect enduring statewide change without leadership on accomplishments that relate specifically to state systems. Supported employment creates new roles for state agencies. Even though local providers actually find jobs and provide employment support, state systems can either foster or hinder that development. A state management system must be present that directs development, provides for ongoing funding, and supports local government units.

Developing a specific measure of success for progressive management seems much more difficult than defining measures for the first two accomplishments discussed (the creation of employment opportunities and the development of local service providers). Even so, several features of a measure can be identified. First, such a measure might include clear identification of barriers (e.g., funding systems, case management systems) that act as disincentives to statewide development of supported employment. A second feature of a measure relates to the percent of major barriers removed at the state level. A final feature might be a checklist of the minimum quality levels for various state mechanisms such as the funding system, service coordination system, and local evaluation systems.

Important strategies related to state systems include defining responsibilities and authority for supported employment among involved state agencies, establishing supportive funding formulas and mechanisms, managing a statewide referral and service coordination system that fosters supported employment, and supporting local government units that administer local operations and evaluation components.

Define Agencies' Responsibilities and Authority for Supported Employment In all states, responsibility and authority for developing supported employment involves the mental retardation agency, the mental health agency, and the vocational rehabilitation agency. In many cases, the involvement of the schools and state public instruction departments is needed to support transition from school to work and adult life. Although any agency might provide primary leadership, it is critical that all roles be clearly specified. A clear division and coordination of responsibilities among agencies can operate to the benefit of local service providers. States must decide which agency will manage the development of supported employment. The specific decision may vary from state to state, yet the outcome is the same—a focus of responsibility and central leadership in a state's supported employment initiative. Interagency agreements are required that specify the role of each agency and the type of coordination needed. These agreements can prevent duplication of effort and send a clear signal to the business community, consumers, advocates, and service providers that supported employment is here to stay.

States also will need to address public policy issues, including dealings with authorities who have an impact on supported employment. Comprehensive state plans are needed to coordinate effective use of resources to address existing barriers and ensure systematic implementation of supported employment. State leaders must ensure that state statutes, regulations, and policy not only permit, but promote, widespread development of supported employment. For example, in some states, service process regulations have been replaced by service guidelines (e.g., State of Washington, 1986). Those guidelines focus on the outcomes of supported employment and provide guidelines on how the outcomes might be accomplished. This approach spurs creativity and encourages innovation.

Clear statements of agencies' responsibilities, the development of statewide supported employment plans, and attention to state-level laws and regulations can remove important barriers and thus facilitate the development of innovative employment options in local communities.

Establish Funding Formulas and Systems In many states, current funding strategies and formulas are the result of many years' accumulation of approaches and priorities. The focus on supported employment in states now provides a unique opportunity to rearrange funding systems to promote supported employment. As measures for successful supported employment emerge, the possibility of new funding mechanisms is created. Funding incentives may be tied to improved outcomes. Start-up and capitalization funds may be arranged around new developments and business incentives. Present systems may be streamlined to respond to innovative proposals from local government units and community service providers.

An important development that has emerged recently in some states calls for the sharing of funding responsibilities by the vocational rehabilitation agency and the mental retardation agency, or another long-term funding agency. This strategy calls for funding for an individual with disabilities for 3–6 months by the vocational rehabilitation agency, which is followed by a commitment by the mental retardation or mental health agency to provide the subsequent systems support and long-term funding for the individual. Such a solution provides for long-term success and allows each agency to plan effectively for financial commitments.

Perhaps more than any other single strategy, the arrangement of funding contingencies can do much to encourage the development of quality supported employment programs statewide. Nationwide, individual programs have shown the capacity to respond to the employment needs of people with severe disabilities. Funding systems that employ existing resources can encourage just that kind of development.

Implement Referral and Service Coordination Processes State systems and local provider systems have meaning only when individuals are referred who need employment with long-term support. Although state policy and funding mechanisms are important for systems change, it is at the level of individual need that supported employment takes on real meaning. As such, the processes for individual referral and service coordination are critical if specific supported employment opportunities are to be matched with individuals with severe disabilities. At issue is the referral of individuals to supported employment programs who need long-term support for successful employment. It is inappropriate to refer and provide service to persons for whom short-term intervention can be expected to result in successful employment. The importance and value of time-limited intervention, which leads to competitive employment, should not be overlooked in the present development of supported employment. This issue points to the need for skilled and knowledgeable personnel to coordinate services in all parts of a state. Attention must be given to individuals who are unemployed and need supported employment, as well as those who are underemployed or inappropriately served by existing programs. Supported employment shifts the focus of service coordination from evaluation to choice among options.

Provide Support to Local Government Units Responsible for Service Management In many states, the primary system for funding, monitoring, and managing service providers is the responsibility of local government units. In some states, individual counties have this responsibility; in others, community service boards or other local governmental units are responsible. Although a state-level initiative can produce initial policies, incentives, and guidelines, it is at the local government level that most supported employment programs will be planned, funded, administered, and monitored. Therefore, it is important that these local government units be capable of planning and maintaining local supported employment developments.

A number of efficient processes are needed at local levels if new supported employment programs are to emerge and existing agencies are to switch to supported employment. Local governments require the capacity to implement RFP processes, provide operating guidelines to service providers, help resolve funding issues, create incentives, monitor services, troubleshoot problems, and organize community members.

State-level planners and administrators can do several things to provide guidance and to support the local government administrative structure. First, state leaders can establish guidelines for quality that provide a blueprint for the development of local supported employment programs. Second, procedures and policies for managing local RFP processes can be offered. Third, training and inservice opportunities can be arranged for local government administrators in both the outcomes and processes for developing supported employment options. Finally, training and assistance can be provided to county or community services boards, which will need to make important decisions related to local change.

Evaluate Local Services The fifth and final major responsibility within the accomplishment area of state management relates to data collection and evaluation. In a systems change of this magnitude there is no substitute for accurate, timely, and relevant information for decision-making. Information on progress and quality is needed at many levels, including information on individual programs, local government units, and the state as a whole. Information must be collected, summarized, and reported regularly to support relevant decisions. Data also allow decision-makers to respond to opportunities and problems that arise as widespread implementation proceeds.

A quality evaluation system must also include standards for local program performance and a system for assessing program outcomes and quality at regular intervals. State leadership, along with participants from many roles in the employment system, can generate acceptable statewide standards for evaluating local services. Although occasionally viewed as unnecessary or solely as a policing function, evaluation systems are more appropriately viewed as indicators that provide the chance to capitalize on opportunity and to correct system problems as rapidly as they arise.

Using state management systems to promote supported employment is a task of some magnitude. However, by aggressively attacking systems such as these, state agencies can provide leadership and guidance to develop supported employment in local communities.

Build Consensus and Participation

Long-term local success in supported employment is possible only when broad consensus supports its development. The fourth accomplishment area concerns the importance of widespread participation and development of consensus among stakeholders as supported employment emerges in a state. Although less precisely defined than other accomplishments, change will be difficult without broad support, participation, and consensus-building.

Measures of success for participation and consensus are difficult to define under any circumstances. Even so, several indicators are possible that may point to the presence of such an accomplishment. First, backing of supported employment by major interest groups is desirable, if not required. Second, the extent of positive media coverage can indicate successful efforts to attain participation and consensus. Third, the volume of participation in state conferences and consensus-building events can indicate if consensus is building on major issues. Finally, the volume of responses to RFPs in communities statewide can indicate the extent of participation in the development of supported employment options.

Encourage Participation of Individuals with Disabilities and Their Advocates Individuals with disabilities, as well as their families and advocates, should have an important role in the planning and development of supported employment. Persons with disabilities and their families are the people who will benefit from this initiative, and their participation is needed if supported employment is to emerge and improve the quality of life. Persons in need of supported employment and advocates must be involved not only in the delivery of supported employment services; participation and consensus-building must also occur in the development of supported employment. Persons with disabilities and their families can help guide state systems, local government, professional groups, and service providers to the most acceptable outcomes of supported employment.

Participation by individuals with disabilities, family members, and advocates is needed at both the state and local levels. Participation is needed in planning supported employment, implementation, monitoring for ongoing evaluation, and adjustment of strategies to achieve supported employment. Planning and implementation councils must include individuals with disabilities and their advocates. Existing advocacy groups should be included in each step of the process. Strategies for the involvement of parents and advocates are explored in Chapter 10.

Provide Public Information Individuals with severe disabilities represent only a small minority of the general population. Largely because of a lack of information, many community members may have misconceptions about people with disabilities. Therefore, accurate information must be provided to the public about the competence of people with disabilities and the importance of supported employment.

Strategies for disseminating information to the public have been developed in many states, and include television coverage, videotapes, news releases and other concise written matter. Such materials can be formulated from existing information, but must be developed with the general public as the target audience. Public information can change general perceptions and the kind of information made available to the public. However, the most effective strategy for increasing public awareness of the ability of persons with disabilities is one that is at the heart of supported employment. That is, public information is best delivered by providing opportunities for community members to work beside and interact with persons with severe disabilities in regular work settings.

Support Professional Consensus-Building A third area of opportunity in building statewide consensus and participation relates to encouraging consensus-building among professionals involved in supported employment. Service providers, state and local government agency personnel, and university and training groups are stakeholders with long-standing commitments to persons with disabilities. Even so, recent experience has revealed both consensus on the value of supported employment and differences concerning strategies to foster its successful development. Strategies for building consensus about the shape of supported employment in the future can only enhance the opportunity currently available.

Central to professional consensus-building are strategies such as holding statewide and regional forums and conferences. These events provide the opportunity to do at least three things: 1) disseminate information and materials concerning effective practices, 2) offer opportunities for discussions among peers with the purpose of sharing values and building agreement on strategies, and 3) directly create, coordinate, and sustain a focus on supported employment.

SUMMARY

The state context in which local supported employment services are developed can enhance or hinder the delivery of supported employment outcomes. The task of implementing statewide systems to promote supported employment is substantial, with numerous complicating issues relating to policy, funding, coordination, and development. Activities must encompass a combination of many strategies. Leaders in states now have an opportunity to take advantage of emerging consensus, federal policy initiatives, and recent innovations. Statewide change is not a goal that can be attained quickly. A plan for state change must be systematic and gradual as policy is shaped, funding is redefined, personnel are trained, and statewide participation is developed.

The structure presented in this chapter offers one approach to the range of issues and opportunities that must be considered. Individual states will find idiosyncratic opportunities and barriers in each area. Therefore, regular review is required to determine how state resources may best be invested. Although the focus of developing state systems may shift from year to year, it appears that each of the accomplishment areas deserves long-term attention. The ultimate outcome from the vantage point of state management must be supported employment as the status quo, accessible to all persons with disabilities in communities throughout the state.

REFERENCES

Cawood, L. (Ed.). (1979). *WORDS: Work-oriented rehabilitation dictionary and synonyms* (2nd ed.). Seattle: Northwest Association of Rehabilitation Industries.

Noble, J. H., Conley, R. W., & Elder, J. K., (1986). Where do we go from here? In W. E. Kiernan & J. A. Stark (Eds.), *Pathways to employment for adults with developmental disabilities* (pp. 85–102). Baltimore: Paul H. Brookes Publishing Co.

O'Neill, H. (1985). *Creating opportunity: Reducing poverty through economic development*. Washington, DC: The Council of State Planning Agencies.

State of Washington (1986). *1987–89 Guidelines for county developmental disabilities services*. Olympia, WA: Department of Social and Health Services, Division of Developmental Disabilities.

Chapter 9

Preparing
for Supported
Employment
The Role of
Secondary Special
Education

Barbara Wilcox, John J. McDonnell,
G. Thomas Bellamy, and Heidi Rose

This chapter addresses the general question of how special education can best prepare adolescents with severe disabilities for supported employment. Unlike adult services available after graduation, high school special education programs are usually rich in resources and available as an entitlement to all students with disabilities. Consequently, the limited time spent in secondary special education is critically important in the lives of persons with severe disabilities. How should this instructional time be used? What kinds of training objectives are most appropriate? What kinds of staff roles are most useful? Where should training occur? Across the country, school districts deal with these questions daily as they plan, organize, staff, and administer high school programs for special education students.

The goal of this chapter is to discuss how secondary programs for students with severe handicaps structure vocational preparation in high school. The chapter first explores the logical implications of supported employment for vocational preparation in high schools. Naturally, radical changes in the structure of posteducational opportunities affect how individuals are prepared for those opportunities. The chapter then describes an approach for organizing and operating vocational preparation programs that lead to supported employment for students with moderate and severe disabilities.

Why should supported employment, which represents a change in the delivery of adult services, affect special education programming? For some time, model secondary programs for students with severe disabilities have abandoned developmentally sequenced programming, choosing instead a "top-down" or "future-oriented" approach (e.g., Brown, Nietupski, & Hamre-Nietupski, 1976; Williams & Gotts, 1976). This approach develops educational goals by defining the environments in which an individual is expected to live or work in the future, analyzes the demands of those settings, and organizes the school's instruction with the objective of teaching required skills and activities. Consequently, by redefining the future for which students should be prepared, supported employment has a major impact on curriculum and organization in vocational preparation programs.

Despite the appeal of the future-oriented approach, this training for the next environment has always created a dilemma for vocational preparation programs. If training were directed toward existing opportunities for adults with severe disabilities, most communities' secondary programs would likely include few vocational objectives. If current day-activity and work-activity programs represented the future for which students should be prepared, secondary education would place little value on either integration or employment skills. However, if training reflected a commitment to actual employment and integration, students would be prepared for employment opportunities that do not exist but that might become available as today's students entered adulthood.

Supported employment offers a comprehensive foundation for the development of future-oriented employment preparation in the secondary school. With a clear national policy on supported employment, it is now possible to build a systematic and logical employment preparation program. Such an approach was not feasible when teachers and administrators could only be distressed at the nonvocational nature of postschool services or guess how employment opportunities and services might be structured for persons with severe disabilities in the future.

The opportunity to adjust schools' employment-preparation programs comes just as secondary special education is faced with other pressures for broad reform. Secondary programs for persons with severe disabilities are expanding rapidly in most states as the first full generation of students to enjoy the right to education becomes old enough to leave school. Now that public education is available, more children with severe disabilities are growing up in their own communities and fewer are being placed in institutions during adolescence. School districts nationwide are expanding their secondary services and developing staffing and program models for secondary special education for these students. This development is supported by the national attention to the transition from school to work and adult life for all students with disabilities, and by the pervasive concern for excellence in American public education. Together, these forces provide a context for change that may facilitate implementation of an employment preparation program that builds toward a future that includes real employment with long-term support.

CURRICULUM GOALS
UNDERLYING SUPPORTED EMPLOYMENT

What future does supported employment create for students with severe disabilities? What skills and activities will be required? Supported employment is defined in Chapter 2 as paid employment in integrated work settings, with ongoing support as needed to maintain performance. Since, with ongoing support, work can be performed in virtually any regular work setting in the community, supported employment actually imposes no constraints on the content or context of work. Given seemingly limitless opportunities, how is high school special education going to provide organization and effective vocational preparation for adolescents with severe handicaps? Despite the variability of potential jobs, all supported employment opportunities share some basic requirements that structure the curriculum goals of high school programs. Five common requirements are briefly described below.

1. All jobs require that an employee perform to the specifications of the employer. A student will maintain paid work after graduation only if she or he works in a way that meets the employer's standards for accuracy, quality, and rate of production. A high school program to prepare students for supported employment would ensure that students learned actual appropriate work behaviors. Though no program could teach work skills for all possible supported employment options, a program can ensure that the skills students are taught are real—that tasks are actually completed in an work setting rather than in a classroom work simulation. Vocationally prepared high school students with severe handicaps can learn to handle a variety of tools and machinery, make discriminations that are basic to the performance of any job, and behave as their work tasks require. After vocational training, a student

should be able to run a dishwasher, bus tables, use a soldering iron, or price and shelve groceries. He or she should also be able to work at a normal pace for the job. It is important to note, however, that working slowly is less likely than working inaccurately to prevent an individual from participating in supported employment, because payment can be arranged that matches the individual's work rate.

2. Work-support behaviors constitute a second requirement common to the many possible supported employment settings. The literature on competitive employment placement is replete with data on people who often lose their jobs because they do not get along with their coworkers, do not control their behavior, spend too much time away from their task, are chronically late, or do not follow instructions (Greenspan & Shoultz, 1981). Different jobs have somewhat different requirements for work-support behaviors, but these are similar enough that they have frequently been viewed as prevocational skills that should be developed prior to work training (Mithaug, 1980). However, because ongoing support is available in supported employment, an individual need not be competent in all of these behaviors before getting access to real work. The cost of support should be less and the likelihood of uninterrupted employment greater when the work-support skills needed in a particular job are present.

3. Preparing for supported employment will also require that students choose among jobs in a community. If the high school curriculum teaches only those skills common to all jobs, the student will remain incompetent at all jobs. Until there is a basic decision about what kind of job an individual is preparing for, preparation is impossible. Choosing to develop work skills in one area precludes opportunities to develop skills in another area. Whereas this narrowing of opportunities is especially apparent among students with severe handicaps who typically require extended training to master any one skill or activity, virtually the same dilemma faces all people preparing for work. Choosing involves decisions not only about what will be done but about what will *not* be done. A clear choice of a job area or cluster allows the resources of the preparation program to be concentrated on the job skills and work support behaviors most important to that occupation.

4. Like most jobs, those in supported employment will require some flexibility. In today's economy, it is only reasonable to assume that the tasks required in any job will change greatly over time, and that the nature of jobs available in any community will also

change. Sustained supported employment in the current market will require a breadth of skills within the chosen work specialization, so that job mobility and advancement will be possible. Narrow vocational preparation may render a student's skills obsolete before he or she even enters the marketplace.

5. Finally, the future offered by supported employment is available only to those students for whom a paid job is found. Placement in a paying job is a prerequisite to participation in supported employment. Because education presently is the individual's last employment-related service entitlement, it is reasonable to ask the school to share responsibility for this placement, or to graduate students with paying jobs. The ongoing support available to the student after he or she leaves school may or may not be sufficient to produce the needed job placement.

These five requirements of supported employment—job skills, work-support behaviors, a choice among the many possible jobs, sufficient breadth of skills to ensure job mobility, and placement in a paid job—are much the same as those required for normal employment. The opportunity for employment with ongoing support, however, means that students need not be independent in each of these areas before employment can succeed. Instead, ongoing support can enhance performance of critical job skills (e.g., by developing fixtures that make the movements or discriminations easier), develop special programs to eliminate problems with work support behaviors, and retrain an individual as jobs change, thereby ensuring job mobility. Available support in the adult service system is finite, so the more that required skills can be developed during high school, the more likely an individual student will be to enjoy sustained supported employment after graduation.

ORGANIZING EMPLOYMENT PREPARATION

How should special education programs for students with severe disabilities be structured to achieve the five curriculum objectives derived from supported employment? Most current efforts to provide adequate vocational preparation to students with severe handicaps have developed in response to a history in which adults with severe handicaps were denied access to vocational training that focused on meaningful work, wages, and integration. Many share the belief that vocational preparation models found in conventional vocational education programs and those that have emerged in services for students with mild disabilities are inappropriate or insufficient for less able students. As described elsewhere (Bellamy, Wilcox, Rose, & McDonnell, 1985), these traditional models of vocational preparation often treat the five curriculum goals as sequential elements of a program. All too often, mastery of prevocational skills (the work-support behaviors in this chapter's analysis) is treated as a prerequisite to on-site vocational experience and training (Brolin, 1976). For students with severe disabilities, this means that training aimed at the other equally important goals is unnecessarily delayed, and that instruction in work-support behaviors relies on the unlikely generalization of behavior from school settings to the workplace. The result is a readiness trap, in which access to employment training is contingent on mastery of presumed prerequisite skills taught with inefficient procedures.

One early alternative to traditional classroom models involved bringing work tasks into the classroom, where the developing instructional procedures could be applied and competence demonstrated. Bicycle brakes, tool-use packages, and kits for sorting and assembly tasks were first described in the research literature, and later appeared for commercial distribution. At a time when the best hope for the future was to help students avoid nonvocational day programs by ensuring access to sheltered work programs, simulating sheltered work in the classroom was a useful way to implement the emerging instructional technology. In light of the requirements for success in supported employment, however, this type of preparation is restrictive in itself. Neither the job skills nor the work-support behaviors required in integrated job settings can be efficiently taught in high school classrooms. The machinery for social interactions and the pace of a real job cannot be simulated. Simulated tasks taught and performed in classrooms provide little realistic information to students and their families who must choose among job clusters, and do little or nothing to promote eventual placement in a paying job. In keeping with the developing literature on the use of simulation in teaching students with severe disabilities, classroom simulations are probably useful only as supplements to on-site training, and then only when the critical aspects of a required skill can be effectively and economically presented in the classroom (Horner, McDonnell, & Bellamy, 1986).

A second approach to organizing employment preparation that has been prevalent in practice, if not in the professional literature, has been long-term training for students at a single job site in the community. This approach has the advantage of teaching work skills and required support behaviors at the same time in a real, integrated context, and providing sufficient training and support to develop independence in job performance. To the extent that long-term placements in single jobs have often precluded training in several job sites, the approach has done little to support experience-based choice among jobs or to develop the breadth of skills needed for job mobility. Furthermore, unless work at the training site can be converted to a paying job on graduation, the single-site training model does little to assist job placement. The student's resumé remains short, and he or she has had the opportunity to demonstrate vocational competence to only a few potential employers.

Some of the shortcomings of a single-site approach are avoided by the use of a centralized training site (Mithaug, 1980). This approach, enables several students to gain experience in a single company, a university cafeteria, a hospital, or another setting that offers several jobs in which training can occur in relative proximity. A central site allows for training across jobs to support both choice and breadth of skills, and maintains many of the advantages of training in real work settings. What students with disabilities have often lacked at central sites is the opportunity to learn and practice a full range of work-support skills because of the presence of more than one such student at these sites. The lack of training, which is evident to many different potential employers, may also hinder placement in paying jobs upon graduation.

Another approach to employment preparation has involved searching for paying community jobs as early as possible in students' secondary school career, and placing students in these jobs. Although this represents a direct investment in the ultimate goal of placement, it may also mean sacrificing needed attention to the variety of job experiences that fosters choice and breadth of skills. Without a well-documented work history, some students may also appear too severely handicapped to be credible candidates for paid employment and may thus be denied work training opportunities altogether.

In light of emerging supported employment opportunities and the inadequacy of existing models to prepare students for those opportunities, the designers of high school programs for students with severe handicaps will be forced to devise new vocational models. Earlier models are not necessarily ill-suited to the requirements for sustained supported employment, as much as they are incomplete. A model that would meet the goal of sustained supported employment for students with severe handicaps would likely include the following features:

1. Simultaneous programming for all five curriculum goals so that students are not caught in a readiness trap that postpones training opportunities until certain goals are mastered

2. Training in job skills that are relevant to the changing local economy so that the skills remain marketable in the student's home community
3. Training in several different jobs, so that informed choices about specialization can be made and a breadth of skills developed
4. Training in regular job sites where persons without disabilities work, so that work-support behaviors can be learned and practiced in natural settings
5. Use of different training and support formats (individual and group training, independent performance) to vary the required work-support behaviors
6. Use of effective instructional procedures so that the skills and activities required for sustained supported employment are actually mastered by students
7. Use of the *individualized education program* (IEP) process for choices about job specialization
8. Use of unpaid jobs as training to expand the range of settings in which training can occur
9. Distribution of secondary classrooms throughout the high schools in a district so that sufficient jobs will be available for training in proximity to the school
10. Training in visible community settings so that student competence at work can be observed by potential employers
11. Development of a resumé for each student, so that he or she can market training experiences to best advantage with potential employers
12. Direct assistance in a paid job placement as the goal of special education, so that this task is not left dependent on the availability and orientation of local adult services
13. Advocacy of adult service improvement, so that the needed support for former students will be available in integrated settings, not just in sheltered programs

THE OPPORTUNITY SCHEDULING APPROACH

This section outlines the framework of one approach to preparation for supported employment that incorporates these program features. The *Opportunity Scheduling Approach* was developed in conjunction with the Oregon High School Model (Wilcox & Bellamy, 1987a; Wilcox & Bellamy, 1987b), a standardized model that focuses on preparation for work, leisure, and independent living in integrated school and community settings. Each component of the Opportunity Scheduling Approach is described in this half of the chapter.

The Opportunity Scheduling Approach was designed initially for students who entered secondary school programs at ages 14–15 along with their age peers, and remained under the auspices of those programs through age 21. The employment preparation aspect of their high school program is divided into three components: 1) sampling and teaching of vocational alternatives, 2) selection and teaching of a job specialization, and 3) placement in paid employment. Although a student's progress through these components is partly influenced by age, the central organizing variable is the potential employability of the student at graduation. Contrary to traditional practices, students with the most severe handicaps are likely to spend less time sampling options, and have placement as a goal earlier than their more capable peers.

Employment Preparation

Sample and Teach Vocational Alternatives   When a student with a disability enters high school, his or her vocational capacity is unknown. Despite the presence of a severe handicap, there is virtually no basis for deciding what jobs a student can or cannot do or the type of support he or she will require to maintain employment. Sampling a range of vocational options allows teachers and parents to assess the student's employment capacity across various *job clusters* (e.g., construction, domestic, or office services), various *training support formats* (e.g., work crews, enclaves, individual employment with indigenous support), and various *dimensions* (e.g., of the complexity and stability of job duties, physical working conditions, transportation, and amount of public contact). During the first few years in high school (ages 15–18), students' IEPs include objectives that sample from six to eight jobs and settings (this presumes two placements each year). With each placement, the teacher and the parent gain additional information about the potential success of the student under particular work conditions. At the same time, the student builds job skills and work-support behaviors, and demonstrates competence to potential community employers.

Select and Teach a Job Specialization   When the student is about 18, he or she, the parent, and the school program select a job cluster as the target for specific job training. This selection reflects the student's previous work history and preferences, parent values, and the potential for job placement at graduation. While a specific job (e.g., dishwasher at Howard Johnson's) may not be identified at this point, the general type of job and support format can be defined. The target for a student might include, for example, a janitorial job in a work crew, an individual job placement with indigenous supervision as a dishwasher in a restaurant, or work as a day care assistant with occasional external support. At this point, the selection and training process results in the limited sampling of various work conditions within a desired employment option. The intent is to identify the specific job performance adaptations and support that will be required to ensure the student's success in this type of employment setting and to teach the work skills and support behaviors that may be required in the chosen job area. On-site training continues to allow the student to demonstrate competence and develop relationships with potential employers.

Place in a Paid, Supported Job   The IEP for a student's final year of school identifies placement in a specific job as the annual goal. Training is designed to develop the work and work-support skills required by the particular support format and employment setting. The choice of job and setting is based on the student's work training history and the local employment opportunities. If the training is successful, the job will be, in effect, the student's first postschool employment. Ideally, the transition from school to adult services would be invisible to the student. Only the school or the receiving supported employment program would be aware of the transfer of responsibility. The student could continue on the same job or as part of the same enclave, but, after graduation, responsibility for support and retraining would be shifted to a developmental disabilities service agency.

As students progress through a series of job training sites and support formats, they encounter different demands for work skills and support behaviors. To make the most of the training opportunities provided by these demands, the program seeks to select and schedule these opportunities in a way that reflects programming and value decisions about individual students. The following section provides a discussion of the issues associated with four of the critical organizational features: the development of job training sites, assessment and individual planning processes, staffing and vocational training efforts, and procedures for informing and involving parents.

Developing Work Training Opportunities in the Community

Although it is hard to imagine that any vocational preparation model could operate without job training sites, the availability of such sites is specially crucial to the Opportunity Scheduling Approach. This approach includes the expectation that all students with severe handicaps will have out-of-school work training objectives on their IEPs, and that each year every student will have at least two different work training opportunities lasting 10–12 weeks. Consequently, a high school program will need a pool of potential job training opportunities larger than the number of secondary students with severe handicaps. A ratio of three job training positions for every two students will provide the necessary flexibility for individualization. Responsibility for developing work training sites may fall to the classroom teacher, his or her teaching associates, a job developer, or a vocational trainer, depending on the resources or staffing pattern of a district. It is less important who does the work than that it be done. Individuals who are comfortable in such social situations or who already have connections with the business community may find the task somewhat easier.

While the absolute number of job training opportunities is important, several features of the total pool of sites and of individual sites are equally important to the Opportunity Scheduling Approach.

Job Training Sites Should Sample Job Clusters Represented in the Local Economy No one would ever consider that all regular high school graduates of a community would enter exactly the same line of work. Nonetheless, we often unwittingly prepare all students with severe handicaps to enter the same "profession" by limiting the work training opportunities available during high school. If the only training opportunity is doing dishes in a local restaurant, students will hardly develop the work and work support skills that might enable them to work as assemblers in an electronics plant, shelf stockers in a local grocery, baker's assistants, or groundskeepers for the county parks system. Developing training opportunities in a range of job clusters is critical if students and their families are to enjoy choice as an outcome of vocational preparation. The particular job clusters in which training opportunities can be developed will naturally be a function of the economy of the community. In some locations, many kinds of work are available, whereas in others the economy is less diversified. Table 9.1 presents general descriptions of job clusters in which work training opportunities have been developed for high school students with severe handicaps.

The more a work training site requires job skills similar to those expected by other employers in the community, the more useful the site is to the overall training effort. Although "one of a kind" training opportunities need not be dismissed, a job developer would do better to invest his or her efforts in seeking training opportunities that are representative of local manpower needs.

As a student has the opportunity to sample jobs from various clusters, his or her performance data provide teachers and parents with valuable information about the type of work the student likes best and the type of job to which he or she is best suited.

Table 9.1. Definitions of job clusters

Definition	Examples	Nonexamples
1. AGRICULTURAL/ NATURAL RE-SOURCES includes activities concerned with propagating, growing, caring for and gathering plant and animal life and products. Also includes caring for parks, gardens, and grounds.	Strawberry picker Henhouse worker Greenhouse worker Groundskeeper Tree planter	Food processor (distribution)
2. CONSTRUCTION includes any activities concerned with fabricating, erecting, installing, paving, painting, and repairing structures such as buildings or roads.	Construction worker Road construction worker Painter's helper	Yard maintenance worker (agriculture/natural resources)
3. DISTRIBUTION includes any activities concerned with handling, processing, or retailing materials. Machinery may be involved in handling or processing operations.	Vegetable processor Shelf stocker Bottle sorter Sales clerk	Food preparer Kitchen helper
4. DOMESTIC AND BUILDING SERVICES includes activities concerned with providing domestic services in private households or lodging establishments, maintaining and cleaning clothing/apparel in a commercial establishment, and cleaning or maintaining the interiors of buildings.	Janitor Maid Laundry worker Drycleaning worker Window washer	Busperson (food preparation/ services)

(continued)

Table 9.1. *(continued)*

5. FOOD PREPARA-TION AND SER-VICES includes activities concerned with preparing food and beverages and serving them to patrons of establishments such as hotels, clubs, and restaurants. Also includes activities that maintain kitchen work areas and equipment or that maintain customer eating areas.	Busperson Dishwasher Food counter person Kitchen helper	
6. HEALTH OCCUPA-TIONS include any activities concerned with maintaining the health, comfort, or safety of individuals. Also includes activities that involve the handling of medicine or materials used in hospital care.	Day care attendant Nurse's assistant Nursing home volunteer Child care helper	Hospital kitchen worker (food preparation/ services) Hospital laundry worker (domestic and building services)
7. MANUFACTURING/MACHINE OPERA-TIONS includes activities concerned with using tools and machines to fabricate, inspect, or repair products.	Mechanic assistant Dryer operator Heat-seal machine operator Quality controller	Packager (distribution)
8. OFFICE AND BUILDING SER-VICES includes activities concerned with recording, transcribing, reproducing, organizing, and shipping goods and materials from an office business.	Filing clerk Mailroom worker Messenger Copy machine operator	Stocking shelves (distribution)

Job Training Sites Should Sample Training/Support Formats
Because high school programs for students with severe handicaps seldom have the training resources available to support all students in individual jobs, there should be an effort to develop sites to support work training for several students simultaneously. Work crews (Sprague, Paeth, & Wilcox, 1983) and enclaves (Rhodes & Valenta, 1985) are also effective formats for providing work training to groups of students. Equally important, they are effective organizational strategies for providing supported employment to adults with disabilities. Developing a pool of working-training sites that includes individual jobs, work crews, and enclaves is appropriate to the logistical reality of school programs. As students try out formats, they provide teachers and others with valuable information about the level of supervision and the type of support that may be most appropriate during later employment. Table 9.2 describes three formats for providing work training to high school students and briefly describes the advantages and disadvantages of each.

Job Training Sites Should Require a Range of Work-Support Behaviors If there are training opportunities that represent various job clusters and include different work training formats, those opportunities will demand different work-support behaviors. Some locations may feature high contact with customers or other coworkers while others are low contact positions or involve working alone. Some job-training sites may require students to use mass transit, while others are within walking distance of the school. Student performance data on work-sites that vary in the work-support skills they require provide decision-makers with valuable information to aid in the design or selection of an appropriate supported employment program.

Training Sites Should Sample "Employer Motivation" Both common sense and professional advice (references) suggest that when high school programs recruit work-training sites, they should stress the training function. Employers are being asked to provide work and space and to tolerate training; they are *not* being asked to provide employment per se. Many businesses that may be reluctant to hire individuals with disabilities may be willing to serve as work-training sites, and thus provide an important opportunity to youth with handicaps. Such sites are useable term after term (presuming that arrangements remain mutually satisfactory). However, because an intended outcome of vocational preparation is a job, the school program should also develop sites in the community where employers are interested in hiring a student once he or she has mastered the job duties. These sites are, in effect, used up once the employer hires someone to fill a permanent supported position. The pool of work-training sites should include "potential employers" as well as permanent training sites.

Table 9.2. Vocational training formats for high school students with severe handicaps

Format	Definition	Advantages	Disadvantages
1. Individual job stations	A work training station in a public or private sector, service, or industrial setting designed to accommodate a single student. Supervision and training is initially provided by school personnel who have completed a comprehensive job analysis. Student performance is maintained through daily contact with indigenous supervisors and coworkers, and systematic follow-up by school personnel. May be used in any job cluster.	1. Opportunity to provide regular and frequent training in actual work environments 2. Training may lead to employment in the work-site 3. Regular and frequent contacts with nonhandicapped coworkers	1. Staff-intensive training format 2. Requires high proportion of staff time to complete job development and analysis
2. Community work crews	An instructional and organizational format designed to provide training for up to four students in multiple settings. Supervision and training are provided by school personnel who have completed a comprehensive analysis of job tasks at each work-site. Student performance is maintained through regular and	1. Efficient utilization of staff for vocational training 2. Opportunities to teach generalized work skills across sites 3. Opportunities for job expansion within and across work-sites 4. Regular and frequent contacts with nonhandicapped coworkers	1. Difficult to schedule sufficient training time for all students during crew start-up 2. Limited opportunity to remove trainer presence 3. Resources required for travel 4. Many work opportunities limited to nonschool hours

(continued)

197

Table 9.2. (continued)

Format	Definition	Advantages	Disadvantages
	frequent contact with school personnel. Crews may be utilized in any job or job cluster that allows division of job requirements into functional work tasks. Crew contracts to complete designated tasks; assignment of duties to individual students is done by crew leader/trainer.	5. Can accommodate very heterogeneous groups of students	
3. Enclaves or centralized work training sites	An instructional and organizational format designed to provide vocational training for multiple students in a single setting. Supervision and training is provided by school personnel, with assistance from indigenous supervisors or coworkers. Job assignment and design is based on a comprehensive analysis of jobs in the work-site. Site may provide multiple jobs within same cluster or single jobs in several different job clusters.	1. Efficient utilization of staff 2. Opportunities to teach generalized work skills 3. Opportunities for job expansion within work-site 4. Regular and frequent contacts with nonhandicapped coworkers 5. Training not limited to a single job cluster 6. Work tasks may be designed to match post-school employment opportunities.	1. Difficult to schedule sufficient training time for all students during start-up 2. Requires staff assignment to central site

Training Sites Should Make Realistic Work Demands There should be enough work to occupy students for at least one school period a day, at least 5 days a week. Jobs that require less work time pose problems for a classroom schedule and provide insufficient practice for actual skill development by students.

Assessment and Individual Program Planning

The variables that guide decisions about vocational objectives must be balanced and rebalanced throughout a student's high school career. This is a complex decision process whose objective is to ensure that all job alternatives have been considered and evaluated, and that the job which best suits the student's interest and capacity is selected. Such decisions cannot be based effectively on popular vocational evaluation devices or standard vocational curriculum sequences. Instead, decision-making is best viewed as an iterative process in which information from each successive year of training is considered along with family values in the IEP meeting to gradually bring occupational choices and training needs into focus. In the Opportunity Scheduling Approach, this process comprises five steps, each of which is described below.

Review Student's Work Training History to Date Vocational objectives should be derived from data on student performance in previous work settings. When a student is young and has had limited work training, the initial selection of training targets is more flexible. Choices naturally become limited near the end of schooling, when career decisions must be made. What a student has done, what he or she has done well, or what he or she has enjoyed all influence decisions regarding future training or placements. In reviewing a student's work history, parents and teachers should attend to several variables, including the level of task completion, the quality of tasks completed, and rate- and work-related skills (e.g., behavior problems, ability to self-manage, ability to use transportation).

The use of student data to make decisions about vocational goals is highly dependent on a systematic tracking format that allows teachers to identify student training needs. Figure 9.1 presents a sample format. The column headings represent the type of variation that must be sampled in order to ensure broad-based preparation. This form is completed after the student's experience at each work-site. In the first column, the teacher enters basic information on the training site, dates worked, number of hours, and days per week the student worked at the site. In the second column, the teacher simply describes the type of work the student did at the site. Column 3 is for recording the format of the training that occurred at that particular site, such as

Student:
Social Security number:
Telephone number:

School:
Date entered:
Graduation:

Basic information	Job cluster	Training format	Job skills	Work-support skills	Transportation	Supervision	Integration	Performance summary
Location: Dates: Hours/ Day: Days/ Week:								
Location: Dates: Hours/ Day: Days/ Week:								
Location: Dates: Hours/ Day: Days/ Week:								
Location: Dates: Hours/ Day: Days/ Week:								

Figure 9.1. Community work training site feasibility analysis.

individual placement, community work crew, or enclave. Columns 4 and 5 are for descriptive information on the specific job skills and work support skills taught at that site. Column 6 is where the teacher records the method of transportation required to get to and from the job. The next column allows the teacher to describe the type of supervision the student received at the work site. This includes conditions such as working only with indigenous supervision, working with supervision provided by a coworker, and working with supervision from the school program. Column 8 provides space for the teacher to summarize the level of contact the student had with nonhandicapped customers or coworkers. In the last column the teacher provides an evaluation of the work placement, specifying the student's success or failure. Specific work training data is available to supplement this narrative summary.

This tracking format follows the student throughout high school and serves as a cumulative record of work training, substituting for separate vocational evaluation reports. This record—in effect a resumé—provides the basis for targeting a specific postschool job.

Review Available Work Training Sites   Before the IEP meeting, the teacher reviews the log of available work training sites to identify which sites are potentially appropriate for the target student. Figure 9.2 presents a page from a job site log, with instructions for completing the form. The entry specifies the work and work-support skills that could be taught in the setting, a list of job duties across days, the type and amount of supervision available, opportunities for job expansion and advancement at the site, and an estimate of the work experience's potential to lead to full-time employment upon graduation.

An "appropriate " site is one that would expand the student's repertoire, or that would support any of the five vocational training outcomes. If no appropriate sites can be identified, the teacher must either develop additional work-training sites that do meet student needs or expand the training formats available within existing work-training sites (e.g., develop an individual job station where there had previously been only a crew).

Select a Training Opportunity That Expands the Student's Repertoire   At the IEP meeting, the teacher presents the list of potential work training opportunities for the coming year. The set of alternatives is narrowed to a single job that best suits the student's age and work history, performance characteristics, and preference, as well as the parents' preferences. The selection of a particular work training opportunity may be based on student performance under certain work conditions or the lack of previous opportunity to sample a specific job cluster, training format, or particular setting characteristics.

Site name:

Address:

Phone:

Contact person:	Fill in the name of the person at the site with whom you are developing the training possibility.
Travel logistics:	List all the travel details necessary for the student to get from school to this site (e.g., buses and transfers student will need to take, the route the student will walk to this site, the time required to travel from school to the site).
Job cluster(s):	List all the job clusters that offer training possibilities at this site.
Work support skills:	List work support skills that may be taught at this site.

Job activity	Constraints
List all the tasks included in the overall job at the site by day (e.g., the tasks for stocking shelves at Safeway may include loading a cart with boxes of goods to be stocked, putting price tags on each item to be stocked, putting items on appropriate shelf, tearing down and disposing of cartons). Include information on possible opportunities for job enlargement and advancement at this site.	List any details necessary for the student to perform the job; for example, for a janitorial job, the student may need to supply his or her own cleaning supplies. For students with physical disabilities, you may want to comment on the accessibility of this site. Specify time limits/days, and additional supervision.

Previous placement history at this site			
Date	Job(s)	Job supervisor	Comments
List the date(s) this site was used for training.	List the job(s) the student(s) did at this site.	Fill in the name of the person(s) from school and from the training site (if applicable) who supervised the student(s) during training.	Include any pertinent comments about the student's performance, the quality of the training site, etc.

Figure 9.2. Vocational placement record form.

For example, a student may have performed well on a janitorial work crew near the school. For the next school year, the choice might be to have the student bus tables in an individual work placement far enough from the school that he or she will have to take the bus. Such a decision samples different work and work support skills, as well as a different training format. Alternatively, if the student were 19 years old, the choice might be a position on a custodial crew at the municipal hospital, because he or she seemed to like janitorial tasks and worked well on a crew, and because the student's parents were pleased at the opportunity for him or her to work where a former classmate had been hired.

Identify Performance Adaptations Many students with severe handicaps will lack the academic, language, or motor skills necessary to perform target tasks at the work-site in the "normal" way. Consequently, teachers need to design the performance adaptations or other logistical supports required to ensure student success at the site. Such adaptations may include self-monitoring systems, job fixtures, transportation alternatives, and communication notebooks. The student can then be trained to use these aids independently, within the context of the work setting.

Write Goals and Objectives Following the IEP meeting, the teacher writes specific vocational goals and objectives for the student that specify the intended outcome of instruction, systems of measurement and evaluation, and criteria for performance. For example, a vocational goal statement might specify, "John will sweep classrooms and halls with a 36-inch dust mop, empty trash cans in all classrooms, and spot-wax hall and classroom floors . . . " Because vocational objectives often reflect very sophisticated and complex behaviors, the criteria established for evaluating student performance must reflect the actual demands of the workplace. Most activities require that a student not only master the vocational skills, but also perform over time and meet the social expectations of the job. For that reason criteria such as "100% correct on 4 out of 5 trials" or "90% correct on three consecutive sessions" are less useful criterion statements.

STAFFING FOR VOCATIONAL PREPARATION PROGRAMS

Managing a high school program that prepares students with severe handicaps for supported employment will require staff with broad competence to recruit work-training sites in the community, analyze the technical requirements of the available jobs, assign tasks to students within various training and support formats, provide effective training, manage public relations with employers, students, and coworkers, and coordinate with adult service agencies and supported employment programs as students near graduation. Until recently, few special education programs trained personnel in such competencies. Indeed, few high school teachers in special education were trained directly for their roles (Halpern & Benz, 1984), or have reported receiving either inservice or preservice training related to preparing students for employment (Arness, Black, & Wilcox, 1985).

The tasks necessary to design, implement, and maintain effective vocational prepraration can be performed by individuals in many roles: teacher, instructional assistant, vocational coordinator, and work study coordinator, among others. Who does what job and with what title will in large part be a function of the local district. Urban districts with relatively large numbers of high school students with severe handicaps may elect to create a specialist position or assign a supervisor particular responsibilities for vocational preparation. In smaller or less affluent districts, the role requirements of existing positions may be expanded. Some programs take the position that for older students, vocational training is more important than traditional therapies, and have shifted staff resources away from occupational therapist, physical therapist, or speech pathologist positions to vocational or community trainers. Alternatively, related service personnel in traditional roles have expanded their responsibilities to include work training.

By using crews and central sites, in addition to individual job training sites, and by using regular student body members as peer tutors, programs can provide out-of-school work training to all students with minimal additional paid staff. Programs with a high concentration of students with multiple handicaps, or programs in high schools located far from any real "community," face unusual problems and may require additional staff to implement the target program.

Informing Parents about Postschool Services

Parents' knowledge, attitudes, values, and actions have an important impact on the supported employment options available to sons or daughters after high school. For example, parents may not believe that their son or daughter can be productively employed, may fear for safety in an individual job placement, or may place a low value on employment outcomes such as wages and integration. Or, parents may provide the direction and pressure needed to establish supported employment programs as an alternative to existing adult day programs, may assist in developing training and supported work placements, and may effectively advocate integrated training opportunities.

Whatever the interests and values of parents, it is critical that the school program supply them information about employment opportunities in the community, the nature and availability of local adult services, and the performance of their son or daughter in work training. This information is best supplemented by descriptions of service approaches so that potential employment opportunities can be more readily defined and established as objectives for both the school's preparation and the family's advocacy efforts.

The Opportunity Scheduling Approach provides the needed information to parents in three ways: a transition manual, parent information events, and individualized meetings. A transition manual describes existing local services and provides data on the wage and integration outcomes achieved by these programs. The manual begins to teach parents how to evaluate service programs and how to get access to valuable generic services. Annual parent information events supply information on model programs and possibilities for post-school employment and support. If parents are to advocate supported employment rather than an expansion of existing nonvocational service, they will need a clear vision of what is possible in supported employment. Finally, individualized information about student performance is provided in the context of the IEP meeting.

WORKING WITH RELATED AGENCIES AND SERVICES

The impact and effectiveness of supported employment preparation in the high school can be increased by collaboration with adult service agencies and existing supported employment programs. If the purpose of school and transition is to provide services in adult life, it is especially important to ensure coordination with the adult service system. This includes both direct service providers and local government officials. If the transition process is already established, these forums and opportunities should exist for movement into the adult system. At the individual level, four strategies can be used to support coordination between the school system and the adult system.

1. Involve case management in the student's individual planning process as soon as the student enters school. This ensures that the adult service system knows and can plan for the needs of the student when he or she leaves school.
2. Formally include transition planning as a part of the student's IEP development. If the IEP provides appropriate vocational objectives and includes adult service personnel, then the transition from school to work is more likely to be smooth.
3. Provide and update data to the adult service system on the ex-

pected nature of the employment needs of students still in the school system. Adult service planners are faced with the need to predict what employment options should be developed in upcoming months and years. This can be done better with accurate information from school personnel about the nature of the employment needed by those leaving school.

4. Coordinate between the school personnel and the adult services personnel with responsibilities related to the development of paid jobs for individuals leaving school. Depending on resources and personnel, it may be most appropriate for an adult service agency to develop a paid job opportunity for students with disabilities, even though training and support may be provided by school personnel until the student leaves school. This strategy should allow any supported employment providers to get to know the student before graduation. The supported employment provider may be more likely to be skilled in developing paid jobs and in dealing with employer incentives.

CONCLUSION

The opportunity for supported employment gives new direction to the design of employment preparation efforts in high school programs for students with severe handicaps. To ensure that students are equipped to take advantage of this employment prospect, vocational preparation during high school must include the development of job skills, work-support behaviors, individual choice, and a breadth of skills. A paying, supported job must also be secured before a student finishes school.

Accomplishing all these objectives requires a blend of strategies from earlier training models. The Opportunity Scheduling Approach achieves this blend by using a variety of community job training sites and different support formats throughout the high school years. It is an iterative process of training and decision making within the IEP. Educational objectives target work skills and support behaviors required for jobs that increasingly reflect the choice of a job specialization. Finally, a specific, paid job is developed in which the student is expected to work after completing school.

When preparation for supported employment is effective, the transition from school to adult services should not even be noticed by the person with a severe disability. The responsibility for supporting the individual in his or her job simply shifts from the school to the adult service agency. This process spares adult services the expense of initial job placement and training. Instead, they can simply provide the needed ongoing support. With this savings, it may be possible, even within limited state budgets, to offer adult services to many who leave school only to languish on waiting lists.

At present, such smooth transitions are far from being possible. Some of the responsibility rests with the schools, which do not always have students working in feasible jobs at the close of their school careers. Part of the responsibility rests with adult service agencies that lack the necessary service models to support individuals with severe handicaps in jobs that provide wages and foster integration. An effective high school program makes it clear that students with severe handicaps can work in regular work environments, given necessary support. Such a program should provide powerful impetus to establish supported employment alternatives for students upon graduation.

REFERENCES

Arness, K., Black, C., & Wilcox, B. (1985). *Work preparation for high school students with severe handicaps: A survey of teacher practices in Oregon.* Unpublished manuscript, University of Oregon, Specialized Training Program, Eugene, OR.

Bellamy, G. T., Wilcox, B. L., Rose, H. E., & McDonnell, J. J. (1985). Education and career preparation for youth with disabilities. *Journal of Adolescent Health Care, 6,* 125–135.

Brolin, D. E. (1976). *Vocational preparation of retarded citizens.* Columbus, OH: Charles E. Merrill.

Brown, L., Nietupski, J., & Hamre-Nietupski, S. (1976). The criterion of ultimate functioning. In M. Thomas (Ed.), *Hey, don't forget about me!* (pp. 2–15). Reston, VA: Council for Exceptional Children.

Greenspan, S., & Shoultz, B. (1981). Why mentally retarded adults lose their jobs: Social competence as a factor in work adjustment. *Applied Research in Mental Retardation, 2,* 23–38.

Halpern, A., & Benz, M. (1984). *Toward excellence in secondary special education.* Unpublished manuscript, Oregon Department of Education, Salem, OR.

Horner, R. H., McDonnell, J. J., & Bellamy, G. T. (1986). Teaching generalized skills: General case instruction in simulation and community settings. In R. H. Horner, L. H. Meyer, & H. D. Fredericks (Eds.), *Education of learners with severe handicaps: Exemplary service strategies* (pp. 289–314). Baltimore: Paul H. Brookes Publishing Co.

Mithaug, D. (1980). *Prevocational training for retarded students.* Springfield, IL: Charles C Thomas.

Rhodes, L. E., & Valenta, L. (1985). Industry-based supported employment: An enclave approach. *Journal of The Association for Persons with Severe Handicaps, 10*(1), 12–20.

Sprague, J., Paeth, M. A., & Wilcox, B. (1983). *Community work crews for severely handicapped high school students.* Unpublished manuscript, University of Oregon, Specialized Training Program, Eugene, OR.

Wilcox, B., & Bellamy, G. T. (1987a). *The Activities Catalog: An alternative curriculum for youth and adults with severe disabilities*. Baltimore: Paul H. Brookes Publishing Co.

Wilcox, B., & Bellamy, G. T. (1987b). *A comprehensive guide to The Activities Catalog: An alternative curriculum for youth and adults with severe disabilities*. Baltimore: Paul H. Brookes Publishing Co.

Williams, W., & Gotts, E. A. (1976). Selected considerations on developed curriculum for severely handicapped students. In E. Sontag, J. Smith, & N. Certo (Eds.), *Educational programming for the severely and profoundly handicapped* (pp. 221–236). Reston, VA: Council for Exceptional Children.

Chapter 10

Parents, Advocates, and Friends

Personal Strategies to Foster Supported Employment

Translating public policies concerning supported employment into real opportunities for people with severe disabilities requires community-level action to create new programs or adjust existing ones. The local effort and leadership needed to bring about this change seldom exist without the active participation of the parents, relatives, guardians, advocates, and friends of persons with disabilities. This chapter is intended as a guide for parents, family members, and others who want to help develop supported employment opportunities in their communities. Although the chapter emphasizes the critical role played by parents and families, others such as guardians, advocates, and friends may also use many of the strategies discussed. The chapter builds on the basic information provided earlier in the book about how to start and manage supported employment programs, and adds a more direct discussion of what parents and others can do to foster supported employment opportunities for their sons, daughters, and friends.

The unique perspectives and support strategies that parents, relatives, and friends bring to service development are critical to each community's efforts to implement supported employment. With a longer view of the individual's future needs and a better memory of past accomplishments and problems, families and friends bring a perspective to service development rarely matched by that of even the most sensitive program managers and professionals. This lifelong view of the service system is complemented by a broader concern for quality of life, a concern which transcends service categories and professional specializations (Turnbull & Turnbull, 1986). This focus is seldom restricted to the family member with a disability, but also includes how that person's experiences affect the whole family. With this frame of reference, parents and other family members may be in the best position of anyone in a community to advocate development of supported employment as one component of a local service system.

Parents and relatives have a special interest in service development. When a community's services are incomplete or inadequate, parents and relatives must either provide the needed support through the family's own resources or cope with the incompleteness they see in their relative's life. Low-quality services or the absence of a particular service aggravate family stress. What is difficult, of course, is that the participation necessary to develop services is usually needed exactly when the family is under the greatest stress from lack of services.

Families naturally differ from each other. Participation in the development of supported employment may be critically important to some, important but impossible for others, and of less importance to others. Location, financial resources, schedule, family needs, and many other factors affect the reasonableness of assisting in service development efforts. For those who become involved in promoting supported employment, the initial targets for program development may vary considerably. This may depend on whether one's son, daughter, or friend is in a day activity program or workshop, which the family would like to change to a supported employment program, at home with no service or on a waiting list for adult services, or still in school, with a little time before adult services—including supported employment—are needed.

Several broad strategies are available for promoting supported employment, and at least some activities within each may be appropriate whatever the family's circumstances. Six personal action strategies are illustrated in the following sections:

1. Set family goals
2. Participate in individual program planning
3. Develop and share an information base
4. Influence program management
5. Influence the system
6. Provide supports directly

1. SET FAMILY GOALS

The first step for any family or advocate interested in promoting supported employment is to develop a vision of an employment future that is appropriate for the family member with disabilities. Ideally, how will working fit into his or her life? What activities will complement work? What kind of work schedule and situation will fit best? What kinds of work will build on existing skills and interests? How important is it to be around many other people at work? What kinds of activities will his or her income support? How much income will be needed? What kind of support will be needed to ensure success in this job? A vision of the employment future is a statement of beliefs about what is possible for the person with disabilities, as well as what seems to be best suited to the person's own interests and adult life-style.

The different supported employment approaches described in Chapter 2 provide a useful beginning for brainstorming by families, advocates, and friends. Would the individual be the most successful and satisfied in a competitive job with support from a service as needed, or would working as a part of a small group with continuous supervision be more appropriate to his or her support needs? A sample guide to setting goals is included in Figure 10.1.

A clear vision of what employment future is possible and desirable is important for several reasons. It provides a basis for selecting objectives in individual program planning meetings in school and adult services. Families and friends can advocate goals that are directly related to performance in the work settings they envision, rather than simply agree to the program goals suggested by teachers. Similarly, a clear employment goal facilitates selection among service possibilities. Adult service programs differ in the extent to which they focus on the opportunity to work, in the kinds of work usually performed, in the extent of social integration, and in the types of support provided. An individual's employment future may be greatly affected by which adult service he or she enters. It is also easier to plan the personal support roles of family members or friends when there is a clear notion of the desired employment future. Depending on the kind of job, the individual's support needs, and the quality of local services, families and friends may need to plan, for example, for transportation supports, assistance in locating job opportunities, and ongoing encouragement of job success. Finally, a vision of the individual's desired employment future gives the family an opportunity to provide experience in responsibilities around the house, and, while the individual is still in school, to arrange for normal teenage

A. **Type of work**

1. How important is work to my child's quality of life?	
2. What work experience, including chores, has my child had?	
3. What kinds of work does my child like?	
4. What kinds of work would build on existing skills?	
5. What kinds of work would I like my child to try?	
6. What kinds of work does my child dislike?	
7. Is it important for my child to be around people at work?	
8. What kind of work schedules could fit my child's life?	

B. **Finances**

1. How much income will my child need?	
2. What kinds of activities will my child have to be able to support financially?	
3. Is loss of Social Security or other benefits a problem?	

C. **Support**

1. What kind of supports will my child require to keep a job?	
2. What kind of organization might best provide this support?	
3. How will my child get to and from work?	

Figure 10.1 Sample guide for family goal-setting.

volunteer roles, summer jobs, and training programs. These experiences provide an opportunity to examine expectations and assumptions. One family's assumption that earning money would not be necessary for their son because of their own resources quickly changed when they saw his satisfaction in managing his income from a brief job after school. Another pair of parents changed their idea that their daughter would have to work in a protected setting when they saw how well she interacted with the public while working at a concession stand at high school basketball games.

Developing a vision of what is possible is important, but difficult, given the pace of recent developments in employment services. High-quality programs now enable persons once considered too disabled to learn complicated tasks to work beside employees without handicaps, and work quickly enough to meet job demands. However, implementation of these model programs has been limited, so parents and others may not have the opportunity to observe such successes in their own communities. Consequently, planning an optimal employment future may require asking questions of professionals in the service system and advocating program development. It might be important to visit distant supported employment programs, talk with other parents and professionals at conferences, and collect written information about employment options.

Great expectations often create great services. The greatest barrier that many people with disabilities must overcome is the belief among others—parents, professionals, and neighbors—that they cannot learn or perform well enough to work. Time and again, these visions of the future have proven unnecessarily restrictive.

2. PARTICIPATE IN INDIVIDUAL PLANNING

Individualized program planning has become a hallmark of modern special education and adult services, providing an organized structure for family members, advocates, and service providers to negotiate service objectives for individuals with disabilities. Whereas the Individualized Education Program (IEP) process in special education offers parents more process rights, the systems in many adult programs also provide an important means of influence over services (Turnbull, 1985). Individualized program planning meetings are an opportunity for family members and advocates to promote supported employment if they participate regularly in these meetings and negotiate effectively for educational or service objectives that reflect the requirements and results of supported employment. Somewhat different objectives are appropriate for school programs, in which the goal is preparation for later employment.

In IEP meetings, families may best promote future supported employment by ensuring that precious instructional time is used as efficiently as possible to develop the skills and experience needed to achieve their vision of the student's employment future. As suggested in Chapter 9, high-quality school programs address five kinds of employment-related objectives: teaching work skills, developing work-support behaviors, facilitating choice among types of jobs, building a breadth of skills within chosen job areas, and obtaining paid employment for each student upon graduation. These are not sequential goals, but ongoing features of a well-designed program; a student's educational objectives at any point should relate to all five goals. For example, an objective for work preparation might involve developing the skills for clerical occupations. In order to build work support behaviors simultaneously with work skills, parents might request placement for their son or daughter in the city library or school administration building, where normal social demands of the workplace provide the context for teaching nonwork skills. Work outside the school also might contribute to later job placement by helping the student build a work history and making him or her known to potential employers. Choice and breadth are facilitated by changing job training sites over time. As this analysis suggests, time spent in training and supervised performance on regular job sites contributes most to the development of skills for future supported employment options. Conversely, prevocational training that involves development of personal "prerequisite" skills before on-site training is allowed, training that involves tasks for which a person probably could not be paid in a community setting, or training in settings where interactions with nonhandicapped persons are not available probably contribute little to a student's ultimate success in supported employment. Good school-based preparation should foster skills, contacts, and experience, three things that most people seek when looking for a job. Family involvement in school-based individual educational planning should promote such objectives, thereby facilitating later success in supported employment.

In adult service programs, individual program planning meetings can foster supported employment by shifting attention away from preparation objectives and toward actual employment outcomes. When individualized plans in adult services designate work or social skills as necessary prerequisites for work, this usually means that fewer program resources are spent in ensuring work opportunities, and more in instruction or therapy that will have little impact on future employment. Since these prevocational objectives can often be maintained indefinitely, a useful individual planning strategy for families and advocates is to argue against these readiness objectives and for objectives that include real employment. For example, parents of a young adult might propose objectives like, "Joe will be earning an average of $100 per month by next July," or, "by next August, Susan will spend at least 20 hours each week working for pay in an integrated setting," or, "Harold will average no disputes with non-handicapped coworkers during work each day." Each of these objectives makes it clear that paid work in regular work settings is the outcome that the family wants from the service, and that presumed prerequisites like learning particular work skills, behaving better in the day program itself, volunteering, or other "readiness" activities are considered inappropriate goals by the family.

Whereas individual program planning offers an important strategy for influencing services to provide supported employment options, such planning is insufficient by itself. Individual planning strategies are useful in gaining access to existing services or resources; they are seldom successful when the barriers to employment require program changes such as different use of staff or changes in program structures.

3. DEVELOP AND SHARE AN INFORMATION BASE

Becoming informed and informing others about local employment programs and possibilities are potentially powerful strategies for fostering supported employment in a community. The objectives of these information strategies are threefold: 1) to help families understand exactly what services are offered by local programs, so that they may make sound decisions concerning service selection, individual planning, and other advocacy efforts, 2) to build a broad base of support among elected officials, advocacy groups, and the general public for developing supported employment, and 3) to describe expectations and perceived problems to service providers in a way that motivates improved performance. A mix of information strategies may be helpful in pursuing these objectives.

The first information strategy is for family members and advocates themselves to learn about local service options and other public programs that affect employment. This process might start with visits to adult service programs arranged for one or more families, or with the creation of a "program fair" where providers are asked to illustrate and describe their services to parents and advocates. These get-acquainted approaches may be particularly helpful to parents whose children with disabilities are still in school, because they provide an orientation to existing postschool options.

Just as important as information on available services is knowledge about how employment affects other services and benefits. It is important to get good local advice on how supported employment would affect medical services, income support, case management, residential services, and other relevant factors. At present, the security associated with continuing access to these other services and benefits in some states is important enough to many families to limit an individual's earnings or work hours in order to maintain eligibility.

A second information strategy is to share the family's vision of what is possible and desirable as an employment future. The public is continually confronted with images of persons with disabilities who are dependent, segregated from the mainstream, and in need of pity or charity. Even professional efforts to gain employment options often reinforce this deviant imagery by emphasizing that only some people with disabilities are "job ready." Counteracting the public images of deviance and dependence is an important element of fostering supported employment. Helping other families to visit model programs, describing effective services in conferences or meetings, and promoting media reports that highlight successes in supported employment are all useful strategies for broadening community support for improving employment and day services. It may be helpful to respond with letters to the editor when new stories create undesirable images. Even in feature stories designed to promote a positive image of people with disabilities, the media often emphasize incorrectly the level of dependence of individuals served. It will be difficult to turn the attention of public officials and business leaders to supported employment when their evening newspapers and televisions broadcast the message that the problems of disability are to be solved by charity and caring services. Work opportunities and work-related support will be forthcoming only when enough people see supported employment as a life-enhancing, realistic, affordable option for persons with severe disabilities.

A third important information strategy involves making a directory of local service and employment programs publicly available. Because many adult services have several program components, a visit, tour, or brief description will seldom tell families all they need to know. To get more details on the employment options in various programs or components of programs, local parent groups have used short questionnaires which all the service providers in an area are asked to complete. By asking about such variables as average monthly wages of program participants, amount of time spent in integrated work settings, type of work done, and average number of hours paid work available to each participant, parents and advocates can compare the actual employment experiences their children might have in different kinds of programs. One such sample survey is included in Figure 10.2.

When providers in one state answered the questions about their

Basic information

Program: _____

Target respondent: _____

Phone number: _____

Date: _____

QUESTIONS	RESPONSE
1. What type of service would you provide my child?	
2. What sort of work/vocational training is provided?	
3. (a) How many people are served in the program?	
(b) What is IQ or functioning range of the people currently served?	
(c) What is their age range?	
4. What are the entrance requirements of the program?	
5. (a) Do people earn wages?	
(b) What is the average monthly wage per person?	
6. (a) What was the average *annual* wage of individuals in the program during the last calendar year?	
(b) What is the average gross commercial revenue of the program for the last 6 months?	

(continued)

Figure 10.2 Sample day program survey.

Figure 10.2. *(continued)*

QUESTIONS	RESPONSE
7. (a) How many staff are employed by your program?	
(b) What are their roles?	
8. (a) What community activities are available from the work site?	
(b) How often do people go into the community during program hours?	
9. (a) How long do people stay in the program?	
(b) During the last 2 years, how many people left your program?	
(c) Where did they go?	
10. If my child were signed up today, how long would it be until he or she received services?	
11. What is the application procedure?	
12. Miscellaneous comments (whatever you are interested in highlighting)	

employment services, the parent group asking the questions published a small guidebook that compared the practices and results of all the services in the area. An excerpt from this directory is included in Figure 10.3. This information serves several functions. It helps other parents who have not had direct contact with the programs decide which may be most appropriate for their sons or daughters. If made available with updates every 6 to 12 months, for example, it could provide important information to service providers about how they stand in relation to each other. Information showing improvement over time and comparisons with other programs can provide strong motivation for programs to improve. The information also provides a way for parents to communicate to legislators and other plicy makers about what improvements are needed for local services to support the employment future they envision for their relatives with disabilities. Regular information describing the employment outcomes of all the day services in an area or state could make for an effective column in a parent association newsletter.

Information-gathering should not be limited to local programs. Families and friends should also obtain information on successful model supported employment programs in other communities. Such information arms parents with a knowledge of what is *possible* as well as what is available.

4. INFLUENCE PROGRAM MANAGEMENT

Most community-based day and work services are operated by private, non-profit corporations under contract to public agencies responsible for administering services. The structure of these corporations, largely determined by Internal Revenue Service regulations for tax-exempt organizations and by state laws concerning governance of non-profit organizations, offers important means for concerned parents to influence program direction. Indeed, the reliance on the non-profit delivery system simply underscores the importance of parental involvement: delivering services in this way, rather than through direct management by government agencies, is supposed to make the service system more flexible, more responsive to innovation, and more sensitive to local priorities. Governance of these nonprofit corporations legally rests with a volunteer board of directors. By serving on these boards, interested and concerned parents can play a powerful role as advocates of alternatives to traditional programs. There are at least two useful approaches: serving on the board of an existing organization in order to help it change its services, or starting a new board which will compete with existing organizations for public funding.

As a member of the board of directors of an existing day program or work service, a concerned parent, relative, or advocate can exert the greatest influence by convincing other board members to refocus the organization's development plans, policies, or program objectives. Development plans of local organizations often include efforts to build new facilities, expand services to different groups or locations, or purchase major pieces of equipment related to contract work. Because many of these plans focus on expanded service in segregated facilities, it is important to argue for alternative development strategies that involve individual or small-group, community-integrated employment for service recipients. Chapter 7 provides general and specific ideas for plans to shift agencies from day service to supported employment.

Figure 10.3 Day programs in XYZ County.

	AB Day Center	CD Work Activity Center	EF Development Center	GH Rehabilitation Center
1. What type of service would you provide?	Skill training work access	Work-oriented activity center, vocational training, paid work, supervised work-site in community	Vocationally oriented work activity center, 1 small community enclave	Classroom instruction, vocational assessment, mobility training, counseling, work experience
2. What sort of work/ vocational training is provided?	Primarily crew labor in community—cleanup, some benchwork at center	Subcontract for firms in community, simulated work when no pay available, 1–8 ratio	Hand packaging, glove recycling, mailings, microfilming, sorting	Simulated work, contract jobs, prevocational skill training, problem resolution
3. (a) How many people are served in the program?	28	44	37–39 in-house, 2 enclave	16
(b) What is IQ or functioning range of the people currently serviced?	30–70 IQ, some severe behavior or emotional problems	25–80	21% mild retardation 36% moderate retardation 33% severe retardation 10% other	Mildly mentally retarded with emotional problems
(c) What is the age range?	21–59	23–60	18–59	20–56
4. What are the entrance requirements of the program?	Self-care, hygiene skills, not dangerous to self or others	County mental health criteria	County mental health criteria	Willingness to participate, adults 18 +, trainable, adequate self-help, not dangerous

5. (a)	Do people earn wages?	Yes, sporadically	Yes	Yes	Yes
(b)	What is the average monthly wage per person?	Varies widely, $0–$50	$35–$50	Average monthly $42.36 Average productivity 17.6% Productivity range 0.1%–45%	$0–$30
6. (a)	What was the average annual wage of individuals in the program during the last calendar year?	$100–$200 (Next year will be better.)	$400	$367.29 per fiscal year (July 1–June 30)	New program begun in September.
(b)	What is the average gross commercial revenue of the program for the last 6 months?	Commercial income minimal; much of work involves direct pay to workers from company	$10,000	$3,330 average monthly	Not reported
7. (a)	How many staff are employed by your program?	4, plus director	7	7.5	3 full-time 1–8 hours/week

(continued)

Figure 10.3. *(continued)*

	AB Day Center	CD Work Activity Center	EF Development Center	GH Rehabilitation Center
(b) What are their roles?	1 instructor, 3 aides	Director, client service coordinator, production coordinator, 4 supervisors	Director, program manager, office manager, 4 floor supervisors, 0.25 FTE quality control, 0.25 FTE clerical	Instructor, vocational aide, coordinator, relief
8. (a) What community activities are available?	Library, bowling, field trips/crew work off-site	Special Olympics, exercise class, mobility training	Few: annual employee party, Christmas party, annual open house	Exercise class
(b) How often do people go into the community during work hours?	Once every other week	Once each month	Not reported	Four people go once each week.
9. (a) How long do people stay in the program?	Few "graduate," 2 are entering "work enclave."	Very little movement at this time	Years	New program
(b) In the last 2 years, how many people left your program?	About 6	3	8	New program

(c)	Where did they go?	Other activity centers, some terminated/violence	1—senior citizen 2—other workshops, Sheltered Services programs	2—institution, 1—married 1—out of state, 4—other programs	New program
10. (a)	If my son or daughter were signed up today, how long would it be until he or she received services?	3–8 years, possibly more	2–8 years	Waiting list has 40 + people; last year we had 1 actual opening for an employee.	Not reported
11. (a)	What is the application procedure?	Contact County Mental Health	Contact County Mental Health	Contact County Developmental Disability	Contact County Mental Health
12. (a)	Miscellaneous comments	Better vocational access anticipated. We do not wish to provide "pre-vocational" experience.	Community work-sites being developed—we want to help provide some movement in system.	(none)	(none)

Influencing services through organization policies involves developing or revising broad policies that guide day-to-day operation. For example, a policy that created equal access to all available work, regardless of the nature or degree of disability, could alter the traditional practice of giving work to the most capable participants while those with more severe disabilities are only assigned to "readiness" activities.

A third influence strategy available to persuasive board members involves development of an annual plan with specific monthly objectives for the organization. Such a plan is described in Chapter 5, and includes establishment of monthly targets for program participants' wage and integration levels. Regular board review of performance measures in response to such a plan provides a powerful incentive for program innovation.

There are many situations in which membership on the board of existing service organizations is impossible, or opportunities for individual board members to effect change are unlikely to arise. In these circumstances, program management strategies involve creating new non-profit organizations that compete with existing programs for service resources and employment opportunities. Creating new organizations can have several advantages for parents interested in developing supported employment opportunities. A new organization offers the possibility of developing a specialized service that uniquely fits a community's employment opportunities, and that is not weighed down by the overhead costs of an unnecessary facility or by staffing costs not directly related to program objectives. It may be easier to develop a supported employment program from scratch than to make gradual changes in an existing service. Finally, creating a single new organization can add enough competition to the service system to induce other organizations that previously resisted change to try supported employment programs. A process for developing a new service organization is described in Chapters 3 and 4.

5. INFLUENCE THE SYSTEM

System-influence strategies are efforts to redirect government administration of day and work programs so that they promote the development of supported employment. The inherent concern of system-influence strategies can be boiled down to one question: "What resources will be made available to whom and for what purpose?" "What resources" refers to the appropriation of funds by elected officials to meet the needs of adults with disabilities. "To whom" refers to the process through which these resources are allocated to individuals and agencies. "For what purpose" refers to the kinds of programs that are funded, and the regulations, evaluation criteria, and training events through which government agencies influence the nature of programs.

System-influence strategies related to resource allocation are important because of the number of adults with severe disabilities who receive no daytime services and are simply on waiting lists for those services (McDonnell, Wilcox, & Boles, 1986). Besides these persons, the thousands of individuals who comprise the first cohort of students to enjoy the right to a free, appropriate public education now complete special education programs each year and require services in the community. Funding for any service for these individuals— either expansion of existing day activity programs or development of supported employment alternatives—requires legislative action. Decisions to continue or expand existing programs or to establish new programs directly affect how quickly supported employment options will be developed in a state. Clearly, additional development of supported employment is required if these employment needs are to be met.

Influencing system decisions has become critical, as state and local agencies attempt to redesign services to accommodate an influx of persons with severe disabilities who leave school. This growth pressure, in tandem with national policy initiatives that emphasize supported and competitive employment, provides the incentive for program philosophies, service definitions, regulations, and evaluation criteria to change. Without active participation by advocates for persons with severe disabilities, this change may produce, as it already has in some states, improved employment services only for persons with mild handicaps. Supported employment will be fostered when program funding is at least partially dependent on a program's success at providing work opportunities, wages, and integrated settings to individuals with severe handicaps.

Strategies to change systems may proceed in several ways, and several excellent guides are available to help parents influence the public decision-making process (e.g., see Biklen, 1974, 1983; Des Jardins, 1984). Some common approaches are making one's views known through letters, calls, or other means, participating in hearings, work groups, and planning committees, building a coalition by identifying other groups with similar interests, and lobbying the legislature through speakers, media campaigns, and parent meetings. A sample format for a letter to a legislator is included in Figure 10.4.

Mary Smith
123 Main Street
Anytown, Oregon 97000
February 20, 1988

The Honorable John Doe
Oregon State Senate (or) Oregon House of Representatives
(Room Number)
State Capitol Building
Salem, Oregon 97310

Dear Senator (or) Representative Doe:

I am the parent of a 13-year-old girl who is mentally disabled and I am also a resident of your district.

I am writing to request your "no" vote on Senate Bill 107, on which you will be voting on March 3 in the Senate (or) House Education Committee.

I believe you should oppose this bill because _____
_____.

It will affect handicapped children in your district in the following ways: _____.

I personally know that the effect of this bill on my daughter, should it pass, would _____.

Advocacy organizations that oppose this bill include ___
_____.

Please inform me on your position and let me know if there is any additional information you might need on this issue. Feel free to call me, by phone: (phone number).

Warm regards,

Mary Smith

Figure 10.4 Sample letter to a legislator.

6. PROVIDE SUPPORTS DIRECTLY

However well-funded or well-provided, services can never substitute for the range of supports available from families and friends. Families often find that they must supplement inadequate employment services or compensate for unavailable ones with help from siblings, parents, relatives, and neighbors. Sometimes, families may be more effective than services. In a survey of special education graduates in one state, Hasazi, Gordon, and Roe (1985) found that more young adults with disabilities found jobs through what Hasazi et al. labeled a "self-family-friend" network than through traditional adult services.

Family support may be helpful or necessary for each of these crucial aspects of employment services: preparation for employment, location of employment opportunities, and support in employment. When school-based vocational training programs do not address the five goals of vocational preparation to a family's satisfaction, and when needed adult employment services are unavailable, families may be able to contribute substantially to their child's employment preparation (e.g., see Moon & Beale, 1984). This involves creating opportunities for employment in regular work settings, and includes part-time jobs, chores for neighbors, normal volunteer jobs in hospitals or churches, and regular responsibilities at home. In each case, there is a multifaceted goal, involving practicing and maintaining skills, developing work-related social behaviors through contact with people who are not disabled, expanding experience, and demonstrating competence to potential employers in the community.

A second critical family support strategy may involve actually locating a job opportunity. The major barrier to successful employment of people now served in day programs is neither skill deficits nor behavior problems, but rather the lack of an opportunity to work. When a work opportunity is available, service resources can be focused on teaching specifically required skills, rather than on development of general work competencies that may or may not be relevant to any particular job. Consequently, when a work opportunity becomes available to an individual, his or her services often become much more focused and efficient. Family and neighborhood contacts are a typical source of job opportunities in a society; the same process applies to identifying supported employment opportunities for persons with severe disabilities. This strategy may be especially important if the individual is leaving school and is suddenly faced with the prospect of no service because there are lengthy waiting lists for all existing services. Family development of a job opportunity can change the bleak prospect of no services now faced by too many students currently growing past the age limit for school programs.

A third aspect of services that may be supplemented by family effort involves the ongoing support that is provided once a supported employment opportunity has been located. Keeping a job once initial training is completed sometimes depends on support from home. This support might include helping to purchase a wardrobe that is compatible with what others in the work place wear, avoiding schedule conflicts that force the individual with a disability to choose between work and family vacations, medical appointments, or recreational events, encouraging the individual by asking about each day's work or providing incentives at home to maintain work performance, helping to resolve transportation difficulties, and suggesting how to handle difficult social situations, personal crises, and other events that might affect work performance.

SUMMARY

Families, advocates, and friends of persons with severe disabilities have an important role in the implementation of supported employment within a community. This chapter summarizes the special interest in service development and quality shared by relatives and friends and describes several strategies they may use to facilitate the development of supported employment options in their communities. Strategies discussed include individual advocacy, family goal-setting, individual planning, and system influence strategies such as legislative lobbying. This chapter details how individuals with a personal interest in the quality of adult employment services can affect the quality and availability of supported employment.

REFERENCES

Biklen, D. P. (1974). *Let our children go: An organizing manual for advocates and parents*. Syracuse, NY: Human Policy Press.

Biklen, D. P. (1983). *Community organizing: Theory and practice*. Englewood Cliffs, NJ: Prentice-Hall.

Des Jardins, C. (1984). *How to organize effective parent/advocacy groups and move bureaucracies*. Chicago: Coordinating Council for Handicapped Children.

Hasazi, S., Gordon, L., & Roe, C. (1985). Factors associated with the employment status of handicapped youth exiting school from 1979 to 1983. *Exceptional Children, 51*, 455–469.

McDonnell, J. J., Wilcox, B., & Boles, S. M. (1986). Do we know enough to plan for transition? A national survey of state agencies responsible for services to persons with severe handicaps. *Journal of The Association for Persons with Severe Handicaps, 11*(1), 53–60.

Moon, M. S., & Beale, A. (1984). Vocational training and employment: Guidelines for parents. *The Exceptional Parent, 14*, 35–38.

Turnbull, A. (1985). From professional to parent: A startling experience. In A. Turnbull & H. Turnbull (Eds.), *Parents speak out: Then and now*. (2nd ed., pp. 127–135). Columbus, OH: Charles E. Merrill.

Turnbull, A. P. & Turnbull, H. R., III (1986). *Families, professionals, and exceptionality: A special partnership*. Columbus, OH: Charles E. Merrill.

Competency-Based Staff Training for Supported Employment

Jay Buckley, Joyce M. Albin, and David M. Mank

The most powerful tool of organizations engaged in supported employment of persons with severe disabilities is the effective use of staff time. If supported employment is to become widespread, effective and competent staff must be available to find jobs, train people to do these jobs, and maintain people in their jobs. Therefore, a critical factor in achieving the goals of federal- and state-supported employment initiatives is the collective ability to produce trained personnel to provide supported employment.

Supported employment presents significant challenges to those who train professional staff for schools and community employment programs. As discussed in other chapters, supported employment can be implemented through a number of diverse program structures, including individual placements in community businesses, small enclaves within industries, work crews, and other small enterprises. Each structure places unique demands on program staff relating to organizational management. Furthermore, each of these approaches is influenced by a seemingly limitless variety of industries in which employment can be found. Staff must be skilled in the type of work being performed and be sensitive to the nature of the business and the needs of the employer. The individuals for whom supported employment is designed present additional challenges to program staff. Staff must be prepared to provide training and ongoing support to individuals experiencing one or multiple severe disabilities, including physical, sensory, intellectual, and behavioral disabilities. Individuals with severe disabilities will probably require different types of initial and ongoing support to perform to employers' specifications and at the same time participate fully in integrated settings. As a result, supported employment professionals must be prepared to assume a number of unique business and habilitation roles. The task for preservice and inservice staff training projects is to provide trained program staff to deliver supported employment through a variety of supported employment approaches.

This chapter provides a discussion of issues in personnel preparation for supported employment. The first section of the chapter summarizes a competencies approach to staff development. This is followed by a section on the delivery of staff training, with emphasis on the outcomes that can be expected from various training formats. The final portion of this chapter concerns methods of evaluating staff training.

A COMPETENCIES APPROACH TO STAFF TRAINING

Both the world of business and the world of vocational habilitation encompass an extensive array of skills and knowledge that is useful to the personnel who work in these two fields. Supported employment represents a marriage of these disciplines in that it requires quality training and support of individuals with disabilities in regular business settings. Those responsible for training staff for supported employment programs need research and evaluation specific to supported employment. The competencies required of staff who work in supported employment include skills similar to those needed by other trainers of individuals with disabilities. However, the integration of habilitation and the private sector business community in supported employment presents real differences—staff need additional competencies that meet the needs of the business world, and because training and support take place in public and in the midst of an ongoing business, staff need to adopt practices that fit the culture of the regular workplace. From the array of potential training objectives, professionals who assume personnel preparation roles need to identify the specific competencies that staff will need to enable individuals with severe disabilities to succeed in paid, integrated employment.

Staff trainers have traditionally drawn upon one or more sources to identify the requisite competencies for personnel working with individuals with disabilities. One source is "expert opinion." Although subjective, expert opinions usually reflect the experience of respected and able professionals. A second source is empirical research aimed at identifying variables that prove to be statistically or practically significant in achieving desired outcomes. Well-designed research is certainly a less subjective source than expert opinion, but using it is a much more formidable strategy. Studies aimed at identifying competencies require numerous primary and secondary subjects and extensive longitudinal measurement. A third source of assistance, social validation, provides a "research" methodology for removing some of the subjectivity from expert opinion. In social validation, knowledgeable members of society select the more significant and important competencies from a comprehensive list of skills. The quality of the results of social validation studies depends on the universe of those surveyed, the validity and reliability of the "ballot," and the nature of the analyses of data.

The goal of training must be exemplary staff performance, that is, accomplishment of the objectives of the organization and the specific job with minimum effort and cost. Therefore, to achieve the desired outcomes of supported employment, the training objectives that lead to quality job performance can best be determined by analyzing and identifying the competencies shown by exemplary staff. Such a process can lead to a more rational judgment of the training that supported employment professionals will or will not need. A number of institutions of higher education have very successfully developed and implemented supported or transitional employment programs. From these programs, personnel preparation programs have been developed. Among these nationally recognized institutions are the University of Illinois, the University of Vermont, the Rehabilitation Research and Training Center at Virginia Commonwealth University, and the Rehabilitation Administration at the University of San Francisco. As a result of their experiences, each of these institutions has identified competencies needed by supported employment professionals. Many of the competencies included in this chapter are drawn from the work of these programs.

AN ORGANIZATIONAL
APPROACH TO IDENTIFYING COMPETENCIES

Efforts to bring about change are sometimes characterized by a tendency to oversimplify complex realities (Case, 1980; Howey & Corrigan, 1980a). This is especially true in staff training. Case (1980) points out that personnel trainers seldom translate competencies into roles within an organization. Recent publications in both organizational development and staff training stress the concept of the organization as the learner. Effective staff training takes this into account. Organizations that attempt to provide employment support to workers with disabilities, as well as the organizations that attempt to engage in personnel preparation, might consider that organizational behavior is learned behavior, shaped by the actions and experiences of its members and those served by it (Case, 1980). An appropriate focus of training for supported employment personnel is organizational development and the skills needed to make it happen. Agencies that develop and conduct staff training may be most successful if they are able to diagnose and respond to identified needs within the framework of a comprehensive organizational model.

One way to approach the task of identifying the competencies needed by staff in supported employment programs is to specify what an organization must do to be successful at supported employment. A comprehensive diagnosis of agency needs depends on identifying specific supported employment outcomes. The features and details of an organizational model can then be translated into specific staff knowledge and performance competencies (Paine, 1984). In Chapter 2, an organizational model for supported employment based on accomplishing five specific outcomes is introduced. Table 11.1 provides a list of these outcomes and describes staff competencies needed for each. Tables 11.2 through 11.6 list specific responsibilities related to each accomplishment. Each listed competency can be elaborated by criterion statements that reflect exactly what a staff person can do to turn a particular activity into a valued accomplishment.

A supported employment organization must design staff roles to

Table 11.1. Supported employment organization outcomes

Paid Employment Opportunities Available—includes the staff competencies needed to generate paid work opportunities for persons with disabilities.

Work Analyzed and Employees Trained—includes the staff competencies needed to ensure that work is organized for performance and that employees with disabilities learn and perform work to employers' specifications.

Individual Service Coordination Provided—includes the staff competencies needed to support employees with disabilities, and encompasses all features of service planning and evaluation.

Integration Achieved—includes the staff competencies needed to ensure that integration with persons who are not disabled occurs in and around the work site.

Support Organization Maintained—includes the staff competencies needed to manage a nonprofit organization providing supported employment services.

Table 11.2. Organizational competencies: Paid employment opportunities available

---

A. Generate work opportunities.
1. Survey local labor opportunities.
2. Identify marketing targets.
3. Develop marketing strategies and materials.
4. Develop sales presentation.
5. Develop network of contacts.
6. Conduct marketing.
7. Conduct thorough job analysis.
8. Negotiate agreement with employer.

B. Maintain access to employment.
1. Provide follow-up contact with employers.
2. Expand work opportunities with existing customers.
3. Obtain and maintain employer satisfaction feedback.

---

ensure that each responsibility is discharged competently, in order to meet the organization's objectives. This definition of staff roles, therefore, may be used to identify the knowledge and skill needed by staff, and to form the basis for staff training.

A recent study identified the need for two main roles for staff within supported employment organizations: professional trainers who provide work opportunities, training, and support for persons with disabilities, and managers of organizations specializing in supported employment services (Harold Russell Associates, 1985). Job enlargement literature and the experience of many demonstration projects in supported employment suggest that staff roles should include both direct service and management components. Whereas the manager of a support organization must possess, or at least be able to evaluate, all the competencies required to accomplish the organizational outcomes needed for supported employment, other jobs within the organization may be designed to include only some of these. An organization may decide to ask these staff to demonstrate competence in a minimum number of areas or to be competent in several.

Within any organization there are staff who have experience or interest in, or aptitude for, some of the competencies that are typically viewed as beyond a traditional direct service role. The design of staff roles within supported employment organizations should take this into account as well. Enabling interested staff to develop and demonstrate the competence to fulfill responsibilities typically performed by a manager accomplishes two things—it allows staff to perform roles that they find particularly satisfying, and it frees the general manager to invest more time in other critical areas.

Table 11.3. Organizational competencies: Work analyzed and employees trained

A. Organize jobs and tasks for performance.
1. Develop process design.[a]
2. Develop facility floor plan, work flow.[a]
3. Develop task designs.
4. Adapt and modify tasks and settings as needed.
5. Use job analysis information to develop a task sequence and task analyses for direct and indirect work behavior.
6. Use task analyses, performance data, prompting and reinforcement to teach specific job skills.
7. Establish inventory and purchasing system.[a]
8. Establish quality control system.[a]
9. Establish work scheduling and allocation system.[a]
10. Establish shipping and invoicing procedures.[a]
11. Establish production information system.

B. Maintain work performance.
1. Collect and analyze performance data.
2. Increase and maintain production rates.
3. Set up self-initiation and self-monitoring systems.
4. Maintain behavior management procedures.
5. Promote maintenance and generalization of skills.
6. Instruct employers on supervising the workers.[b]
7. Conduct retraining if worker performance falls below criteria or if job changes.
8. Set up system to collect data after trainer has decreased his or her presence.
9. Maintain scheduling, quality control, inventory, and other production systems.[a]
10. Maintain production information.
11. Provide other ongoing support.

[a]Needed primarily by staff in entrepreneurial organizations.
[b]Needed primarily by staff in personnel support organizations.

DELIVERY OF TRAINING

The current national expansion of supported employment creates a major staff training and retraining need. No doubt this need will be filled through a combination of federal personnel preparation programs, college and university efforts, state training and technical assistance projects, and local staff development programs.

Preservice versus Inservice

Community supported employment professionals may be trained through either preservice or inservice training programs, or both. The functions of each differ, as do the problems associated with each. Preservice training is defined as the "substantial beginning of a life-long program of professional education" (Tyler, 1978, p. 138). In most

Table 11.4. Organizational competencies: Employees integrated

A. Identify and gain access to integration opportunities.
1. Identify integration opportunities in and around the work place.
2. Identify normal company routines and social integration demands on the job site.
3. Design and implement needed performance adaptations to facilitate integration.
4. Arrange access to integration activities.
5. Analyze activities and design training strategies.

B. Maintain employee integration.
1. Design system to collect integration data.
2. Assess integration levels.
3. Assess performance.
4. Provide training and support to improve integration activities.
5. Provide and increase employee integration.

Table 11.5. Organizational competencies: Individual service coordination needs met

A. Hire employees.
1. Develop hiring policies and procedures.
2. Define support services for prospective employees/guardians.
3. Obtain historical information on applicants.
4. Interview prospective employee/family/guardian.
5. Match individuals' abilities/needs to available job; select employees and jobs.
6. Arrange transportation and other pre-employment logistics.
7. Inform consumers/parents/advocates/other public agencies of contribution they can make to job success.
8. Develop employee orientation process.

B. Deliver employee services.
1. Identify individual competencies, support network, and support needs.
2. Match individual needs with public and community resources.
3. Implement transportation system.
4. Provide family support and training.
5. Develop individual habilitation plan.

C. Maintain employee services.
1. Develop/implement advocacy strategies to enable the worker to keep the job.
2. Develop/implement a management information system (MIS) to track worker outcomes.
3. Provide support in response to MIS data.

D. Provide transition from school programs.
1. Describe the organization's support services to parents, secondary personnel, and students.
2. Work cooperatively with school and community agency personnel to place, train, and support secondary students making the transition to adult life.
3. Develop and implement individual transition plans.

Table 11.6 Organizational competencies: Organizational capacity maintained

---

A. **Establish organizational capacity.**
1. Follow state and federal supported employment regulations.
2. Complete planning activities and submit proposal for funding.
3. Establish and operate a legal nonprofit agency.
4. Work effectively with allied organizations.
5. Advocate state/local systems change.
6. Obtain Department of Labor certification as appropriate.
7. Establish and implement personnel policies.
8. Establish and implement financial systems.
9. Hire staff.

B. **Manage organizational capacity.**
1. Develop and monitor budget/finance functions; maintain contract for funding.
2. Monitor staff resource allocation.
3. Identify and meet staff development needs.
4. Establish and maintain a public relations program.
5. Interpret evaluation/management information system (MIS) data.
6. Establish and use annual plan and MIS data to improve project outcomes.
7. Work effectively with board of directors; maintain board functions.
8. Obtain external evaluations.
9. Satisfy requirements of external regulatory agencies.

---

fields, the issue is not whether preservice is apt to be more effective than inservice training in effecting competent performance. Many professionals who achieve competence do so as a result of some preservice education supplemented by ongoing inservice opportunities. To achieve significant and lasting change, therefore, both preservice professional preparation programs and inservice training programs should include training for the competencies needed by staff to implement supported employment. Both must include the business and organizational management competencies required for supported employment as well as the more conventional training in habilitation competencies. Preservice training offers potential supported employment professionals the opportunity to develop the required skills and knowledge in a comprehensive and organized manner. However, if undergraduate and graduate preservice training programs changed their curricula today, it would still require several years for these programs to graduate professionals trained in the competencies required for supported employment. Furthermore, it will require several years for professionals with preservice training in supported employment competencies to assume a majority of the positions in emerging supported employment organizations.

There are several compelling reasons why inservice training is required for creating change in the services offered to adults with disabilities:

Currently Operating Programs Have Staff That Could Benefit from Inservice Training Organizations that make the commitment to convert to supported employment have a valuable asset in the staffmembers who share this commitment. Incumbent staff are familiar with the individuals who receive services through the organization. Staff probably also possess some of the skills required for implementing supported employment. An inservice training approach provides opportunities for staff to supplement existing skills with the competencies required for supported employment at minimum cost.

Incumbent Staff Exhibit Diverse Training Needs Related to Supported Employment The personnel from school and rehabilitation programs have had a mixture of preservice training, inservice training, and experience. Certified classroom teachers, vocational rehabilitation counselors, vocational evaluators, classroom aides, and placement counselors all possess some of the knowledge and skills required to perform as exemplary employment training specialists. However, a vocational evaluator is likely to have different retraining needs from a high school teacher's. An inservice training strategy permits individualization of training.

The Incentives That Promote Changes to Supported Employment Are Immediate Transitional and supported employment programs are emerging in every part of the United States. Several major research institutes and more than 100 other employment projects have been funded by state and federal sources. The U.S. Office of Special Education and Rehabilitative Services (OSERS) has provided funds to a number of states to convert existing day services to supported employment (*Federal Register*, 1985). Therefore, decisions made in the next few years will have enduring consequences for the quality of services in many communities. Existing programs need to build competence quickly to take advantage of current incentives.

These few points lead to the conclusion that inservice is an effective and expedient means of helping organizations and their staffs develop the competencies needed to support individuals with disabilities in paid and integrated employment. Comprehensive preservice programs based on the competencies needed by commmunity employment professionals must also be designed to enable training of new professionals entering the work place. Competency-based preservice programs offered by institutions of higher education will help change the inservice training needs of employment specialists over time.

Instructional Modalities and Outcomes

The most important variables to consider in choosing instructional modalities are the outcomes that can be expected of each modality (Baldwin, Campbell, & Fredericks, 1982). Preservice or inservice training for supported employment professionals can be expected to result in increased *awareness*, that is, the perception that procedures exist for arriving at particular outcomes, or that those outcomes are desirable; *knowledge*, that is, the ability to remember previously learned material such as trends, criteria, principles, and theories (Gronlund, 1982); or *skills*. Skills may be viewed as *immediate, enduring,* or *generalized* (Baldwin et al., 1982). An immediate skill is defined as the ability to perform a task according to a set criterion before the end of training. Enduring skill implies that an individual maintains the skill beyond the training period. Generalized skill represents the ability to adapt and demonstrate performance across novel conditions. Skills endure when individuals are provided repeated opportunities to practice with feedback. Skills transfer best to other settings when opportunities for practice are provided across a variety of settings. The choice of a specific training format for use in a particular preservice or inservice training session, therefore, should be based on the desired outcome.

Table 11.7 presents these potential training outcomes and lists training formats that may be used to achieve such outcomes. These formats are commonly used training modalities in quality preservice and inservice training programs.

Table 11.7 Training formats and expected outcomes

Expected outcomes	Formats
A. Increased awareness	Lectures Tapes and films Written materials
B. Knowledge	Lecture and discussion Demonstration and discussion Programmed videotapes and written materials Interactive software
C. Skill	
1. Immediate skill	Practice with feedback
2. Enduring skill	Repeated practice with feedback in natural setting
3. Generalized skill	Follow-up observation and instruction across conditions

Too often, the selection of training formats is not based on realistic objectives. For example, Howey and Corrigan (1980a) report that the results of a national survey on preservice and inservice training for special educators indicated that the most common, yet least preferred, modality of instruction is the lecture-discussion format. Although it is the most common format, lecture-discussion cannot be expected to result in increased skills for the learners. The only outcome that realistically can be expected is increased knowledge or awareness. Table 11.7 serves as a reminder of the limits of certain training modalities and explains why competent performance is not always the outcome of traditional staff training.

Table 11.7 also provides staff trainers with a suggested sequence of training activities that can lead to improved competence. Feedback should be provided during activities aimed at building skill (Baldwin et al., 1982; Inge & Snell, 1985). Follow-up observation and instruction in the natural setting should be included if enduring skills are expected (Baldwin et al., 1982; Weisman-Frisch, Crowell, & Inman, 1980). Finally, for generalized skills, training must include the opportunity to practice in settings that best approximate the conditions under which trainees will later be expected to perform (Baldwin et al., 1982).

Training can be structured so that competent performance is developed over a series of cumulative sessions. Brief introductory sessions might be used to build awareness that will set the stage for further training in which knowledge and specific, enduring skills can be developed (Baldwin et al., 1982; Howey & Corrigan, 1980b). The goal and outcomes of specific training sessions should be made public so that supported employment organizations can plan for and select staff training opportunities that lead to specific, needed organizational competencies.

Incentives to Increase Staff Competency

The cumulative arrangement of training activities according to expected outcomes may not be sufficient to ensure that trainees acquire, maintain, and generalize needed competencies. Competent performance will not occur if the individual performer does not value the accomplishment (Gilbert, 1978). Thus, attention must be paid to staff motivation and incentives in building competence (Gilbert, 1978; Seekins & Fawcett, 1984). Howey & Corrigan (1980b) identify four types of incentives that should accompany staff training. Table 11.8 lists these incentives and suggests how each can be applied to staff training for supported employment organizations. Management staff can facilitate the development of staff competence by ensuring that

Table 11.8 Incentives and their application to supported employment staff training

Incentives[a]	Applications to supported employment staff training
Economic	Pay raises can relate to mastery of certain competencies.
Technical	Increased knowledge and skills enable staff to reach organizational outcomes more efficiently. Improved worker outcome measures relate directly to staff competencies. Improved competency reduces burnout.
Contextual	Mastery of certain competencies leads to a reduction in the effort required to enable workers to succeed and to an increase in employers' ability to supervise workers. Competent staff have better working relationships with their supervisors and employers.
Professional	Competence leads to enhanced status and autonomy. Status can be tied to certification based on mastery of competencies. Opportunities for professional advancement can be tied to documented performance.

[a]The incentives listed were suggested by Howey and Corrigan (1980b).

training is accompanied by professional, conceptual, technical, and financial incentives.

The Responsibility to Provide Training

Professional trainers usually come from two distinct backgrounds: personnel preparation and vocational habilitation. Personnel preparation staff, per se, may not be perceived as credible if they lack skills in specific content areas. Conversely, vocational service staff may be perceived as lacking the expertise to design and carry out well-organized personnel training (Baldwin et al., 1982). One solution lies in a training partnership of staff from backgrounds that include content expertise as well as personnel training competencies (Baldwin, et al., 1982; Freagon, 1982; Helge, 1981). A training staff composed of individuals with experience in personnel preparation and vocational habilitation will be more likely to prepare supported employment professionals successfully.

EVALUATION OF TRAINING

Although gauging the impact of training on individuals and organizations is difficult, most organizations involved in supported employment are committed to using staff training to change employment opportunities for persons with disabilities. The question is: How can the effect of staff training be measured?

Staff training programs typically seek feedback by asking participants to rate their satisfaction immediately after training (Howey & Corrigan, 1980b). This form of evaluation, although important, measures satisfaction rather than the full impact of training. Ideally, evaluation must include measures that determine the degree to which training has enhanced the agency's ability to reach its organizational outcomes. The organizational outcomes listed in Tables 11.1 through 11.6 form a basis for assessing organizational performance before and after staff attend training. This method of organizational evaluation requires that agencies receiving training cooperate in measuring performance changes (Gilbert, 1978). There are two steps in this process. First, the organization conducts internal evaluations of staff achievements in each of these five performance outcomes prior to staff training. Then, after training, the organization assesses the improvement in specific competencies within a particular outcome area. For this to happen, the agencies must make potential recipients aware of the expected outcomes of training, and of the formats that will be used to achieve these outcomes.

Although the organizations receiving training should participate in the evaluation of training, the primary responsibility for assessing the impact of training rests with the agency offering training. There are at least seven major evaluation concerns for staff training organizations. These concerns include the social validity of seminars, the utility of the content of seminars, the effectiveness of seminars, the quality of seminars, the impact of seminars on the performance of participants, the impact of seminars on the performance of the supported employment organization, and the impact of seminars on individuals with disabilities. Table 11.9 presents these concerns, along with possible evaluation questions, data sources, and measures for each.

The evaluation of the impact of training according to the major outcomes of supported employment organizations should provide the feedback required to assess the validity of individual competencies selected for training, the quality and performance of the personnel who provide training,and the value of instructional modalities used during training. The variety of data sources and measures listed in Table 11.9 is required to accomplish this level of evaluation. Without this level of effort, the purpose of staff training—change—is extremely difficult to measure. With ongoing evaluation and adjustment, training organizations can best help supported employment organiza-

Table 11.9. Specific evaluation concerns for supported employment staff training

Evaluation concern	Evaluation question	Data source (instrument)	Measure
Social validity of seminars	Is the proposed content perceived as useful to the range of professionals sampled?	Written ratings of competencies by local administrators, consumer advocates, schools, and supported employment agencies.	Percent of proposed competencies retained by external panel after validation process
Utility of seminars' content	Do the training seminars address content that is useful to participants in their job roles?	Participant/organization satisfaction evaluation form	Likert scale ratings for each session
Effectiveness of seminars	Do participants meet the competencies set for each seminar?	Seminar products and tasks	Percent of skills acquired by participants
Quality of seminars	Are seminar participants satisfied with the quality of the seminars provided?	Participant satisfaction evaluation form	Likert scale ratings for each session
Impact of seminars on participants' performance	Are adult service agencies satisfied with the competencies gained by seminar participants from their agencies?	Agency satisfaction survey form	Likert scale ratings
Impact of seminars on performance of supported	Do organizations report that the seminars have en-	Survey	Likert scale ratings

(continued)

Table 11.9. *(continued)*

Evaluation concern	Evaluation question	Data source (instrument)	Measure
employment organizations	abled them to change or improve on organizational outcomes?		
Impact of seminars on individuals with severe disabilities	How many individuals with severe disabilities are served by seminar participants?	Participant registration form	Number of individuals with severe disabilities who are served by participants
	Do participants report improved vocational performance by their students as a result of training?	Survey	Likert scale ratings

tions identify the changes required to enable individuals with severe disabilities gain access to employment in integrated settings.

SUMMARY

In every state, personnel preparation is emerging as a central issue in systems change of supported employment. The supported employment initiative depends, in part, on the availability of training that helps develop competent staff. Skilled and competent staff will likely make the difference between the widespread achievement of supported employment, and a situation in which a few individuals with severe disabilities have access to paid and integrated work while the vast majority remain underemployed in segregated day programs.

Those assuming responsibility for providing staff training must develop competency-based training programs in which training consists of activities that lead to enduring skills. Consumers and providers of training must be able to relate individual competence to the organizational outcomes required for supported employment. The responsibility for success in staff training is shared by the agencies receiving training and the institutions providing it. However, institutions looking to provide staff training must be willing to assume responsibility for the outcomes realized by supported employment organizations. To offer training is to make a commitment to the success of supported employment.

REFERENCES

Baldwin, V., Campbell, B., & Fredericks, H. D. (1982). The application of inservice training technology. In B. Campbell & V. Baldwin (Eds.), *Severely handicapped/hearing impaired students: Strengthening service delivery* (pp. 23–32). Baltimore: Paul H. Brookes Publishing Co.

Case, C. W. (1980). Schools as social systems: Applying organizational and development concepts and practices to inservice education. In D. C. Corrigan & K. R. Howey (Eds.), *Special education in transition: Concepts to guide the education of experienced teachers* (pp. 87–103). Reston, VA: Council for Exceptional Children.

Federal Register. (1985, June 18). Speech projects and demonstrations for providing vocational rehabilitation services to severely handicapped individuals, 50(117), Part 373.

Freagon, S. (1982). A commentary response. In B. Campbell & V. Baldwin (Eds.), *Severely handicapped/hearing impaired students: Strengthening service delivery* (pp. 33–45). Baltimore: Paul H. Brookes Publishing Co.

Gilbert, T. F. (1978). *Human competence: Engineering worthy performance.* New York: McGraw–Hill.

Gronlund, N. E. (1982). *Constructing achievement tests.* Englewood Cliffs, NJ: Prentice-Hall.

Harold Russell Associates. (1985). *Final report: Consensus seminar, proceedings and recommendations.* Unpublished manuscript.

Helge, D. (Winter, 1981). Multidisciplinary personnel preparation: A successful model of preservice team training for service delivery. *Teacher Education and Special Education, 4*(1), 13–17.

Howey, K. R., & Corrigan, D. C. (1980a). Overview. In D. C. Corrigan & K. R. Howey (Eds.), *Special education in transition: Concepts to guide the education of experienced teachers* (pp. 3–14). Reston, VA: Council for Exceptional Children.

Howey, K. R., & Corrigan, D. C. (1980b). The school based teacher educator: Developing a conceptual framework. In D. C. Corrigan & K. R. Howey (Eds.), *Special education in transition: Concepts to guide the education of experienced teachers* (pp. 15–32). Reston, VA: Council for Exceptional Children.

Inge, K. J., & Snell, M. E. (1985). Teaching positioning and handling techniques to public school personnel through inservice training. *The Journal of The Association for Persons with Severe Handicaps, 10*(2), 105–110.

Paine, S. C. (1984). Standardized program models in human services: The user's perspective. In S. C. Paine, G. T. Bellany, & B. Wilcox (Eds.), *Human services that work: From innovation to standard practice* (pp. 209–215). Baltimore: Paul H. Brookes Publishing Co.

Seekins, T., & Fawcett, S. B. (1984). Planned diffusion of social technologies for community groups. In S. C. Paine, G. T. Bellany, & B. Wilcox (Eds.), *Human services that work: From innovation to standard practice* (pp. 247–260). Baltimore: Paul H. Brookes Publishing Co.

Tyler, R. W. (1978). Accountability and teacher performance: Self-directed and external-directed professional improvement. In L. Rubin (Ed.), *The in-service education of teachers: Trends, processes, and prescriptions.* Boston: Allyn & Bacon.

Weisman-Frisch, N., Crowell, F., & Inman, D. (1980). Inservicing vocational trainees: A multiple perspective evaluation approach. *Journal of The Association for Persons with Severe Handicaps, 5,* 158–172.

Chapter 12

Business Participation in Supported Employment

Larry E. Rhodes, Kenneth D. Ramsing, and G. Thomas Bellamy

As the primary source of work opportunities, private companies and their managers are essential to the implementation of supported employment. This chapter addresses the question of how private employers can participate in supported employment. The intent is both to offer ideas for business participation and to make service agencies sensitive to issues of concern to employers. Employers have been hiring persons with disabilities for years. Supported employment is not a substitute for these activities. Rather, it is intended to increase employers' involvement so that persons are given consideration who, until recently, have not been part of the work force.

Supported employment is discussed in this chapter from the perspective of private sector businesses. Many of the issues and strategies addressed here may also pertain to employers in the public sector, but such employers are not addressed separately. Also not included in the discussion of employers are those nonprofit service agencies that provide employment in combination with publicly funded rehabilitation services.

EMPLOYER INTEREST IN PERSONS WITH DISABILITIES

Contemporary business managers face challenges that threaten the existence of their companies. Overseas competition, lagging productivity, product innovations, management-union conflicts, and fluctuating currency values provide the context within which day-to-day management decisions must be made. Like other management choices, a decision to employ someone with a disability must reflect a business interest.

The prospect of employing persons with severe disabilities has often raised employer fears such as lower productivity or increased industrial insurance rates (Vandergoot & Worrell, 1979). In an uncertain economy, companies go to great lengths to explore new ways of increasing profitability. However, any approach perceived to conflict with this goal is likely to be ignored. There is little question that employing people with disabilities can be a sound decision leading to increases in productivity.

The business interests that are served by hiring persons with disabilities naturally vary from one company to another. Nevertheless, there are at least six good reasons why employers have chosen to participate in efforts to employ persons with disabilities. Although an exhaustive review is beyond the scope of this chapter, these reasons are briefly described next.

The Company Benefits from Having Good Employees

For years, successful employment placement programs have been stressing the value to the company of hiring employees with disabilities. Benefits that have been identified include low absenteeism (Rhodes & Valenta, 1985), high motivation, and reduced turnover (E. I. du Pont de Nemours & Co., 1982). Benefits also include job performances that reflect the competence and social adjustment of persons with disabilities (Hill & Wehman, 1980).

Hiring People with Disabilities Benefits Community Relations

A second benefit is a positive public image associated with hiring persons excluded from the traditional work force. It is difficult to determine the precise impact of positive public relations on profitability. However, companies routinely go to considerable effort and expense to generate a good public image. Although the specific public relations messages may vary, most organizations desire name recognition and a positive image within their respective communities. Successful public relations makes it easier to recruit qualified applicants and demonstrates the social responsibility that may be a part of the organization's mission. A company's concern for its community is often expressed through an effort to put resources back into the area where it does business.

Hiring Persons with Disabilities Enriches a Company's Culture

A company's culture consists of the combination of values and beliefs that govern its personnel and organizational structure, thereby producing behavioral norms. Concern about the nature of the culture that exists in organizations has followed directly from concern about productivity. To build an effective corporate culture, a business must respond to an increasingly heterogeneous work force, demonstrating its interest in and support for all its employees. Hiring and incorporating persons with disabilities into the work force serves as a visible demonstration of a company's concern for its employees.

The Capability to Hire Persons with Disabilities Gives Companies an Edge in a Labor-Short Economy

The successful economic development of many communities has led to labor shortages (Wingate, 1985). Shortages are expected to continue and spread as the size of the young adult population declines through 1995. These shortages, frequently found in service industries, represent major opportunities for companies with expertise in employing persons with disabilities. Consequently, a company that builds experience in incorporating persons with disabilities into its work force is investing in its own future.

Business Taxes Are At Least Partially Affected by the Efficiency of Social Service Delivery

Businesses fund services with their tax dollars. More tax money is required when these services are ineffective or inefficient. Because the opportunity to work often reduces social service needs, it is in the interest of the business community to ensure that as many potential service recipients as possible have job opportunities.

Employing Persons with Disabilities Improves a Company's Capacity to Respond to Government Regulation

Affirmative action is now a part of everyday business for many of the nation's organizations in both the public and private sectors. Employing persons with disabilities demonstrates responsiveness to affirmative action expectations, helps an organization meet other public contract requirements, and allows a company to take advantage of various government initiatives. Federal law also requires many companies to make reasonable efforts to hire people with disabilities.

CURRENT EMPLOYER PARTICIPATION

Efforts to employ persons with disabilities have always included private employer involvement. In recent years, emphasis on this role has increased. Government priorities have focused on employment and reduced dependence on public assistance, with greater reliance on the private sector for the achievement of these social policy objectives. More complete information on employer practices toward persons with disabilities is greatly needed. Although the extent to which employers hire individuals with disabilities cannot be determined, four current methods of participation can be identified in addition to work subcontracted to sheltered workshops.

Direct Employment of Persons with Disabilities

Survey data on the number of persons with any type of disability who are placed in competitive jobs are not conclusive. It has been estimated that the actual number is far less than the number reported (Levitan & Taggart, 1982). Nonetheless, the competitive job market accounts for many thousands of job placements per year.

Reasonable Accommodation

The Rehabilitation Act of 1973 mandates accommodation to an employee's or job applicant's physical limitations with architectural modifications that effect "reasonableness" of access and facilities. Businesses have made giant strides in accommodating persons with disabilities, although a U.S. Department of Labor survey reported as recently as 1980 that 91% of the companies surveyed were not in compliance with the 1973 act (Pati & Adkins, 1980). Participation in supported employment provides a way for employers to show commitment and build skills in employing many people with disabilities.

Participation in Special Employment Projects

One of the most successful participatory programs has been the Projects With Industry (PWI) program authorized in 1968 to provide funding to help persons with severe disabilities obtain competitive employment. PWI programs have pioneered the use of strong links with industry through rehabilitation-industry councils and a preparation strategy to place persons in desirable jobs in competitive environments. PWI programs have demonstrated that it is possible to rely on volunteer employers for the primary "marketing" of the program to other businesses (Geletka, 1982). This partnership between industry and rehabilitation service is based on the assumptions that actual work places provide the most reliable setting for evaluating the skills and attitudes of potential employees, assistance in hiring and training workers with handicaps is useful to employers, employers can best identify possible jobs for handicapped workers and define the qualifications for those jobs, and instituting programs to employ such workers is in industry's best interest (Pati & Morrison, 1982).

Charitable Contributions

Business has played and will continue to play a role in services to persons wtih disabilities through charitable contributions. The actual amount of funds generated through industrial contributions and gifts to day programs for people with disabilities is unknown. Perhaps the greatest contribution is the unrecorded contribution of time from "loaned executives" and business managers who sit on the boards of directors of nonprofit service providers. Loaning executives is becoming an increasingly important aspect of companies' community relations.

SUPPORTED EMPLOYMENT: A NEW OPPORTUNITY FOR BUSINESS PARTICIPATION

As successful as employer programs have been in creating opportunities for persons with disabilities, they have had little immediate impact on those for whom supported employment is designed. This has been a natural consequence of the pursuit of reasonable business interests. Employers usually select the most traditionally "qualified" candidate for a job, and even when hiring persons with disabilities, choose the most capable and least disabled. Publicly funded vocational services are thus encouraged to follow this lead by serving persons thought to be likely job candidates, while screening out those with more severe disabilities (Levitan & Taggart, 1982). Those left out of this process constitute the primary group for whom supported employment is intended: individuals who frequently receive nonvocational services because they are considered unable to work at expected production levels with conventional employer supervision.

Supported employment differs in three important ways from conventional business efforts to employ persons with disabilities. Supported employment: 1) involves an ongoing relationship with a support organization, 2) may involve employment at subnormal productivity levels and wages, and 3) requires social integration of the work place, whether work is done within a host company or under contract with a vocational service. Each of these differences is briefly described next.

Ongoing Involvement of Public Agencies

The people for whom supported employment is designed have different needs from those served by most rehabilitation services. Traditional rehabilitation services have been time-limited. An individual is trained, retrained, or otherwise prepared for a job. He or she is placed on the job, performance is monitored during a short follow-up period, (usually 3–6 months), and then the case, considered successful, is closed. Although many persons with disabilities need such a short-term employment preparation service, it does not serve all persons who can work. Supported employment provides an alternative for persons who can work but require continuing assistance. In supported employment, a support organization, usually a nonprofit service provider, receives public support to provide whatever assistance the individual needs in order to do the job for as long as he or she is employed.

This arrangement for sustained support changes typical employer participation in three ways. First, the employer will always have assistance available when a supported employee has difficulty meeting workplace demands or requires assistance in coping with other personnel issues. Second, this assistance is available because of the presence of an independent support organization, so the employer maintains an ongoing relationship with that organization. Third, the support organization generally provides a formal link between the employer and residential support or social service funding agency. This permits the company to focus on business and employment issues while the support organization manages any social service issues that arise.

Productivity and Wages

The purpose of supported employment is to hire persons who could not work in regular employment environments without continuing public support. The need for ongoing support is not necessarily related to productivity, but many persons requiring support may also work at levels less than typical for other employees. It is possible under U.S. Department of Labor regulations for employers to pay wages based on an individual's actual productivity level even when the resulting pay levels are less than the statutory minimum wage. Taking advantage of this provision enables employers to offer jobs to persons with significant productivity limitations, and to benefit from the positive economic contribution these individuals make. In this situation, the individual's income may be supplemented through continued receipt of income transfer benefits at a level reduced in proportion to earned income.

Emphasis on Integration

Supported employment emphasizes work in the natural workplace as critical to achieving the normal social benefits of working. Although contracting with large sheltered workshops has generally been considered a strategy for helping persons with disabilities obtain work, this does not necessarily contribute to the development of supported employment. Supported employment exists only when persons with severe disabilities work beside coworkers who are not disabled. Work performed by groups of more than eight people with disabilities is not integrated, according to current definitions of supported employment. Because of this emphasis on integration, employers wishing to participate in supported employment must know about the circumstances under which any contracted work will be performed.

INDUSTRY PARTICIPATION

Industry participation in supported employment offers the same opportunities for community leadership, demonstration of social consciousness, and commitment to affirmative action that is involved in other strategies for employing persons with disabilities. There are three specific ways in which industry participation will create opportunities for supported employment.

1. Hire an Individual in a Supported Job

Given the availability of a local service organization with ongoing funding to support people in jobs, it may be in a company's interest to employ a person with severe disabilities who would not otherwise be hired. The employment support organization can provide training and supervision so that the employer incurs no costs beyond that required for other employees. The support organization then continues to provide support as needed to maintain the employment of the individual. Industries wishing to create a supported job usually need to perform at least three steps:

1. Identify a job or set of tasks within the company that needs to be performed. This may constitute a full-time or part-time job. The selected tasks might generally require only a few hours of work a day. When performed by someone working at a reduced productivity level, however, they could provide full-time work.
2. Locate a vocational service provider with the capacity and expertise to train and support an individual in the company. Because the concept of supported employment is relatively new, not every community has such providers at this time, although this is rapidly changing.
3. With assistance from the provider, select an individual who fits into the company and who needs the ongoing support that the provider is funded to offer.

By employing a person in such a supported job, the company creates an opportunity for someone who otherwise would be unlikely to enter the work force. The ongoing support protects the employer from the risks of unexpected or unreasonable costs. Furthermore, the presence of a work opportunity reduces the overall public cost of service to the individual.

2. Start an Enclave

One promising idea for developing employment opportunities is to provide several individuals with severe disabilities highly specialized training or other job supports and allow them to work within a company. The company adopts this strategy as a means of employing persons who otherwise would be unable to work within the company, even with frequent outside support. The basic strategy is for a private, nonprofit corporation to provide ongoing support to the company. This employment support organization may be responsible for many functions, including the provision of special training and supervision. The most desirable approaches are those that maximize company involvement and minimize the intrusiveness of outside support, while maintaining the long-term supervision and training structure that makes the employment possible. This approach uses company effort, organization, and activities to increase the likelihood of integration with peer employees. Ideally, the individuals with disabilities will be physically integrated with other employees, and employed directly by the company rather than by the support organization. It is through the employment support organization that training can also be provided to other company employees to help them feel comfortable about, and skilled at, working with people with disabilities.

The employment support organization is of key interest to many companies, in part because it reduces the risks they perceive as associated with employing persons with severe disabilities. The employment support organization can troubleshoot issues both within and outside the workplace, such as those that frequently arise concerning transportation. The organization can provide a buffer between the firm and the various state and county social service organizations that regulate or fund services. Finally, it helps complete a framework for planning and program implementation that allows the interests of the company to be balanced with those of the service purchasers and consumers.

3. Form an Employer Group to
Facilitate Supported Jobs or Enclave Formation

Companies can help supported employment develop by providing leadership within the business community, in addition to offering employment to persons with severe disabilities. An employer group can do far more than most service providers to identify employment opportunities and communicate the advantages of supported employment to other potential employers. A group of employers participating in the development of supported employment can take the lead in informing the private sector of effective service models that benefit both the business community and individuals who otherwise would be economically dependent. In Portland, Oregon, a business group that was formed to develop prospects for supported employment became a principle component of the employment support organization. This relationship is depicted in Figure 12.1.

An industry-led process offers several advantages. It recognizes the diversity of local communities and companies. It is cost-effective in that it employs volunteers from the private sector who can most readily identify work force needs and opportunities. It also offers the potential for large-scale dissemination because it reaches enough companies to have an industry-wide impact, rather than focus on developing opportunities in single companies. In addition, it takes advantage of existing networks in social services and trade associations.

SUPPORTED EMPLOYMENT: GOOD FOR BUSINESS

The logic of supported employment is straightforward. Rather than supporting persons with severe disabilities in endless preparation for employment, public funds now committed to day programming are shifted to provide support while people work. When this is done, an individual with a severe disability may earn wages based on his or her

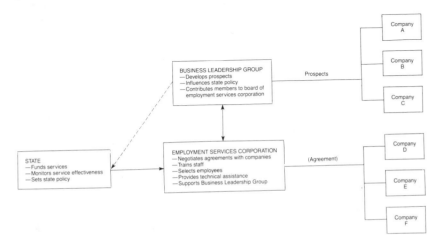

Figure 12.1. Industry-led organizational strategy.

productivity, with a resulting reduction in dependence on income transfer payments and public medical assistance. The employer gains the benefits associated with employing persons with disabilities while being protected from excess employment costs by the presence of ongoing support. There is strong evidence from demonstration programs that supported employment is cost-effective for most adults with severe developmental disabilities, when compared to day care and extended sheltered employment programs (Hill & Wehman, 1983; Rhodes & Valenta, 1985; Noble, 1985). The same evidence points to cost-effectiveness when service costs are contrasted, and when service costs are measured against outcomes.

But is supported employment really good for the employer? Although data is scarce, preliminary reports are positive. Many of the tangible benefits of hiring persons with disabilities are discussed earlier in this chapter. With adequate support to the company and its employees, businesses engaged in supported employment may expect employee stability, increased worker heterogeneity, low absenteeism, high work quality, and labor costs commensurate with the work performed. Businesses may also expect monetary supports from the government to offset the additional costs that may be associated with hiring persons with disabilities. Employees who require extensive, sustained training and supervision, those who have difficulty adapting to the company environment, or those who work at greatly diminished productivity levels do represent additional business costs (Cho & Schuermann, 1980). In supported employment, these costs may be paid through government subsidies and contributions, just as public funding supports sheltered workshops. Tax credits are one common vehicle for initial support; another is public fees paid to either the support organization or the company to cover other identified costs of employing persons with disabilities.

Identifying or quantifying extra costs to the company often presents a difficult problem. Figure 12.2 provides a worksheet for considering the financial impact of a program on a company. It will not be possible to quantify all of the effects. Many—or most—of the possible effects may not be of interest to any particular company. However, areas in which costs are identified may pinpoint needs for public funding or shape the design of the program. If financial impact is planned, initially perceived costs to the company can become benefits. For example, specialized training costs the company nothing when carried out as the responsibility of the support organization, and may even provide the company directly beneficial training and job analysis technology. With careful planning, costs can become a benefit or at least be neutralized by public funding.

In assessing the costs and benefits of supported employment in your company, it may be helpful to review the following topics. For each item, attempt to rate the cost/benefit high, medium, or low. It may not be possible to put specific costs on most of the items. For companies considering employment, it may be helpful to consider the experiences of other companies.

Possible effect	Cost	Benefit	Comments
Absenteeism			
Cost of training			
Cost of supervision			
Personnel costs			
Affirmative action			
Community reputation			
Production stability			
Tax credits			
Benefits to employees			
Cost of manufacturing			
Materials, work stations			
Fixture development			
Consistent quality			
_____			
_____			
_____			

Figure 12.2. Worksheet for consideration of the financial impact of supported employment on a company.

Table 12.1 provides an example of how the financial impact worksheet has been applied to Physio Control, a company whose plant in the state of Washington employs about one thousand persons. Twelve of Physio Control's employees have developmental disabilities, including eight who work under special supervision. Summing up the issue of profitability, Director of Production Dave Jay said:

> Our program makes a legitimate contribution to the company's operation; no one was interested in setting up a charity operation . . . But, we also looked beyond the profitability and saw that the enclave participants, the company and the community are enhanced in so many ways. When we presented the original plan to Physio's senior managers, it took only a short time for them to say yes. We had done our homework and shown that a program like the enclave is good business. ("Enclaves," 1986, p. 2)

ROLE OF THE SUPPORT ORGANIZATION

The ongoing support in supported employment is typically provided by an independent nonprofit organization with funding from a public

Table 12.1. Impact of an enclave on a Redmond, WA, company, Physio Control, after 3 years

Possible effect

Absenteeism	The program has experienced less than 1% absenteeism, while the company's average is 2%.
Training and supervision	The individuals in the program require more training and longer training time than most other employees. This additional staff cost was initially covered by public funds, but the company may have benefited by having a highly qualified trainer available. All training and supervision costs are now assumed by the company. Ongoing expenses relating to training company supervisors and peer employees have been covered by public funds.
Personnel costs	Screening potential employees is a cost of the nonprofit support organization. No additional personnel costs have been determined.
Affirmative action	Federal law requires many companies to make "reasonable accommodation" for hiring people with disabilities. This program provides dramatic enhancement of the affirmative action program, yet both the cost and benefit are difficult to quantify.
Community reputation	The company's reputation is enhanced, an effect that is believed to be translated into economic benefits by helping to attract the most qualified personnel available.
Tax credits	The company was eligible for $8,550 in tax credits.
Benefits to employees	The company believes that overall employee morale is heightened by the program.
Cost of manufacturing	Employees are paid only for their output. There should be no difference in manufacturing costs. If additional costs are identified, these costs are borne by public funds. Set-up costs, materials costs, and work station costs have had no discernable negative impact on company costs.
Fixture development	Extra expenses for fixtures could be appropriately paid with public funds, rather than by the company, and should therefore not represent any additional cost to the company. These fixtures at Physio have been very inexpensive, and have not been valued.
Consistent quality	Is quality better or worse, in general, than among other employees? Precise training and more intense supervision has kept production quality at company standards.

agency. The quality of this support organization is critical and has much to do with the benefits actually experienced by a participating company. Employers have a right to expect much from today's service providers. A good supported employment organization will do the following:

1. Act in Accordance with the Economic Interests of the Employer

A good supported employment organization will not rely on industrial charity as the basis for the employment of persons with severe disabilities. This implies that the support organization is obliged to understand the employer's product and the business demands associated with that product.

2. Fit within Company Policies

For enclaves and supported jobs, it is important that the program procedures complement company procedures. Reasonable accommodation does not include rewriting company policies that do not interfere with the essential characteristics of the program. For example, one manufacturer with more than 70,000 employees made the point of not filing for targeted job tax credits, even though several thousand of its employees were eligible. The reason: the load of paperwork and changes in procedures amounted to more trouble than the tax credits were worth.

3. Facilitate Employee Screening

A key feature of supported employment is that it is not limited to those considered "job ready." However, there must still be a process for matching potential employees with a place of work. Many employers will have some requirements that will not suit all referrals. For example, it remains a common desire among businesses to protect peer employees from individuals who are potentially disruptive of the working environment. A good support organization will insure success from the perspective of both the employer and the employee through careful planning and assessment of the company's environmental constraints. By screening potential employees for the company, the support organization ensures an appropriate match between the working environment and the employee.

4. Attend to Skill Deficits and Problem Behaviors

Inappropriate work behaviors and skill deficits are among the common effects of disability that have obstructed employment in the past. The concept of supported employment does not include the assumption that an employer must now shoulder the responsibility for, or cost of, these behaviors. A good support organization will be able to provide the support a company needs to overcome performance problems that otherwise would be untenable. This may be done in many ways, including the provision of training to the employee's supervisors and coworkers or direct supervision of the employee by the support organization.

5. Deal with All State and Federal Agencies

Employers are already faced with governmental regulations that lead to costly paperwork. Programs for persons with disabilities carry the potential to burden the employer with even more regulations and paperwork. Contracts to receive public support funding, certification or accreditation of the program, and Department of Labor subminimum wage permits provide examples. The support organization should assume responsibility for such requirements whenever possible.

The support organization exists to ensure that an employer is only required to make reasonable accommodation in successfully employing persons with disabilities. As more employers initiate innovative hiring programs, they may choose to assume more of the traditional responsibility of the service providers. For now, it is imperative that good support organizations emerge to support business in these new endeavors, by bringing the best of habilitation and training technology to the business, and by removing the troublesome barriers that have led to past exclusion of persons with severe disabilities.

SUMMARY

This chapter provides a discussion of active participation by the business community in the development of supported employment opportunities. Potential benefits to companies have been identified, substantiated by emerging examples of employer participation. Businesses can choose to become involved in supported employment through one or more of several strategies, including hiring persons with disabilities, starting an enclave, or forming an employer group. A company willing to engage in a supported employment project might expect to realize tangible benefits such as reduced turnover, assured productivity standards, possible tax credits, increased employee heterogeneity, low absenteeism, and high-quality work.

Finally, the role and importance of the employment support organization has been discussed. It is only with access to work through business, along with organized long-term support, that employment benefits result for individuals previously excluded from the workplace.

REFERENCES

Cho, D. W., & Schuermann, A. C. (1980). Economic costs and benefits of private gainful employment of the severely handicapped. *Journal of Rehabilitation. 46*(3), 28–32.

E. I. du Pont de Nemours & Co. (1982). *Equal to the task: 1981 du Pont survey of employment of the handicapped.* Wilmington, DE: E. I. du Pont de Nemours & Co.

Enclaves can fit into any company's culture. (1986, May/June). *Monitor,* p. 2 (Physio Control, Redmond, WA).

Geletka, J. R. (1982). *A creative partnership: Guidelines for the development of a project with industry.* Washington, DC: Electronics Industries Foundation.

Hill, J., & Wehman, P. (1980). Employer and nonhandicapped co-worker perceptions of moderately and severely retarded workers. *Journal of Contemporary Business, 8*(4), 107–112.

Hill, J., & Wehman, P. (1983). Cost benefit analysis of placing moderately and severely handicapped individuals into competitive employment. *Journal of The Association for Persons with Severe Handicaps, 8*(1), 30–38.

Levitan, S., & Taggart, R. (1982). Rehabilitation, employment and the disabled. In J. Rubin (Ed.), *Alternatives in rehabilitating the handicapped* (pp. 89–150). New York: Human Science Press.

Noble, J. H. (1985). *The benefits and costs of supported employment and impediments to its expansion.* Richmond: Virginia Department of Mental Health and Mental Retardation.

Pati, G. C., & Adkins, Jr., J. J. (1980, January-February). Hire the handicapped—compliance is good business. *Harvard Business Review,* 14–22.

Pati, G. C., & Morrison, G. (1982, July-August). Enabling the disabled. *The Harvard Business Review, 58*(1), 152–160.

Rhodes, L. E., & Valenta, L. (1985). Enclaves in industry. In P. McCarthy, J. Emerson, M. S. Moon, & J. M. Barcus (Eds.), *School to work transition for youth with severe disabilities* (pp. 131–149). Richmond: Virginia Commonwealth University.

Vandergoot, D., & Worrell, J. (1979). *Placement in rehabilitation: A career development perspective.* Baltimore: University Park Press.

Wingate, A. (1985, December 8). Work-force shortage will worsen. *The New York Times,* p. 38.

Chapter 13

Passing Fad or Fundamental Change?

The logic of supported employment is fundamentally different from that of previous day services. By combining employment services with ongoing assistance, supported employment creates basic changes in both. Traditionally time-limited, employment services have provided relatively brief periods of work preparation with the expectation of future independent employment. Continuous services traditionally have been nonvocational, designed to provide the care and treatment needed by individuals considered incapable of working independently in the competitive labor market. Ongoing support for individuals who work with assistance, but who are not likely to work independently, constitutes both a new type of service and a new opportunity for persons with severe disabilities. Supported employment offers an option between total dependence and independent employment, and thus creates opportunities for persons traditionally excluded from the labor market. It also represents a new type of partnership between the public and private sectors because it involves continuing support after an individual is employed. Supported employment requires ongoing relationships with employers. The economic basis on which businesses make hiring decisions changes because all the costs of training and maintaining the individual on the job are not borne by the employer.

Will this fundamental, logical shift to supported employment create practical differences in the lives of persons with severe disabilities? Or will it, like many other large-scale federal initiatives, result in more rhetoric than substance, more bureaucratic activity than local opportunity? The outcome depends on how the concept is implemented—on what parents, service providers, employers, state agency staff, researchers, and others do with the opportunity provided by federal and state supported employment initiatives.

Passing fad or fundamental change? The difference will largely be determined by how efforts to implement supported employment answer four questions: 1) Can programs that provide supported employment be developed in local communities nationwide? 2) Can these programs actually achieve supported employment objectives while employing persons with severe disabilities? 3) Once available, will employment be valued by and for persons with severe disabilities? 4) Will the anticipated benefits of supported employment really result? This chapter briefly addresses each of these four questions. The first has been the focus of this entire book. The remaining three point to activities that are needed as initial implementation efforts proceed.

CAN PROGRAMS DESIGNED TO PROVIDE SUPPORTED EMPLOYMENT BE DEVELOPED IN LOCAL COMMUNITIES?

If current policy goals concerning supported employment are to create lasting change in services for persons with severe disabilities, the first implementation issue is the extent to which those policy goals affect the objectives of local programs and the public agencies that fund them. Lasting change requires, first of all, that the goal of supported employment be adopted locally, and that organizational structures be established to pursue that goal.

As suggested throughout this book, creating organizational structures to achieve the goal of supported employment is a complex task. Implementation builds on the strengths of an existing network of private, nonprofit, vocational service providers. However, it requires basic changes in the location of those services, whom they include, how their purpose is defined, and how they are managed and staffed. Changes cannot be achieved only from within these programs. Success depends on the active involvement of several groups, each filling specific roles and accomplishing specific tasks in relation to supported employment. The role of parents and other advocates in defining acceptable employment outcomes, the role of employers in providing work opportunities, the task of public agency managers in creating incentives for organizational change and accomplishment, the responsibility of teachers to prepare for supported employment during the school year, and the role of universities in building the personnel capacity to offer supported employment are all critical to a successful transition from prevocational and nonvocational services to supported employment.

As implementation proceeds, the concept of supported employment will become elaborated and improved by local successes. It will also be criticized for local mistakes. Even at this early stage in the implementation process, one can anticipate several local implementation issues that will raise questions about the overall concept of supported employment. First, public investment in the development of new programs creates powerful incentives for current local program managers simply to relabel existing practices, claiming that traditional sheltered work fits within the concept of supported employment and should qualify for the newly available funding. Although some organizations' exemplary practices fit the definition of supported employment, exclusive funding of existing programs would focus services on those individuals who have already gained entry into vocational services, and exclude the many who traditionally have been served in nonvocational and prevocational programs. The result would be a skewing of the concept of supported employment toward more capable individuals, and away from those for whom it was originally designed.

Other communities may make supported employment unnecessarily expensive, perhaps in part by adding it to existing services in day-activity and sheltered workshop programs, instead of replacing those activities. On-site training and ongoing support is indeed expensive, if it must be treated as a supplement to traditional therapy, teaching, counseling, and evaluation services. It is only when the employment training specialist who provides direct training is seen in an alternative role that the anticipated efficiencies of supported employment are likely to result.

In some implementation efforts, rigid agreements among responsible state agencies artificially limit the range of program options that may be effectively used. Different supported employment strategies require different mixes of capital investment, initial training for individual workers, and ongoing funding. Since some approaches appear better at accommodating different individuals, rigid funding strategies may create the impression that supported employment is effective only with persons experiencing particular types or levels of disability. An extreme instance of this rigidity would probably occur if state funding strategies were specifically designed around only one strategy for providing supported employment. No doubt, such a state would ultimately conclude that supported employment was useful for only a small subset of individuals.

Ultimately, the utility and outcomes of supported employment will be determined not by the validity of the concept but by the success of state and local implementation efforts. The concept will naturally evolve during the implementation process, and it is implementation, not the original concept, that will now determine whether the fundamental change promised in policy becomes reality for persons with severe disabilities.

CAN LOCAL PROGRAMS ACHIEVE
THE OBJECTIVES OF SUPPORTED EMPLOYMENT?

As the organizational implementation described in this book proceeds, and as programs are established or altered to provide supported employment, concern will shift to the procedural strategies that those programs can use to develop and support the work performance of persons with severe disabilities. No matter how successful the program-level implementation, supported employment will constitute a fundamental change in services only if a procedural technology emerges for providing training and support to persons with various types and levels of disabilities.

Much of the needed procedural technology that exists results from three broad efforts. First, research on teaching work tasks to individuals with severe disabilities in workshop settings has provided reliable procedures for analyzing repetitive tasks, teaching the required skills, and using the analysis as a basis for data collection and data-based decisions about training (e.g., see Bellamy, Horner, & Inman, 1979; Gold, 1976). The strength of this research is its broad, successful application to persons with severe and profound mental retardation who present significant challenges to trainers.

Second, procedures developed in integrated, community-based secondary school programs for students with severe disabilities have addressed a variety of training needs similar to those found in regular workplaces. Procedures for enhancing social interaction (Bates, 1980; Gaylord-Ross, Haring, Breen, & Pitts-Conway, 1984), developing transportation skills (Marchetti, McCartney, Drain, Hooper, & Dix, 1983; Page, Iwata, & Neef, 1976; Vogelsberg & Rusch, 1979), and responding to the multiple cues in complex community settings are all directly relevant to the demands of regular work settings. Some of the most important recent work has been the development of strategies for obtaining generalized performance by teaching several carefully selected instances of the expected variation in tasks and settings (Horner, Sprague, & Wilcox, 1982). This general-case programming provides a framework for teaching work skills that can be used as job conditions and requirements change.

The third source of important procedural information is the research and development that has accompanied transitional training programs designed to prepare individuals for independent, competitive employment (Rusch, 1986). Whereas most of this work has been done with persons with less severe disabilities than those for whom supported employment was designed, the procedures nevertheless provide a comprehensive view of the concerns to be addressed during training at regular work sites. Particularly important are the procedures for combining work and nonwork instruction in a cohesive set of intervention procedures.

A synthesis of these three sets of procedures will be needed if supported employment is to include all those individuals for whom it is needed. Not surprisingly, many communities have begun implementation of supported employment with persons with moderate or mild disabilities—those who have traditionally been served in sheltered workshops—rather than the less capable individuals in day-activity and prevocational programs. Although this may reflect the current local availability of procedures for training and supporting more challenging individuals, it only partially addresses the goals of supported employment. Full implementation will require continued refinement and dissemination of the procedural technology, to enable more programs to offer services competently to persons with severe disabilities.

Procedures need to be developed in the analysis of the periodic social and vocational demands and opportunities of a job in a way that creates a functional data system for monitoring trainee performance. Previous efforts to analyze these aspects of jobs have largely been designed to structure readiness training or to select individuals who are most likely to succeed in a particular job. Neither of these uses requires the level of analytical precision needed when the goal is to create a structure for collection and use of performance data. Once a practical system is developed, it will help make many of the training and support decisions of employment-training specialists more empirically based.

Supported employment creates a new research and development challenge by emphasizing that all persons, regardless of the level or type of disability, can work for pay on regular work sites. Development, testing, and dissemination of procedures for supporting challenging individuals in such settings will determine whether supported employment provides an opportunity for persons with severe disabilities, or whether, like previous employment initiatives, it will be predominantly for persons with mild and moderate disabilities.

ONCE IT IS AVAILABLE, WILL EMPLOYMENT BE VALUED FOR PERSONS WITH SEVERE DISABILITIES?

The premise of supported employment—and of this book—is that work is desirable for persons with severe disabilities. The research literature and many personal accounts of individuals with disabilities support the value of employment to both the individual and to society as a whole. Despite this support, it seems likely that in the midst of their effort to create supported employment opportunities, advocates, professionals, and others will be asked to address not just whether they *can* offer supported employment to persons with severe disabilities but whether they *should* do so.

Three general arguments are likely to be raised against an employment focus in publicly financed programs for persons with severe disabilities. Although an extensive discussion is beyond the scope of this chapter, brief comments on each may help program advocates anticipate common concerns. The first of these arguments is that in times of high unemployment it is unreasonable to expect employers to offer jobs to persons with severe disabilities. Consequently, it is suggested, public programs should maintain a nonvocational focus that reflects the opportunities available to the individuals served. (For elaborations of this viewpoint, see Parmenter, 1986; Tizard & Anderson, 1979.)

One response to this argument addresses its implications about the value of persons with disabilities and their rights as people and citizens. It is difficult to justify disproportionate joblessness among persons with disabilities without devaluing them directly or by implication. Persons without disabilities do not have a greater claim on available work, any more than do persons of one race, sex, or religion. In addition, by offering ongoing support in the work setting, supported employment makes it easier for an employer to offer jobs. If administered as conceptualized, supported employment should eliminate excess costs an employer might incur as a result of hiring persons with severe disabilities, by allowing the employer to pay the same amount for work performed, whoever performs it. Consequently, the incentives to bypass persons with severe disabilities can be removed.

A second argument against an employment focus in public services for persons with severe disabilities emphasizes the many other services that these individuals appear to need, especially to reduce skill deficits. Developmental progress, it is argued, requires continued training and therapy, which is displaced by programs that focus primarily on providing supported employment. Like anyone seeking or accepting employment, persons with disabilities choose to devote time to productive work that might be used instead to develop skills. Few people are completely qualified for their first job before tackling it; likewise, the acquisition of new skills and ongoing education generally happen concurrently with working. Persons with disabilities should also be entitled to pursue continued development as a discretionary activity that complements work, rather than a required activity that precludes work.

The third argument typically leveled against an employment focus in public services for persons with severe disabilities is that it is possible for persons with disabilities to experience the benefits of working without actually having a paid job. The combination of public income support and volunteer work, for example, is seen by some as an adequate alternative to paid work (Brown et al., 1984). Others argue that work is not necessary in order to achieve a high quality of life.

Although partially true, these arguments do not necessarily support a nonvocational program focus. It is possible for individuals to separate the benefits derived from wages from other benefits of working, although strict reliance on public income supports creates sub-poverty level living. It is also true that life can be satisfactory without work. Many structure their lives quite well around alternatives to employment. However, work remains the most normative way of organizing daily activities and ensuring income for the individual. The least expensive option for society, it leaves the individual in maximum control of his or her own life and least vulnerable to policy changes affecting services and income supports. Work may not be the only way to achieve a high qualtiy of life, but it appears to be a rational objective for government to emphasize in publicly funded services.

However the discussion of these three and other questions proceeds, the outcome is critical to the success of supported employment. Unless a consensus is maintained that work is important for persons with severe disabilities, the federal and state initiatives on supported employment will indeed constitute only a passing fad.

WILL THE ANTICIPATED BENEFITS
OF SUPPORTED EMPLOYMENT BE REALIZED?

Seekins and Fawcett (1986) describe four separate phases in the policy development process: agenda-setting, policy development, policy implementation, and policy review. Recent legislation on supported employment shows that the first two of these phases are largely complete. The current national effort to develop supported employment opportunities falls into the third phase—policy implementation. The analysis by Stevens and Fawcett suggests this while that effort is underway, it is important to look ahead to later policy review. If supported employment is to represent lasting change, information must be collected now to show exactly what benefits and problems result from implementation.

Data from several early supported employment programs provide a basis for estimating the costs and benefits likely to result from national implementation. It is only natural, however, to expect differences between these relatively circumscribed studies and the effects of large-scale implementation. Potential effects of particular importance to sustaining the commitment of policymakers to supported employment include:

1. The effect on federal expenditures and income—Several studies have documented increased governmental income from taxes paid by previously dependent persons, and from savings associated with the discontinuation of social services and income support programs (Smith, 1986). For individuals who remain eligible for benefits, reductions in income support payments will also be important to document when supported employment is evaluated. Because supported employment may be part-time work below minimum wage, the anticipated effect for many individuals is not removal from eligibility for these programs, but rather a decrease in the amount of subsidy received. For example, an individual receiving Supplemental Security Income (SSI) who earns $300 each month would, under current rules, receive about $107 less each month from SSI. Similar reductions for even 1,000 of the almost 200,000 persons with mental retardation now in day services would create an annual saving of $1,284,000.

2. Benefits to state and local governments—These may include additional tax revenues, smaller state supplements to income support programs, and potential savings in program operation. Initial data are not conclusive on the relative costs of traditional day services and supported employment, but there is clear evidence that some supported employment programs are much less expensive in some communities than in others (Rhodes & Valenta, 1985).

3. Anticipated benefits for persons with disabilities—These benefits include increased income, enhanced quality of life because of this income, more extensive social networks because of integration at work, and greater use of normal community resources. Critical evaluation questions concern whether these anticipated benefits for the individual actually result. It is also important to know what individuals with disabilities give up in order to achieve these benefits. Concerns about loss of contact with friends who are disabled, the risk of job loss and consequent disruptions in services, and the deterioration of skills that could be practiced in traditional programs should all be carefully studied and creatively managed.

Supported employment will remain an option for persons with severe disabilities only if a systematic effort is made now to collect, analyze, and report the program evaluation information that will allow Congress, state legislatures, and public agencies to review the established policies and adjust programs accordingly. Because the potential benefits are so great and the costs of alternative service models so high, there should be widespread support for collecting the needed data.

SUMMARY

Is supported employment a passing fad or a fundamental change? The concept is fundamentally different from earlier service efforts, but whether it creates a real and lasting effect on the lives of persons with severe disabilities depends on what local communities do now to implement supported employment.

Fundamental change will result only if federal and state policy initiatives lead to local supported employment programs, if those programs have access to an improving procedural technology that allows them to support all persons with severe handicaps in jobs, if the consensus on the importance of work for persons with severe disabilities prevails, and if continuing evaluation shows that the promised benefits of supported employment actually occur.

Supported employment is an opportunity, not a mandate. How it affects the lives of persons with disabilities in any community largely depends on the efforts of concerned people in that community.

REFERENCES

Bates P. (1980). The effectiveness of interpersonal skills training in the social skill acquisition of moderately and severely retarded adults. *The Journal of Applied Behavior Analysis, 13,* 237–248.

Bellamy, G. T., Horner, R. H., & Inman, D. (1979). *Vocational habilitation of severely retarded adults: A direct service technology.* Baltimore: University Park Press.

Brown, L., Shiraga, B., York, J., Kessler, K., Strohm, B., Rogan, P., Sweet, M., Zanella, K., VanDeventer, P., & Loomis, R. (1984). Integrated work opportunities for adults with severe handicaps: The extended training option. *Journal of The Association for Persons with Severe Handicaps, 9*(4), 262–269.

Gaylord-Ross, R. J., Haring, T. G., Breen, C., & Pitts-Conway, V. (1984). The training and generalization of social interaction skills with autistic youth. *Journal of Applied Behavior Analysis, 17,* 198–199.

Gold, M. (1976). Task analysis of a complex assembly task by the retarded blind. *Exceptional Children, 43*(20), 78–84.

Horner, R., Sprague, J., & Wilcox, B. (1982). Constructing general case programs for community activities. In B. Wilcox & G. T. Bellamy, *Design of high school programs for severely handicapped students* (pp. 61–98). Baltimore: Paul H. Brookes Publishing Co.

Marchetti, A. G., McCartney, J. R., Drain, S., Hooper, M., & Dix, J. (1983). Pedestrian skills training for mentally retarded adults: Comparison of training in two settings. *Mental Retardation, 21,* 107–110.

Page, T. J., Iwata, B. A., & Neef, N. A. (1976). Teaching pedestrian skills to retarded persons: Generalization from the classroom to the natural environment. *Journal of Applied Behavior Analysis, 9,* 433–444.

Parmenter, T. R. (1986). *Bridges from school to working life for handicapped youth: The view from Australia.* New York: World Rehabilitation Fund, Inc.

Rhodes, L. E., & Valenta, L. (1985). Industry-based supported employment: An enclave approach. *Journal of The Association for Persons with Severe Handicaps, 10*(1), 12–20.

Rusch, F. R. (Ed.). (1986). *Competitive employment issues and strategies.* Baltimore: Paul H. Brookes Publishing Co.

Seekins, T., & Fawcett, S. B. (1986). Public policy making and research information. *The Behavior Analyst, 9*(1), 35–45.

Smith, M. (1986). *Supported employment for certain severely handicapped persons* (86–816 EPW). Washington, DC: Congressional Research Service, Library of Congress.

Tizard, J., & Anderson, E. (1979, June). *The education of the handicapped people.* Paris: Organization of Economic Cooperation and Development, Center for Educational Research and Innovation.

Vogelsberg, R. T., & Rusch, F. R. (1979). Training severely handicapped students to cross partially controlled intersections. *AAESPH Review, 4,* 1–127.

__ Appendix _____

Suggested Readings

GETTING STARTED

Allen, L. L. (1968). *Starting & succeeding in your own small business*. New York: Grosset & Dunlap.

Burstiner, I. (1979). *The small business handbook: A comprehensive guide to starting and running your own business*. Englewood Cliffs, NJ: Prentice-Hall.

Goldstein, A. S. (1984). *Starting on a shoestring*. New York: Ronald Press.

Griffin, W. R., (1980). *How to start and operate a successful service business*. Seattle: Cleaning Consultant Services, Inc.

Hummel, J. M. (1980). *Starting and running a nonprofit corporation*. Minneapolis: University of Minnesota Press.

Kamoroff, B. (1980). *Small-time operator: How to start your own small business, keep your books, pay your taxes, and stay out of trouble!* Laytonville, CA: Bell Springs.

Kirk, J. (1976). *Incorporating your business*. Scarsdale, NY: TPR Publishing.

McLaughlin, J. J. (1985). *Building your business plan: A step-by-step approach*. New York: John Wiley & Sons.

Sechrist, T. & Quitzau (1987). *Janitorial Contracting: The complete how-to-do-it guide*. Verndale, MN: RPM Press.

PRINCIPLES OF MANAGEMENT

Drucker, P. F. (1963). *Managing for results*. New York: Harper & Row.

Drucker, P. F. (1967). *The effective executive*. New York: Harper & Row.

Drucker, P. F. (1973). *Management*. New York: Harper & Row.

Drucker, P. F. (1974). *Management: Tasks, responsibilities, practices*. New York: Harper & Row.

Drucker, P. F. (1980). *Managing in turbulent times*. New York: Harper & Row.

Flamholt, E. G. (1985). *Human resource accounting*. San Francisco: Jossey–Bass.

Gilbert, T. F. (1978). *Human competence: Engineering worthy performance*. New York: McGraw–Hill.

Green, G. G. (1975). *How to start and manage you own business*. New York: Mentor.

Haimann, T. & Scott, W. G. (1974). *Management in the modern organization*. Boston: Houghton-Mifflin.

Newman, W. H., & Summer, C. E., Jr. (1961). *The process of management*. Englewood Cliffs, NJ: Prentice–Hall.

Odiorne, G. S. (1965). *Management by objective—A system of managerial leadership*. California: Pitman Publishing.

Reynolds, H., & Tramel, M. E. (1979). *Executive time management: Getting 12 hours' work out of an 8-hour day*. Englewood Cliffs, NJ: Prentice-Hall.

SMALL BUSINESS MANAGEMENT

Baumback, C. M., & Lawyer, K. (1979). *How to organize and operate a small business*. Englewood Cliffs, NJ: Prentice–Hall.

Dollar, W. E. (1983). *Effective purchasing and inventory control for small business*. Boston: CBI Publications.

Small Business Administration (1982). *Cash flow in a small plant*. Washington, D.C.: Author.

Stern, H. H. (1976). *Running your own business: A handbook of facts and information for the small businessman*. New York: Crown.

FINANCIAL MANAGEMENT

Anthony, R. N. (1976). *Essentials of accounting*. Reading, MA: Addison–Wesley.

Bierman, H., & Drebin, A. (1972). *An introduction: Financial accounting*. New York: Macmillan.

Bierman, H., & Drebin, A. R. (1972). *Managerial accounting: An introduction*. New York: Macmillan.

Cashin, J. A., & Lerner, J. L. (1981). *Theory and problems of Accounting II*. New York: McGraw–Hill.

Davidson, S., Schindler, J. S., Stickney, C. P., & Weil, R. L. (1978). *Managerial accounting: An introduction to concepts, methods and uses*. Hinsdale, IL: Dryden Press.

Droms, W. G. (1984). *Finance and accounting for nonfinancial managers*. Reading, MA: Addison–Wesley.

Horngren, C. T. (1977). *Cost accounting: A managerial emphasis*. Englewood Cliffs, NJ: Prentice–Hall.

Kallber, J. G., & Parkingson, K. (1984). *Current asset management: Cash, credit, and inventory*. New York: John Wiley & Sons.

Lipay, R. J. (1984). *Understand those financial reports: Question-and-answer guide for investors and nonfinancial managers*. New York: John Wiley & Sons.

Tracey, J. A. (1983). *Wringing cash flow and other vital signs out of the numbers: How to read a financial report, for managers, entrepreneurs, lenders, lawyers, and investors*. New York: John Wiley & Sons.

Relevant publications are also available from the U.S. Small Business Administration, PO Box 30, Denver, CO 80201-0030:

−MA 1.008 Attacking business decision problems with breakeven analysis

−MA 1.010 Accounting services for small service firms

−MA 1.015 Budgeting in a small business firm

−MA 1.016	Sound cash management and borrowing
−MA 2.016	Checklist for going into business
−MA 2.010	Planning and goal setting for small business
−MA 2.018	Insurance checklist for small business
−MA 2.022	Business plan for small service firms
−MA 4.016	Signs in your business
−MA 5.006	Setting up a pay system
−MA 5.008	Managing employee benefits
−MA 6.003	Incorporating a small business
−MA 6.004	Selecting the legal structure for your business
−87	Financial management
−18	Basic business reference sources
−94	Decision making in small business
−72	Personnel management

MARKETING

Alderson, W., & Halbert, M. H. (1968). *Men, motives, and markets.* Englewood Cliffs, NJ: Prentice–Hall.

Bell, M. (1979). *Marketing concepts and strategy* (3rd ed.). Boston: Houghton Mifflin.

Buzzell, R. D., Nourse, R.E.M., Matthews, Jr., J. B., & Levitt, T. (1972). *Marketing: A contemporary analysis* (2nd ed.). New York: McGraw–Hill.

Garvey, L. K. (1980). *Public relations for small business.* Washington DC: Small Business Administration, Small Marketers' Aides.

Kotler, P. (1980). *Marketing management* (4th ed.). Englewood Cliffs, NJ: Prentice–Hall.

McCarthy, J. E. (1968). *Basic marketing: A managerial approach* (3rd ed.). Homewood, IL: Richard D. Irwin.

McCarthy, J. E. (1971). *Basic marketing* (4th ed.). Homewood, IL: Richard D. Irwin.

Rados, D. L. (1981). *Marketing for nonprofit organizations.* Boston: Auburn House.

Rogers, A. J. (1972). *Elements of markets.* Hinsdale, IL: Dryden Press.

Relevant publications are also available from the U.S. Small Business Administration, PO Box 30, Denver, CO 80201-0030:

−MA 4.001	Understanding your customer
−MA 4.008	Tips on getting more for your marketing
−MA 4.019	Learning about your market
−89	Marketing for small business
−9	Marketing research procedures

__ Index _____

State leadership—*continued*
consensus and participation in,
178–180
employment opportunity creation in, 169–171
local service provider development in, 171–174
state management system establishment in, 174–178
challenges for, 163–167
barriers within day services,
164–165
complexity of relevant services,
165–167
lack of control over employment opportunities, 165
uncertainties in generalizing to
widespread practice, 163–164
importance of, 162–163
State management systems, 174–178
definition of agency responsibilities and authority in,
175–176
funding formulas and systems in,
176
local government support in, 177
local service evaluation in, 178
referral in, 176–177
service coordination in, 176–177
Structural change, 139
Substantial Gainful Activity (SGA),
15
Supplemental Security Income
(SSI), 15
Supported employment
benefits of, 16–17
realization of, 269–271
concept of, development of, 8–9
criteria for, 25–26
federal government and, *see*
Federal supported employment initiative
Supported employment programs,
see Program *entries*
Supported job programs, 20–21
Support needs, ongoing, organizational accomplishment of,
31–32
Support organization
role of, 257, 259–260
see also Program(s)

Surveys in, planning process,
43–45
System-influence strategies,
224–226

"Tall" organizational structure, 144,
145
Target group, identification of, in
program proposal development, 47–48
Tax advantages, to businesses, 249
Technical assistance, for service
providers, state arrangement
of, 173–174
Technological change, 139
Technology transfer, 93
Trainer, in supported jobs programs,
20, 80–81
Training
for secondary school students,
185–186
see also Secondary special
education
staff, *see* Staff training
work performance and, 91–92
Training sites
single versus centralized, 188–189
see also Opportunity Scheduling
Approach
Training staff, 249
Transition variables, work performance and, 92
Troubleshooting tree, 103–106

U.S. Office of Special Education and
Rehabilitative Services
(OSERS), 9, 237

Value, of employment, for persons
with severe disabilities,
267–269
Vocational alternatives, in Opportunity Scheduling Approach,
191
Vocational habilitation staff, 240
Vocational rehabilitation, 14
Vocational Rehabilitation Act of
1954, 141

Vocational training
for secondary school students,
185–186
see also Secondary special
education
work performance and, 91–92
Volunteer board of directors, 219,
224

Wages
productivity and, 252
in work-activity programs, 6
see also Paid employment
Work
access to, 146–148
preparation for, special education
programs in, 187—190
see also Opportunity Scheduling Approach
see also Job entries
Work-activity programs, 5
costs of, 6–7
earnings in, 6
growth of, 6–7
Work crews, mobile, 22–23
Work demands, in Opportunity
Scheduling Approach, 199
Work opportunities
development of, 30, 87–91
change strategies for, 149–151
competition between business
and service needs in, 90–91
expansion and, 88–89
focus on tangible outcomes in,
88

by industry, 253–255
maintenance of clear employment strategy in, 89–90
program quality and, 116–118
state leadership and, 169–171
family location of, 227
lack of control over, state leadership and, 165
prospective, identification of,
71, 73
and quality constraints, 135
see also Opportunity Scheduling Approach
Work performance, 91–94
employer requirements for, 30–31
follow-up support and, 93–94
maintenance of, 92–93
program quality and, 118
self-management and, 93
skill transference and, 93
Workshops, 4–5
Work specialization
in Opportunity Scheduling Approach, 191
preparation for, in secondary special education, 186
selection of, in program proposal
development, 48
staff skills in, employer requirements for, 75, 77, 79
Work stations, 22
Work-support behaviors, preparation for, 186
in Opportunity Scheduling Approach, 196